Dinners with Famous Women

Dinners with Famous Women

From Cleopatra to Indira Gandhi

Eugenia R. Van Vliet

Writers Club Press
San Jose New York Lincoln Shanghai

Dinners With Famous Women
From Cleopatra to Indira Gandhi

Writers Club Press
an imprint of iUniverse.com, Inc.

For information address:
iUniverse.com, Inc.
5220 S 16th, Ste. 200
Lincoln, NE 68512
www.iuniverse.com

ISBN: 0-595-13730-X

Printed in the United States of America

To Andrew Hudson who encouraged me to write a book about the subjects I love best, food and history.

Epigraph

Eugenia Van Vliet graduated from San Francisco State University with degrees in Cultural Anthropology and Classical Archaeology. For the past ten years she has studied Culinary History with an emphasis on recreating meals from the past. She is currently working on classes that combine the culinary history of Food and cooking. This book is the first in a series that she hopes to create for famous people and the cuisine of their time.

Contents

Acknowledgements

I would like to acknowledge the following people for their support in my writing: June Mc Laren Peters, with whom, I have had many discussions of history and women. To Kyle Davidson who edited this cookbook for me, Naomi Kakiuchi who teaches at Sur La Table in Seattle and who shares my passion for recreation of meals from ancient times. Andrew Hudson, who has spent innumerable time carting me back and forth to the library, to pick up all the books I have read for my research.

Introduction

Dinners With Famous Women

The study of culinary history, from both an anthropological and archeological point of view, has occupied my life for many years. When I first received my degree in cultural Anthropology, more than 20 years ago, the material available for research into the history of food was very limited. Today there is a multitude of wonderful, scholarly books on the subject. In this cookbook, you will find a smattering of historical information on the times these women lived, told through first person, fictional accounts of their own life stories, as well as recipes and menus based on the food available at that time. Many of the recipes have been adapted from historical cookbooks and others I have created based on my knowledge of the foodstuffs of each era. Women were the cornerstones of the history of food. Although the more distinguished culinary professions were largely reserved for men, it was women who shared recipes and introduced new foods into each culture. Take for example, the Italian Catherine De Medici, who when she married the King of France, brought with her artichokes, pasta and innumerable other culinary delights that would later become staples of the French cuisine.

Since I wanted to provide the widest ranges of cuisine available in each time period, it was difficult to decide which women to include, as history is rich with women who influenced the culinary arts. So welcome to a widely diverse assortment of infamous and famous women who either affected the course of culinary history, or greatly enjoyed its bounties: from Queen Hatchepsut of Egypt, (18th century), to Indira Gandhi, (1917–1984). Each woman will speak of herself and the epoch in which she lived, including the meals served and the food staples available. Many interesting facts and antidotes will result; that tomatoes did not originate in Europe, but were imported from the Americas; why Queen Elizabeth's teeth were black; and what Catherine the Great ate for Russian Easter.

Increased communication and cross-cultural relations has resulted in a dilution of previous culinary practices. The cuisine of the modern world is a fusion of many different influences, rooted in the incredible abundance and availability of diverse staples and ingredients from all corners of the globe. This dynamic will be reflected in the format of this book. The chapters on ancient women, up until the 20th century, will include a greater wealth of historical, anthropological information, tracing the evolution of culinary practices of old into the present day. Before the modern world could provide for a higher quality of life, methods of food preparation were formed on the basis of survival and practical concerns. The reader will note that the accounts of the more modern women will focus less on culinary history and more on the particular cultural influences which make their particular flavors and cuisine unique. It is my intention to present a book for people interested in something more than simple instructions on how to prepare a certain meal, but rather tasty recipes accompanied by historical references and cultural antidotes, presented in a light, fictional format. This book is for those who wish to enrich their cooking practices with the sustenance of historical knowledge, transforming a mere meal into a method of reaching out to the past.

The preparation of food is the heartbeat of life, for without it we would perish from the face of the earth. It is my sincere hope that in this era of time constraints and busy schedules, when a meal most likely consists of a sandwich from a deli, or a quick dinner out, that more people will take the time to prepare dishes for themselves. The recipes have thus been streamlined for a creature of the modern world, although some require more preparation than others. Cooking inspires us and gives a sense of the continuum of life. Even if the women mentioned below did not always cook their own meals, they certainly were interested in food and the finer points of a good meal. Preparing a meal creates a sense of joy and accomplishment, whether felt by us in today's fast paced, modern world, or by the Renaissance chefs who painstakingly created extravagant wedding banquets.

This cookbook is different than most in its format. The women will be presented in chronological order and a menu and recipes will follow the story told by each. The final chapter consists of basic, supplemental recipes of staple items, such as short crust pastry and white sauce, which are used frequently throughout the various other recipes and require only a single entry. Meals were much larger in content in the past, as a dinner could have up to sixteen courses or more. Prepare the entire course for a dinner party or simply pick a single dish and enjoy!

From Queen Hatchepsut to Indira Gandhi

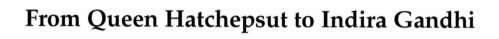

Chapter 1

Hatchepsut

18th Dynasty; Queen and Pharaoh of Egypt

I, Hatchepsut, had the audacity to proclaim myself the first female Pharaoh of Egypt. I acted as regent for my nephew Tutmose the III, but in reality, I and I alone ruled. While I reigned, Egypt became wealthy, providing the privileged class with better houses, gardens and pools, along with their own granaries, bakeries and breweries. While there was a disparity in the diet of the wealthy and the poor, the poor had more vegetables and healthy food in their diet than in previous ages. We of the wealthy class knew no difference in disease from the poor. We suffered from lung disease, the result of breathing the sand, dental abscesses from poorly ground bread and blindness from contamination by flies and their larvae, blown into the eyes by the wind.

Dinners were an important social time. The men and woman sat opposite each other on separate sides of the room, but during banquets I allowed them to sit together. While we owned spoons, we preferred to eat with our fingers, washing them afterwards with water. Sometimes at a very festive event, cones of sweet smelling unguents, where placed atop our heads. They melted and covered our bodies with aromatic odor.

The meal might have consisted of bread, of which, by the time of Rameses the II, there were 46 different types. One particular type was baked in a triangle shape and called the *shat cake*. In fact, grain was so sacred to us, it became the symbol of rebirth. We buried an effigy of Osiris in our tombs, made of wet clay in his shape, upon which seeds of grain had been strewn to germinate and grow in the under-world. Cheese, which we were very found of, was eaten in both the hard and cream cheese forms. As for fowl, we ate ducks and other wild birds sacred to the goddess Satis, the Egyptian goddess of the hunt. We domesticated the goose, and were the first makers of Foie de Gras, or goose liver pate. Meat consisted of beef, lamb and goat, either grilled, roasted or stewed. During my reign, I owned several thousand gazelles, oryx and antelope, which we also ate as a source of meat. We ate vegetables, both cooked and in salads. We had sugar cane, but we didn't know how to refine it, so the main sweetener was honey. We also drank wine, first importing it and then making our own. Beer was the beverage of choice at most events, as we perfected the art of beer making. Unlike the Babylonians, who left the husks of the grain in the beer, we strained them out, giving a smoother taste.

Come join me while I sit at my gaily-painted table, eating bread seasoned with spices, leeks cooked slowly and caramelized, yogurt cheese, and many other delicacies. At the end of the meal, a ritual reminds us of our mortality. A small coffin is carried around the room, bidding us to feast in the moment, for tomorrow we may be seeing Maat, the goddess of truth, and Orisis the god of rebirth, as we journey in the underworld to the next life. But fear not, for death is treated with the same celebration as life. The funeral would be a source of joy and mourning at the same time. Hired mourners would enlarge your entourage and add to the commotion, while others tear at their clothes, ripping their hair and covering themselves with dirt and ashes. The procession carrying your mummified body to the tomb would include all the servants, bringing the many possessions of the departed. When the party reaches the tomb they all follow the body inside and wait as the rituals for a joyful after-life are carried out. Then the entourage would retire to another room in the tomb, where the servants would prepare a banquet for all. At the end of this meal, all the leftovers, plates, drinking cups, flowers would be buried in a cache next to your tomb.

So hail the great gods, Amon-Ra, Ptah, Hathor, Isis, and others who make this stay on the earth such a pleasant one!

*　　　　　　*　　　　　　*

Hatchepsut's Evening Meal

Seasoned Pita Bread
Leek Dip and Onion Dip
Yogurt Cheeses
Cumin Spiced Lamb
Roast Beef with Garlic
Cucumber and Watercress Salad
Apricots with Pomegranate Seeds
Sliced Melons
Beer

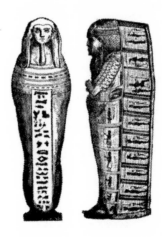

*　　　　　　*　　　　　　*

Seasoned Pita Bread

We were very lucky to have many wild herbs, used to season our food. Crispy flat bread would have accompanied the Leek and Onion Dip in the following recipe. Leeks and onions were some of the oldest vegetables grown in Egypt, dating back to prehistoric times

1 bag Pita bread
4 tablespoons olive oil
1 tablespoon minced cilantro
1 teaspoon ground coriander
1 teaspoon ground cumin
1 teaspoon sea salt

Preheat the oven to 350°F. In a bowl, combine the oil with the cilantro, coriander, cumin and salt. Mix well.

Cut each Pita bread into four sections. Place the sections on a baking pan. Brush with the seasoned oil. Bake until crispy. Remove from the oven and cool.

Serves 6

Leek and Onion Dip

1 bunch Leeks, cleaned and diced
1 small onion, diced
½ cup olive oil
1 teaspoon sea salt
1 tablespoon minced cilantro

In a saucepan heat the olive oil. Add the leeks, onion and the salt. Cook until the leeks and onions have melted to a golden brown color and are caramelized. Remove from the heat and cool. Place in a serving bowl. Sprinkle with the minced cilantro. Serve with the Pita bread.

Serves 4-6

Yogurt Cheese

Our cheeses were mainly made from yogurt or goat's milk, and we preserved them in olive oil. We packed them in clay jars or bags made of animal skins.

1 16 oz container plain yogurt, natural style
4 tablespoons minced dill weed
1 tablespoon minced cilantro
Extra Virgin Olive Oil

For this recipe you must use natural yogurt, as the pasteurized kind will fail to solidify. Line a colander with cheesecloth, and place the yogurt in the middle. Set colander over a bowl and place in the refrigerator. Drain for 24 hours. Remove the cheese from the colander. It should be soft, but solid enough to shape into little balls. Roll each little ball in some of the minced herbs. Place in a jar. Fill the jar with olive oil. Keep in the refrigerator until ready to serve.
Serves 4-6

Cumin Spiced Lamb

Some of the earliest forms of domesticated animals we ate were the goat and the lamb. In fact, we ate so much meat, especially among the wealthier class, that we suffered from a high rate of obesity related diseases, such as hypertension and heart disease.

3 tablespoons olive oil
4 garlic cloves, minced
2 tablespoons minced cilantro
1 teaspoon ground cumin
1 (4 pound) leg of lamb, butterflied (
Arugula

Watercress

Green onions, sliced lengthwise

Preheat the oven to 350°F. In a food processor, combine the olive oil, garlic cloves, cilantro and cumin. Process until pureed. Spread the paste on the lamb. Bake in the oven until the meat thermometer registers 150°F., or about 2 ½ hours. Wash the arugula and watercress. Tear off the tough stems from the watercress. Slice the meat and place on a platter. Surround with the arugula, watercress and the sliced green onions.

Serves 6

Roast Beef with Garlic

We did domesticate several strains of longhorn beef. Beef was available to all classes of people. The choicer cuts were reserved for the artisans who worked on the tombs in the Valley of the Kings, as a bonus for their good work. Only the leg and the beef roast were reserved for the Pharaoh to eat. Beef was considered the sacred food of our goddesses of fertility, Hathor and Isis.

1 (3-4 pound) rump roast

2 heads garlic, sectioned and peeled

4 tablespoon olive oil

1 teaspoon salt

½ teaspoon ground cumin

1 teaspoon coriander seed

4 cups red wine

Preheat the oven to 350°F. In a food processor, combine 1 head of the garlic with the olive oil, salt, cumin and coriander seed. Process to a paste and set aside. In the remaining olive oil, brown the meat in a Dutch oven or large casserole dish. Spread the paste on top of the meat. Sprinkle the rest of the garlic along the side of the beef in the pan. Add the red wine. Cover tightly and bake for 2 ½ hours or until the meat is very tender.

Serves 6

Cucumber and Watercress Salad

This salad combines two of our favorite vegetables. Watercress is favored for its spicy taste while the cucumber is revered for its cooling effect. Some of our medical procedures for bringing down a fever involved using the cucumber in various poultices and drinks.

3 bunches watercress, washed and torn

2 large cucumbers, peeled, seeded and diced

1 bunch green onions, diced

6 tablespoons olive oil

3 tablespoons red wine vinegar

1 teaspoon ground cumin

1 teaspoon salt

In a large bowl, combine the cucumber, watercress and onion. Toss. In a small bowl, whisk together the olive oil, red wine vinegar, cumin and salt. Add to the salad and toss.

Serves 6

Poached Apricots and Plums with Pomegranates

We first imported the pomegranate from our neighbors, the Hittites. Later, we learned how to grow them ourselves. They became a symbol of fertility for us. The invaluable apricot was considered the beloved fruit of the sun god Aten. Served fresh or dried, it provided the Egyptian army with an easily transportable food on their long, grueling campaigns. The plum was first introduced to Egypt during my reign in the 18th century.

8 fresh apricots, halved and pitted
5 large plums, halved and pitted
¾ cup honey
¾ cup water
2 tablespoons fresh mint, minced
2 tablespoons pomegranate syrup
¾ cup pomegranate seeds

In a saucepan, bring the honey and water to a boil. Boil for 5 minutes. Add the apricots and the plumscut side down. Sprinkle with the mint and pomegranate syrup. Simmer for 10 minutes. Remove from the heat and let cool. Transfer the fruit to a serving dish, spoon the syrup over the top, and sprinkle with the pomegranate seeds.
Serves 6
Note: Pomegranate syrup can be found in Arab and gourmet food stores. It has a sweet, yet slightly tangy taste.

*   *   *

Queen Shubad of Ur

2900 BC, Queen of Babylonia

It was Sir Leonard Wooley, who first excavated my tomb at Ur that made me famous. Such an important figure as myself was honored with a large burial site, which included the sacrifices of my servants and many animals. I was buried alongside my exquisite gold headdress, composed of gold leaves and precious stones. Not to mention the numerous possessions I had loved during my lifetime. When Leonard Wooley opened my burial site, he first found the bodies of my loyal servants, buried in the area above my tomb. They too went to their death with all their finery, including headdresses made of carnelian, lapis lazuli, and colored glass beads. In another part of the pit, my oxen and their drivers were found, as well as various soldiers from my husband's army. Yet none of these people suffered a violent death. They were as eager to serve me in death as they had in life.

Music and dancing were a large part of my funeral rites. There was also a meal, consumed by all in attendance, including my servants, before they took their lives by drinking a poisonous draught. This large funeral banquet could last as long as a day, with many courses interspersed with music and oratories for the deceased. I have only included a small fraction of the food served, for in the modern world no one would have the time or energy to cook the 30 or more dishes necessary for such an event. Eunuchs served dark red wines poetically labeled *Divine Liquid* and *Unguent of the Heart,* imported from the vineyards of far off Assyria and our own vineyards in Ur. A heady brew of barley and a wine of date palms stiffened with honey were also offered. As a first course we would sample a salted river perch, garnished with locusts and seasoned with ginger and coriander, followed by roasted ducks and geese from our royal farms, sauced with mint and mustard. A profusion of vegetables-turnips, leeks, carrots and onions, and a salad of cress, lettuce and endive were also served. The meal ended with cakes made of barley sweetened with honey. Now, savor the taste of life everlasting, by partaking of my funeral supper.

*   *   *

Queen Shubad's Funeral Dinner
Flat Bread with Melons, Goat Cheese, and Green Onions
Hearts of Palm Salad
Beans cooked with Turnips and Carrots
Grilled Duck with Pomegranate and Coriander
Grilled Garlic Fish
Onions cooked with Cumin
Honey wine
Molded Barley with dates

*   *   *

Hearts of Palm Salad

Bitter herbs such as arugula, chicory, endive, sorrel and watercress were the main greens used in our salads.

1 head chicory
1 bunch watercress
1 bunch arugula
1 8oz can hearts of palm, diced
1 large cucumber, diced
1 onion, diced
1 small leek, sliced into rings
½ cup olive oil
3 tablespoons red wine vinegar
1 teaspoon salt
¼ teaspoon powdered sumac

Wash and tear the chicory, watercress and argula into bite-size pieces. Place in a large salad bowl. Add the hearts of palm, the cucumber and the onion and the leek. In a small mixing bowl, combine the ingredients for the salad dressing and mix well. Pour over the salad and toss.

Serves 6

Note: The edible sumac in the previous recipe can be found in Arab stores.

Beans with Turnips and Carrots

We cultivated several varieties of beans in Babylon. We especially prized the fava bean and the chickpea or garbanzo bean. Like the Chaldeans, another ancient Middle-Eastern civilization, we believed that one could be reincarnated as a bean in the next life.

1 cup dried garbanzo beans
½ cup skinned fava beans

10 cups water

2 tablespoons olive oil

1/3 cup minced cilantro

3 large turnips, peeled and diced

3 large carrots, peeled and diced

2 large onions, peeled and diced

1 large leek, sliced

1teaspoon salt

½ teaspoon ground cumin

In a large pot, place the beans and the water. Bring to a boil and skim. Then add the olive oil and the cilantro. Bring to a boil again. Reduce the heat and simmer covered for 1 ½ hour. Then add the diced vegetables, salt and cumin. Simmer for 35 minutes. Ladle into soup bowls.

Serves 6

Note: You can by skinned Fava beans at any Middle Eastern Store. I have literally ripped out my hair, trying to soak and skin them myself. Then I discovered that you could by them skinned, what a saving grace!

Grilled Duck with Pomegranate and Coriander

We loved fowl of all different kinds, but the duck was perhaps our favorite. We flavored it with many spices and sweeteners, like the pomegranate syrup in this recipe.

2 large duck breasts

½ cup pomegranate syrup

1 teaspoon salt

½ teaspoon ground coriander

1 tablespoon olive oil

½ cup minced cilantro

¼ cup minced mint

Preheat the broiler. Place the duck breasts on a rack with a pan below. In a small bowl, combine the rest of the ingredients, except for the cilantro and the mint. Brush the marinade on the duck and continue to baste with the sauce while grilling. Grill for 12 minutes. Remove from the oven. Cut the duck breasts in half. Sprinkle with the remaining marinade of minced cilantro and mint.

Serves 4-6

Grilled Fish with Garlic

While this recipe uses snapper, it would be more authentic with perch, a fish we used extensively in our cooking.

6 snapper fillets

6 large cloves garlic, minced

1 teaspoon ground ginger

1 teaspoon ground cumin

½ Teaspoon Sea salt

6 tablespoons olive oil

1 tablespoon minced cilantro

In a small bowl, combine the garlic, ginger, cumin, sea salt and olive oil. Blend well. Preheat the oven to broil and place the snapper fillets on a rack. Brush with the garlic mixture generously. Grill for 3 minutes on each side. Brush more marinade on the top. Transfer to serving plates and drizzle with the remaining marinade. Garnish with minced cilantro.

Serves 6

Onions Cooked with Cumin

Cumin was one of our flavoring agents, used in meat stews, fish and vegetable dishes, or sprinkled over bread.

6 large onions, peeled

3 tablespoons olive oil
1 teaspoon ground cumin
1 teaspoon salt
1 cup sour cream

Preheat the oven to 350°. Grease a large baking pan. Place the onions in first. Sprinkle with the olive oil, cumin and salt. Roast for 45 minutes to 1 hour, or until the onions are soft. Remove to a platter and spoon sour cream on top.
Serves 6

Honey Wine

We learned the art of grape growing from the Sumerians, who lived on the Tigress and Euphrates rivers. Since the wine we made was rather harsh, we preferred to drink it flavored with sweet spices and honey.

1 cup honey
1 bottle red wine
1 cinnamon stick
4 cardamon pods
3 large slices ginger root
¼ teaspoon anise seed

Place the entire ingredients in a saucepot and bring to a boil. Reduce the heat and simmer for 1 hour. Remove from the stove and cool. Strain and serve.
Serves 6

Molded Barley with Dates

Barley was one of our oldest grains. Archeologists have found evidence of the cultivation of barley at Jericho, where a six rowed barley strain has been found. The Date Palm was a sacred tree and was used as a model for decoration on our temples. We ate dates in all forms, fresh, dried and in syrup. We also made a date wine that was reserved for the royalty.

    4 cups cooked barley
    1 cup bulgur
    ½ cup butter, melted
    ½ cup honey
    1 cup pitted dates, chopped
    1 tablespoon pomegranate syrup

Preheat the oven to 350°F. Butter a large springform pan. Mix the barley and bulgur together in a bowl with the melted butter. Add the honey, dates and pomegranate syrup. Mix well. Pat into the spring form pan. Bake for 45 minutes. Remove from the pan and serve.
    Serves 6

            *   *   *

Helen of Troy

Circa 2500 BC, Queen of Sparta

I, Helen of Troy was not allowed to eat at my wedding feast to Menelaus the King of Sparta. For even though I was one of the most beautiful and powerful females in the world, I was not given reprieve from the laws that forbade a woman to eat with men. We the Greeks began the practice of gourmet food preparation, combining many ingredients and elaborate recipes to produce a more sophisticated culinary style. In this new era of culinary richness, we created great sauces, delicate custards, and sumptuous vegetable and egg dishes. As the daughter to the Gods Zeus and his human mistress Leda, my immortal table assumed Olympian heights. Yet since I was forbade to attend, I can only speculate about the food presented to the men on that day. Upon arrival at my wedding feast, each man was given a silver-drinking cup as a memento of the festivities. Then flat loaves of bread were served on bronze plates, upon which each guest could heap duck, chickens and pigeons. A second course of meat was served that included hares, baby goats and partridges, followed by a large pork roast or whole roasted baby lamb. Next a course of seafood was served, and finally a course of greens, fruits, nuts, cakes and sweetmeats.

This party lasted far into the night and even into the next day. The food left unconsumed by the men was given to the dogs that clustered around the table. During the presentation of these different courses of food, slave girls provided singing and dancing. Poetry and great heroic tales were also told. The next day Menelaus, my husband-to-be, could barely take his place at the temple for the marriage ceremony.

*   *   *

Helen's Wedding Feast

Olives
Radishes served with the tops left on
Feta Cheese
Pita Bread
Honeyed Shrimp
Chicken Stuffed with Olives
Cabbage Athenian Way
Leg of Lamb with Dates
Eggs with Herbs and Pine Nuts
Pancakes with Honey and Sesame Seeds
Alexanderian Sweets
Fresh Fruit in Spiced Syrup
Greek Cream Cheese Wedding Cake

*   *   *

Honey Glazed Shrimp

We learned the practice of bee-keeping from Egypt, after her conquest at the hands of Alexander the Great.

    1 pound medium sized shrimp peeled and deveined
    2 tablespoons olive oil
    2 tablespoons red wine
    1 tablespoon honey
    2 teaspoons fresh minced oregano
    1 teaspoon black pepper
    Lettuce leaves

Heat the olive oil, red wine and honey in a saucepan. Add the shrimp and sauté for 3 minutes or until cooked. Remove the shrimp from the pan. Add the oregano and black pepper. Cook for 2 minutes. Remove the sauce from the pan, pour over the shrimp and toss. Serve the shrimp in a large bowl lined with lettuce leaves.

Serves 4

Chicken Stuffed with Olives

Our wealth was founded on the production of olive oil. We imported it to many other countries. The best of our olive oil was produced on the island of Crete.

    1 chicken (3 pounds)
    1 cup kalamata olives, pitted and diced
    ½ cup minced cilantro,
    1 large onion, minced
    1 teaspoon black pepper, ground coarsely
    2 cups red wine

Preheat the oven to 350°F. Mix the olives, onion, and black pepper together in a small bowl. Then stuff the chicken with the mixture. Place in a roasting pan, and cover with the red wine. Bake for 1 ½ to 2 hours.

Remove from the oven and carve. On each plate place a piece of chicken, some stuffing, and spoon some of the pan juices over the top.

Serves 4-6

Athenian Cabbage

There is a Greek legend that associates the origin of the cabbage with the God Dionysos. When Dionysos was traveling around Greece converting people to his religion, he encountered resistance by King Lycurgus of Thrace. The king easily captured Dionysos intoxicated army composed of Maenads and Satyrs. Dionysos was forced to flee to the cave of Thetis. When Zeus found out about the treatment of his son Dionysos, he made Lycurgus go mad and he cut up his own son. Upon discovering what he had done, he cried and his tears turned to cabbages. Thereafter we ate cabbages as a cure for drunkenness.

> 1 small cabbage, cored and shredded
> ½ cup honey
> 4 tablespoons red wine vinegar
> 1 tablespoon minced cilantro
> 1 tablespoon minced parsley
> 1 tablespoon minced mint
> 1 teaspoon salt
> ½ teaspoon pepper

Make the honey vinegar first. Melt the honey in a saucepan and add the vinegar. Stir for about 1 minute. Remove from the heat and place in a small jar. In a bowl, combine the cabbage, cilantro, parsley, mint and the salt and pepper. Toss well. Then add 3 tablespoons of the honey vinegar. Toss again. Serve immediately.

Serves 6

Leg of Lamb with Dates

Lamb was the meat of choice for us and still is today. It is cooked the same way now as it was in ancient times, roasted over a spit whole, or made into stews.

> 4 cups milk
> ½ cup honey
> 1 teaspoon rosemary
> 3 tablespoons olive oil
> 1 (4-5 pounds) leg of lamb

Sauce:

> 2 tablespoons honey

1 ½ cups red wine

1 tablespoon Thai Fish Sauce*

2 tablespoons minced parsley

1 tablespoon minced lovage

1 cup dates, pitted

In a large bowl, combine the leg of lamb with the honey, milk, one tablespoon of the olive oil and rosemary. Let it marinate for 24 hours in the refrigerator. Preheat the oven to 350°F. Remove the lamb from the marinade and place it in a large roasting pan. Sprinkle with the remaining two tablespoons of olive oil. Roast until the leg of lamb is done, thoroughly cooked but still somewhat pink.

Sauce:

Chop the dates, and soak in the red wine overnight. The next day, place the dates, red wine, fish-sauce, parsley, lovage and honey in the food processor. Process until smooth. Serve on the side with the leg of lamb.

Serves 6-8

*Note: Nam Pla or Nuoc Mam, Thai fish sauces, are the closest products we have to the Garum that was used by both the Greeks and Romans as a substitute for salt. You can find them Asian Grocery stores.

Eggs with Pine Nuts and Herbs

Eggs were sacred to us, for they represented the cosmic egg of birth that began the world of the Gods and Goddesses. Lovage is a slightly sweet tasting herb that was used by the Greeks and Romans lavishly as a seasoning.

6 hard cooked eggs

1 cup pine nuts

3 tablespoons olive oil

2 tablespoons minced cilantro

2 tablespoons minced parsley

3 tablespoons minced lovage

1 tablespoon minced mint

1 teaspoon cracked black pepper

2 teaspoons salt

2 cucumbers, peeled and sliced

2 green onions, diced

In the food processor, combine the pine nuts and the olive oil. Process until smooth, then add the herbs, black pepper and salt. Process until smooth. Cut each egg in half and place on a plate. Place a dollop of the pine nut sauce on top of each half. Garnish with cucumber slices and the diced green onions.

Serves 4

Pancakes with Honey, Sesame Seeds and Fresh Figs

Pancakes were another one of our favorite dishes. We sometimes flavored them with cheese, but usually we served them as a dessert, with honey and sesame seeds or sweetened wine and figs.

1 cup all-purpose flour

1 cup milk

1 cup honey

2 tablespoons vegetable oil

3 tablespoons sesame seeds, toasted

4 fresh figs, diced

Mix the flour and milk with 2 tablespoons of the honey. Whisk till smooth batter forms. Heat 2 tablespoons vegetable oil in a frying pan. Pour a quarter of the mixture into the pan. When it sets and bubbles have formed, turn it. Remove from the frying pan, and spread with honey and sesame seeds. Make 3 more pancakes the same way, spreading each with the honey, sesame seeds, and the fresh figs. Then stack them together. Remove to a platter and cut into four pieces.

Serves 4

Alexanderian Sweets

One of our favorite nuts was the hazelnut. We used them in cakes, sauces and candies. This candy is similar to the peanut brittle of today.

1-cup sesame seeds
1 cup hazelnuts, whole
1 cup honey

Toast the sesame seeds and hazelnuts until browned. Remove from the heat and cool. Heat the honey in a saucepan until it foams. Add the sesame seeds and the hazelnuts. Cook for 3 minutes. Remove from the heat and pour into a greased pan. Let it cool until touchable. Roll 1 tablespoon of the honey mixture into a ball, and place on a plate. Let cool.

Serves 16 candies

Fresh Fruit in Spiced Syrup

Fruits were very popular at all meals in ancient Greece. Figs were especially valued and for a time, their export from Greece was banned in the hope that the excellent fig trees of Attica could be preserved.

4 cups apples, peeled, cored and diced
2 cup fresh figs, quartered
1-cup pomegranate seeds
2 cups plums, pitted and quartered
2 cups white wine

3/4 cup honey

1 teaspoon cinnamon

1 teaspoon pepper

In a small saucepan, bring the white wine and honey to a boil. Boil for 2 minutes. Remove from the heat and stir in the cinnamon and the pepper. Place the fruit in a bowl and cover with the syrup. Toss well to coat. Chill until ready to serve.

Serves 6-8

Greek Wedding Cake

To truly make this cake authentic, you would shape it like a female breast, symbolizing the fertility of woman. In Greece, different cakes were made for various religious events to symbolize the different powers of the God's and Goddesses. At a wedding ceremony such as mine, this cake would have been shaped like a woman's vagina, to ensure the couple would have many children.

32 oz cream cheese

2 cups flour

4 eggs

½ cup of honey, melted

1 cup diced dried dates

1 cup diced dried figs

1 teaspoon cinnamon

½ teaspoon coarsely ground black pepper

Preheat the oven to 350°F. In a bowl, combine the cream cheese with the eggs, one at a time, beating after each addition. Sift the flour with the cinnamon and black pepper and add the mixture to the cream cheese and eggs, alternating with the melted honey. Mix in the dried dates, and figs. Remove from the bowl and pour into a greased springform pan. Bake for 45 minutes, or until the top is golden brown. Remove from the oven and cool.

Serves 6-8

*   *   *

Cleopatra

69-30 BC, Queen of Egypt

In the year 325 BC, the armies of Alexander the Great rolled victorious across Egypt, starting 300 years of Ptolemic dynasties. As a descendant of the commanders of the conquering army, my lineage was more Greek than Egyptian. When my father, Pharaoh Ptolemy Auletes died, he named my brother Ptolemy XIII and I co-regents of Egypt. I was forced, according to Egyptian law, to marry my brother in order to rule. I soon dropped his name from any official documents, and had coins minted with my own name and picture. I was a woman who believed Egypt would again be a great nation, but only under my sole supervision. By 48 BC, my brother and many of the court officials were unhappy with the way I governed. They conspired to overthrow me, and I was forced to flee Egypt for many years, while my brother served as the sole ruler, under the protectorate of Rome. When the Roman General Pompey was murdered at Alexandria for conspiring with my brother to assume independent control of Egypt, I knew that it was time to act. I had myself hidden in a rug and delivered to the Emperor of Rome, Caesar. I hoped to convince him that I would make a stronger ruler than my incompetent brother Ptolemy. Caesar soon agreed to ally himself with me against my brothers weakening reign. During the ensuing Alexanderian War, my brother was drowned in the Nile while trying to escape attack and I became the sole ruler of Egypt. I again had to marry another surviving brother, Ptolemy XIV, who I later had killed. Caesar and I became lovers and I bore him a son Caesarion. Caesar went back to Rome and then sent for me. I went to live in Caesar's house. He planned to marry me and make Caesarion his heir. However, he was murdered and I was forced to flee for my life, returning to Egypt from Rome.

In 41BC, Mark Anthony, a general of Caesar's successor Emperor Octavian, invited me to Tarsus. I knew I must do something to capture his attention and thereby insure Egypt's future under my rule, so I sailed down the Nile in a large boat, with silver oars and purple sails, dressed as Aphrodite the Goddess of love. So began one of the greatest love affairs of all time as Mark Anthony and I assumed leadership of Egypt.

There is much to tell of the feast I prepared for Mark Anthony at Tarsus. The other great female Pharaoh, Hatchepsut, would have been amazed at the sheer volume of food we had available for this feast. Egyptian food at this time had many subtle influences from the cuisines of Greece and Rome. Dinner was served on the boat, in elaborate surroundings. Gold and silver dishes had replaced the more common clay plates of the earlier dynasties. Servant girls danced and sang throughout the dinner, which included as many as 100 dishes. Some of the food served included mussels, oysters, venison, lobsters, and capons cooked in spicy sauces. Next came piglets stuffed with quails, and whole roasted peacocks and woodcocks, and a never-ending procession of breads, cakes, salads, fruits, and cheeses. Marc Anthony was impressed by the fastidiousness of our nature, for we washed our hands continuously during the meal, with towels and perfumed water. Wine and beer were served, although by the time of my rule, wine had become the major beverage of the upper classes, for we had perfected the art of winemaking. Bread had also become more refined, as we discovered we could make it lighter with the addition of yeast. This discovery came accidentally when we learned the yeast used in beer making could also be used for raising dough. Cakes were also more elaborate than earlier dynasties and we copied the more sophisticated techniques of the Greeks. With such extravagant tastes, I beguiled Marc Anthony, as the thought of a woman of royal blood becoming his lover appealed to him. The history of the world swung in the balance of this most anticipated gathering.

*   *   *

Feast for Marc Anthony

Pike or Salmon with Sour Cream
Duck Breasts with Hazelnuts`*
Tuna with Mint and Cilantro sauce*
Barley, Beef and Fava Bean Potage
Cucumber Salad with Olives
Red Chard and Watercress, baked with Goat Cheese
Stewed Leeks and Celery*
Millet with Mint and Almonds
Dates stuffed with Honey and Sesame Seeds
Grape Cake*

* Note: Some of the recipes have been adapted from Apicius's Cookery and Dining in imperial Rome.

*   *   *

Pike or Salmon with Sour Cream

There was an abundance of fish available from the Nile and the waters of the Mediterranean Sea, but pike, perch and red mullet were the most common fishes that we ate.

1 (2 pound) salmon fillet

1 teaspoon salt

1 teaspoon ground cumin

4 tablespoons minced cilantro

1 ½ cups sour cream

Preheat the oven to 350°F. Grease a baking dish with olive oil. Place the salmon in the baking dish and sprinkle with salt. In a bowl, combine the cumin, cilantro and sour cream. Spread on top of the salmon. Bake for 30 minutes, or until the salmon is just cooked through. Transfer to serving plates and sprinkle with more cilantro.

Serves 6-8

Duck Breasts Roasted with Hazelnuts*

As Egyptians, duck was one of our favorite fowl. Egypt was fortunate to be located in the middle of the migratory patterns of birds, and was thereby assured an ample supply for our tables. On our tombs we painted many scenes of our Pharaohs and other wealthy Egyptians hunting ducks and other waterfowl.

2 large duck breasts

¼ cup olive oil

1 teaspoon ground coriander

1 teaspoon dried dill

1 cup hazelnuts

¼ cup minced mint

½ cup red wine

¼ teaspoon saffron, dissolved in water

Roast the hazelnuts, and chop finely. In a saucepan, heat the olive oil and add the coriander, dill, hazelnuts, mint, red wine and saffron. Cook for 10 minutes. Grease a large baking pan with olive oil. Preheat

the oven to 350°F. Place the duck breasts in the baking pan and cover with the sauce. Bake for 35-45 minutes, or until the duck breasts are just done. Transfer to a serving dish, and spoon the sauce over the top.
Serves 4-6

Tuna with Mint and Cilantro Sauce*

Tuna from the Mediterranean appeared in many of the meals during my reign. We began to create sauces similar in their complexity and subtlety to those of the Romans.

1-cup mint leaves
¼ teaspoon salt
1 teaspoon black pepper
3 tablespoons minced cilantro
1 /2 large onion, minced
1 tablespoon olive oil
4 large tuna steaks, about 1 inch thick

Place all the ingredients, except for the tuna, in a food processor and coarsely chop. Remove from the food processor and let stand at least 1 hour, long enough for the flavors to mingle. Brush the tuna steaks with olive oil. Broil for 4 minutes on each side until the fish is just done. Transfer to serving plates and spoon some of the sauce on top.
Serves 4

Barley, Beef and Fava Bean Potage,

Barley still continued to be a commonly used grain in most of our stews. We combined it with meat and beans such as the fava.

2 tablespoons olive oil
1 onion, chopped

1 pound beef stew meat, diced in 1 inch cubes

1 cup fava beans, skinned

½ cup pearl barley

6 cups water

1 bay leaf

One head garlic, peeled

Cilantro

Heat the olive oil in a large saucepan. Add the onions, and sauté until limp. Then add the beef stew meat. Sauté until browned. Add the fava beans, water, bay leaf and garlic. Bring to a boil and skim. Reduce the heat and cover. Simmer for 1 hour. Then add the pearl barley and simmer for another hour. Serve in soup bowls, garnished with minced cilantro.

Serves 6

Cucumber Salad with Olives

Cucumbers were one of our favorite vegetables. We loved the way that any number of herbs and spices could enhance their bland flavor.

2 large cucumbers, peeled, seeded and diced

2 tablespoons minced cilantro

2 tablespoons minced mint

1 cup kalamata olives, pitted and diced

½ cup olive oil

¼ cup red wine vinegar

1 teaspoon salt

Place the cucumbers in a salad bowl and toss with the herbs. Add the kalamata olives and toss again. In a bowl, combine the olive oil, red wine vinegar, and the salt. Whisk. Pour into the salad and toss. Serve immediately.

Serves 4-6

Red Chard and Watercress Baked with Goat Cheese

Vegetables like this chard dish would be baked in a clay pot embedded in the embers of a fire. Goat, and sheep cheese were valued highly for their sharp acidic taste.

1 large bunch red chard, stems removed
2 bunches watercress, cleaned and torn
3 garlic cloves, minced
½ cup olive oil
1 teaspoon ground cumin
1 teaspoon salt
3-oz Chevre cut into rounds

Preheat the oven to 350°F. Grease a baking dish. Shred the chard. In a bowl, combine the chard, watercress, olive oil, garlic, ground cumin and salt. Toss to coat. Transfer to the baking dish. Cover with the goat cheese rounds. Bake for 30 minutes. Transfer to serving plates.
Serves 4

Stewed Leeks and Celery*

Vegetables began to be flavored with black pepper, introduced to us by the Romans, who used it generously in many of their recipes.

1 bunch leeks
1 bunch celery
1 cup vegetable broth
1 cup white wine
1 teaspoon black pepper
1 tablespoon honey

Clean and wash the leeks thoroughly. Trim the leeks and split them in half. Trim and clean the celery, removing the strings. Cut into 3-inch lengths. In a large saucepan, heat the vegetable broth, white wine and honey. Add the vegetables and bring to a boil. Sprinkle with the pepper. Reduce the heat and cover with a lid. Simmer until the vegetables are soft. Transfer to a serving dish.

Serves 4

Millet with Almonds and Mint

Millet was considered by the Hebrews as a poor grain not fit for human consumption unless out of necessity. However, during my reign it became an important part of a meal. We liked to cook millet with nuts, broth and herbs. They made a very savory porridge.

1 cup millet
2 ½ cups beef broth
¼ cup minced mint
2 tablespoons olive oil
1 cup slivered almonds
1 teaspoon garlic, minced

In a large saucepot, bring the beef broth to a boil. Add the millet and bring to a boil. Reduce the heat and cook until the millet is done. In a saucepan, heat the olive oil and add the mint leaves, garlic and almonds. Sauté for several minutes or until the almonds are golden. Spoon some millet on each serving plate, and top with the sautéed almonds.

Makes 4 servings

Dates Stuffed with Honey and Sesame Seeds

The date still continued to be one of our most important foods. We especially liked them as a sweetmeat. We stuffed them with honey and sesame seeds. Honey was such a necessary part of our diet, that we placed large quantities in our tombs, as an offering to the God Min.

20 large dates, pitted
1 cup honey
1-cup sesame seeds

Toast the sesame seeds. Bring the honey to a boil and cook until it foams. Then add the sesame seeds and turn off the heat. Let cool. Fill each date with one tablespoon of the honey mixture. Place on a serving plate and garnish with mint leaves.
Makes 20 dates

Grape Cake*

We first imported wine from the Babylonians and the Sumerians. But later we became adept at cultivating our own strains of grapes. We also began the process of refining our wines by learning to age them. We also ate both fresh and dried grapes as a dessert fruit.

2 eggs beaten
½ cup honey
1 ½ cups whole-wheat flour
1 teaspoon baking powder
1 cup sour cream
3 tablespoons butter
1 ½ cups whole grapes, halved

Preheat the oven to 350°F. Using one-tablespoon of the butter, grease a large springform pan. In a bowl, beat together the eggs and the honey and then stir in ¾ cup of the wheat flour. Then mix the baking soda with the sour cream and add to the egg mixture. Mix in well and add the rest of the flour. Spread in the springform pan and then lay the grapes halved side down on top of the cake. Bake for 1 hour or until the cake is browned.

Serves 10

*   *   *

Messalina

20-48 AD, Wife of the Emperor Claudius

I was the great Granddaughter of Octavia. I caught the eye of Claudius, the Emperor of Rome, and he married me in 39AD. Claudius was so in love with me, that he overlooked all of my indiscretions. I fulfilled my duty and gave him two children, Britannicus and Octavia. Bored with Claudius, I turned to taking many men as lovers until I met Gaius Silius, who became my great infatuation. While Claudius led his armies through the British Isles, Gaius convinced me to marry him and rise him to a position of power in Rome. When Claudius found out, it devastated him, and he ordered my execution. I have no regrets about the way I lived nor of the parties I threw while he was gone. These dinners set the stage for my more amorous adventures later on in the evening. I loved to eat a good meal and my sexual appetites were equally undiminished.

Dinner was a grand affair during my time in Rome, as Roman food had become very lavish. For example, a clutch of birds such as larks, were sewn inside a boar, then sewn inside a cow and finally cooked. Sauces were the mainstay of Roman food and composed of many ingredients. Fruits were served in stews with meat, and in omelets for dessert. Wine was aged for two or three years, and was sealed in jars with plaster instead of the pine pitch used by the Greeks.

We ate on beds reclining around low tables, and were provided with water and napkins with which to clean ourselves during the many courses. It was proper etiquette to eat only small amounts of each dish.

While it has been said that we were gluttons, dinner was the only meal, which contained many courses. Breakfast and lunch were composed of lighter food, such as wine and bread for breakfast and a small snack for lunch.

Meals were now easier to cook, since we had invented the kitchen. Previously, food was cooked in an open courtyard. The poor also ate better than before, having a large assortment of foodstuffs available to them. The working class did not have new kitchens, as did the wealthy, so they ate their major meal at a cookshop. They could also take advantage of the many street vendors who sold snacks all day long, including roasted fava beans.

I had many wonderful dinners before cavorting with my various lovers, and while I was a very promiscuous woman, I relieved myself of the tedium that comprised the lives of most Roman women. While we did have greater freedom than our Greek counterparts, we were still pawns for the ambitions of men, and it was only a very cunning woman who could obtain and retain a position of power.

*   *   *

The Roman Prandium
Cheese Round with Herbs *
Olive Paste*
Bread
Fish in Coriander Paste*
Lobster Patties*
Seasoned Oysters*
Chicken Stuffed with Sausage*
Asparagus Patina*
Broccoli in Anchovy Sauce
Artichokes with Herbs*
Farina Pudding*

Honey Custard*

*Note: Recipes with the * have been adapted from "Apicius Cookery and Dining in Imperial Rome":

*   *   *

Cheese Round with Herbs *

With this recipe I will introduce you to Garum, a fermented fish sauce we used on everything. Garum was made by fermenting fish in casks with herbs and salt, and then draining off the liquid to be used as a seasoning. Special areas of the city were put aside for the making of Garum, as the smell was so terrible. Garum was considered to be one of the great gastronomic passions of Rome and could command fantastic prices, such that the prices of caviar and truffles today look like nothing in comparison.

2 cups ricotta
1 tablespoon honey
1-tablespoon Thai Fish sauce
2 tablespoons minced cilantro
1 tablespoon minced parsley
1 teaspoon fennel seed
1-tablespoon minced mint
1 tablespoon minced Chervil
Olive oil

Grease a 9-inch, round baking dish. Preheat the oven to 350°F., and in a food processor combine all the ingredients except for the olive oil. Pour into the baking dish and bake for 35 minutes. Remove from the oven and pile into a serving dish. Drizzle with olive oil and sprinkle with the minced chervil. Serve with flat bread.

Serves 4-6

Olive Paste*

The Romans learned the art of olive growing from the Greeks. By the time I was born we had extensive olive groves of our own. Like our neighbors the Greeks, olives became a passion. This olive paste recipe is the forerunner of the French Tapanade, the modern day olive paste, highly popular in France.

2 cups kalamata olives, pitted
1-teaspoon Thai fish sauce
½ cup parsley
¼ cup mint
1 teaspoon cumin seed
1 teaspoon fennel seed
¼ cup olive oil

Combine all the ingredients in a food processor and process until coarsely chopped. Serve with bread.

Serves 6-8

Fish in Coriander Paste*

We the Romans loved fish. For this reason there was considerable trade during the Roman Empire of young fish used to stock the various ponds in which they were held. Different types of fish prevalent during this time include anchovies, mackerel, snapper, sole, tuna, sea bream, monkfish and halibut.

1 large snapper, (about 3 pounds) boned with the head left intact

1 tablespoon coriander seed
2 small garlic cloves, minced
1-teaspoon Thai fish sauce
1 teaspoon ground cumin
1 bunch parsley
4 tablespoons olive oil
2 tablespoons minced parsley

Preheat the oven to 350°F. In a food processor, combine all ingredients except one tablespoon of the olive oil. Grease a large baking dish with the remaining olive oil. Spread the paste on top of the fish. Bake in the oven for 25 minutes or until the fish is opaque. Remove from the oven and serve on a platter, garnished with minced parsley.
Serves 6

Lobster Patties*

Shellfish, especially the lobster, was an everyday food for the wealthy. Most of the time lobster meat was cooked in delicate patties or rissoles and patinas combined with eggs.

2 pounds cooked lobster meat
1-tablespoon Thai fish sauce
2 large eggs
½ cup breadcrumbs
1 tablespoon minced mint
1 teaspoon pepper
5 tablespoons olive oil

Dice the lobster meat into very small pieces. Place in a bowl with the remainder of the ingredients except for the olive oil. Mix well. Heat the olive oil until very hot. With your hands, form 8 patties with the mixture and fry until golden brown on both sides.

Serves 4-6

Seasoned Oysters*

Before we learned how to cultivate the oyster, we imported them from Great Britain. These oysters were not eaten fresh, but were salted and cured. This recipe is adapted from the cookbook of the great Roman host Apicius, who cooked for the upper crust of Roman society. Sadly, when he found he could no longer afford to put on his dinners, he poisoned himself.

Two jars (8oz each) oysters and their liquid

1 teaspoon pepper

2 tablespoons minced lovage

1 tablespoon minced mint

2 tablespoons minced parsley

1 teaspoon Thai fish sauce

3 cups fish broth

4 egg yolks beaten

1 tablespoon olive oil

Strain the oysters from their liquid and set aside. Pour the oyster liquid, pepper, lovage, mint, parsley, Thai fish sauce and broth into a large pot. Bring to a boil and then reduce the heat and cover. Simmer for 30 minutes. In a separate bowl, beat the egg yolks and the oil together. Pour ½ cup of broth into the eggs, whisking slowly and then pour the eggs into the pot with the rest of the broth. Whisk, until the egg yolks are amalgamated into the soup. Add the oysters and simmer for 5 minutes, or until the edges of the oysters begins to curl. Serve in soup bowls with a sprinkling of minced mint and parsley.

Serves 4

Chicken Stuffed with Sausage*

This elaborate chicken dish containing many herbs, sausage and other exotic ingredients, is indicative of the love affair between Romans and chicken meat. Delicious and easy to prepare, chicken became our most prized type of fowl.

1 (4 pound) chicken
1 bunch parsley
1 bunch lemon balm
1 bunch mint
1 bunch dill
4 small leeks, trimmed
2 pounds pork sausage
1 teaspoon cumin seed
1 teaspoon ground coriander
1 teaspoon salt or Thai fish sauce
2 tablespoons olive oil
1 tablespoon sweet sherry

In a bowl, combine the sausage, cumin and coriander. Mix well. Stuff the chicken with the mixture. Brown the chicken in the oil. Transfer to a large baking dish. Add the combination of herbs to the pan. Along with the leeks and the salt or Thai fish sauce. Add one cup of water to the pot. Cover and bake in the oven for 1-½ hours or until the chicken is tender and the juices run clear when the thigh is pierced with a fork. Remove the chicken from the pan and keep warm. Skim the fat off the pan, and remove the contents of the pan to a food processor. Puree, and add the sherry. Pour into a sauceboat. Carve the chicken and serve with the stuffing and drizzled with the sauce.

Serves 6

Asparagus Patina*

We Romans were the first to domesticate the wild asparagus, which also appears in great many recipes by Apicus.. A patina is a forerunner to the modern day omelette and was a great favorite.

2 pounds asparagus spears, trimmed
5 jumbo eggs
1 tablespoon Parmesan cheese, grated
3 tablespoons minced parsley
1 teaspoon salt
1 teaspoon pepper
3 tablespoons olive oil

Cut the asparagus into bite size pieces. Sauté in a skillet with two tablespoons of the oil for 3 minutes, or until tender, but still bright green. While the asparagus is cooking, beat the eggs in a bowl until foamy, and then add the rest of the ingredients, except for the oil. Beat well. When the asparagus is tender, pour the rest of the olive oil into the pan and spread the asparagus evenly around the bottom. Pour the egg mixture into the pan. Reduce the heat and cover with a lid. Cook over very low heat, until the mixture is set. Remove from the heat and cut into wedges.
Serves 6

Broccoli in Anchovy Sauce

Broccoli was another favorite vegetable of ours. Although in the beginning only the leaves were eaten, this recipe, with its flavorings of anchovy, cumin and pepper, illustrates the love of salty and spicy food that is the mainstay of ancient Roman cookery.

1 pound broccoli, trimmed and broken in florets
1 cup red wine

½ cup olive oil

2 teaspoons ground cumin

1 teaspoon anchovy paste

1 teaspoon black pepper

Steam the Broccoli until just crisp and tender. In a small bowl, combine the rest of the ingredients and whisk. Drain the broccoli and transfer to a serving bowl. Toss with the sauce.

Serves 6

Artichokes Braised with Herbs*

Because we had developed the kitchen with its large fireplaces, we could now braise dishes, by cooking them in large cauldrons. The artichoke and its fellow thistles were perfect for the technique of braising, which we pioneered.

6 large globe artichokes

1 tablespoon minced lovage

1 tablespoon minced mint

3 tablespoons minced cilantro

1 tablespoon fennel seed

1 teaspoon Thai fish sauce

1 cup water

3 cups red wine

Trim the artichokes and place in a large kettle. Sprinkle with the herbs and the fish sauce. Cover with the water and the wine. Bring to a boil and then reduce the heat. Cover the pot, and simmer until tender. Remove the artichokes from the pot and keep warm. Bring the cooking liquid to a boil, and then reduce to one half. Serve the artichokes, with some of the sauce over the top of each.

Serves 6

Farina Pudding*

Puddings like this farina comprised a good part of our desserts. Spelt and or Farina were the major grains we cultivated.

> 1 cup farina
> Boiling water
> 1 cup slivered almonds that have been sautéed in olive oil
> 1 cup raisins
> ½ cup pine nuts
> ½ cup sweet sherry
> ¼ cup honey

Cover the farina with the boiling water and cook until thick. Add the rest of the ingredients, except for the sherry and honey and the ¼ cup slivered almonds. Mix well and pour into a serving bowl. Sprinkle with the rest of the slivered almonds. Mix the honey and sherry together and pour over the top.
Serves 6

Honey Custard*

Honey remained the major flavoring for us as it had been for the Greeks and the Egyptians. We used it in such delicate recipes as this egg custard, flavored by that truly unique Roman addition, black pepper.

> 8 large eggs
> 4 cups milk
> ½ cup honey, melted
> 1 teaspoon black pepper

In a large mixing bowl, combine the milk, eggs, and the honey. Beat well. Pour into 9-inch pie tin, and sprinkle with the black pepper. Place the pie tin into a larger pan filled half way with water. Place in the oven and bake at 350°F. for 40 minutes.

Cut into squares and serve.

Serves 6

*　　　　　*　　　　　*

Chapter 2

Matilda of Flanders

1028-1083, Wife of William the Conqueror and Queen of England

Although I became the queen of England, I was originally born into the House of Baldwin, the royalty of Flanders, in the area now known as Belgium and the Netherlands. Destined to marry someone rich and powerful of royal European lineage, I was initially unimpressed with the courting antics of William of Normandy, the son of the Duke of Normandy who was considered a bastard because of his peasant mother. Although he had been promised the English throne by Edward the Confessor, Saxon King of England, I initially doubted William's stock and potential. But when William sought to strengthen the political ties between Flanders and Normandy and came to the court at Flanders to press his suit for my hand, my father and I soon relented. We were married in 1053 and waited to assume William's claim to the Saxon controlled English throne. However, as Edward the Confessor lay dying, he changed his mind and named his Saxon brother in law as heir to the throne. William set out to reestablish his Norman claim to the throne of England. By 1067, after the battle of Hastings, England had been subdued enough for William to securely crown me queen of his kingdom. During my marriage to William, I gave him ten children, which was no easy feat. We were constantly traveling with his troops from one battle to another, and I was very small for a woman, only 4 foot 2 inches.

In the centuries leading up to our reign, known as the Dark Ages, (500 AD-1066 AD), cultivated food was very hard to find, let alone cook. The destruction of the Roman villas by the Gauls in 500 AD led to a complete collapse in social customs and trade routes in the British Isles. Cooking regressed back to the open hearth, and consisted of whatever one could catch. Ordinary people only ate meat on special occasions, and survived on fish, grain, and wild roots found within a ten-mile radius of their village. The single ray of light on the culinary scene in Europe during the Dark Ages came as the result of the reign of Charlemagne (742 AD-814 AD). The first educated king of the Franks, he modernized the distribution of foodstuffs and resources. This brought great changes to the European dinner table, as well as the world. He ordered the gardens both at his palace and the monastery of St. Gall planted with lettuces, cresses, endive, parsley, chervil, carrots, leeks, turnips, onion and garlic. During our reign in the Eleventh Century, the French and Italians had begun to eat foods of a more healthy variety, including vegetables. However, we the British still lagged far behind the rest of Europe in the diversification of our diet.

Dinner in Anglo-Saxon England was monotonous to say the least. Cooking was done over log fires with spits and cauldrons, especially when I ventured out on campaigns with my husband. Since forks had not yet been invented, we ate with spoons and wooden bowls. The more refined food of the medieval period was yet to come. Dinner on the road was comprised of what could be caught or taken from neighboring farms and woods. After the Romans left England in 410 AD, the carrots, turnips, and onions they introduced to us as vegetable crops remained. Also we used both wild and cultivated herbs, along with nuts, pears, grapes, and apples.

The dinner given below would have been served to us in a great tent, set with a trestle table, sheepskin rugs, and wool blankets to ward off the cold. We would have eaten with our hands and spoons, dipping hunks of bread into the sauces from the cooked stew, eating the fish right off the stick and drinking the soup with our spoons of bone. William would have regaled his fellow lords with stories of past battles, while I nestled in the warmth of animal skins, basking in the glory of his love.

*   *   *

The Camp Dinner

Barley and Nettle Broth
Rabbit Stew
Cheese
Birds Roasted with Bacon
Red Currant Pudding
Apple Crumble

*   *   *

Barley and Nettle Broth

Vegetables were scarce in Anglo-Saxon England. Sometimes, to supplement a diet deficient in greens, we would send our cooks to forage for nettles as an addition to our soups and stews.

Six cups water
2 medium leeks, finely chopped

2 cups nettle tops, finely chopped

1 sprig of parsley

3 sprigs of lovage leaves

1 ½ teaspoon peppercorns

1 teaspoon sea salt

½ cup barley

In a large soup pot, combine all the ingredients, except for the barley. Bring to a boil and reduce the heat. Simmer covered, for 2 hours. Then add the barley and simmer for 1 hour. Ladle into soup bowls.

Serves 6

Rabbit Stew

Rabbits were found in abundance in Anglo-Saxon England, and provided a main source of meat. Cattle were reserved for milk and their hides.

3 tablespoons butter

1 (3 pound) rabbit, disjointed

1 pound leeks, washed, trimmed and sliced

1 small head cabbage, cored and chopped

3 ¾ cups water

3 tablespoons red wine vinegar

2 bay leaves

2 tablespoons minced parsley

Heat the butter in a large soup pot and add the rabbit. Brown on all sides. Add the rest of the ingredients and bring to a boil. Reduce the heat and cover. Simmer for 1-½ hours, or until the rabbit is tender. Ladle into soup bowls and serve.

Serves 6

Birds Roasted with Bacon

Small birds such as quail and guinea fowl constituted a large part our menu. When on campaign with William, the archers would shoot and snare many birds, providing us with one of our main courses. When at home in our castle, birds would be roasted on large spits in the fireplace of the great hall.

    6 small Cornish game hens or quail
    6 sprigs of parsley
    6 bay leaves
    6 slices of thick bacon

Preheat the oven to 375°F. Place the sprigs of parsley and the bay leaves on the Cornish game hens. Wrap with the bacon. Secure the bacon with toothpicks. Place in a large baking dish and roast in the oven for 1 ½ hours, or until the game hens are tender and cooked through.
    Serves 6

Barley and Red Currant Pudding

During the summer months, we were fortunate to make use of the berries that grew in abundance among the hedgerows. Mixed with barley and honey, they made sweet desserts.

    ½ cup barley
    3 cups red currants
    2 tablespoons honey
    2 cups water
    1 tablespoon fresh minced mint
    3 large eggs
    6 tablespoons red currant jelly
    Half and half

In a pot, combine the barley, red currants and water. Bring to a boil and cook for 30 minutes, then add the honey and cook for 10 more minutes, until the barley is mushy. Remove to a food processor and puree, while adding the eggs, mint and jelly. Butter a large pudding basin. Add the barley mixture and cover the top with greaseproof paper and tie firmly. Steam in a saucepan with water filling up the pan by two-thirds. Steam for 45-50 minutes. Remove from the pot and turn over on a serving plate. Cut into slices and serve with cream.

Serves 6

Apple Crumble

To make this dessert, a pot would have been sunk into the coals of a log fire and covered with a lid, with more coals heaped on top of the lid. Apples and other fruit trees grew all over Anglo-Saxon England, a legacy of the Romans, who brought apple seeds along during their colonization of pre-Saxon Britain.

2 ½ pounds apples, cored, peeled and sliced
1 cup honey
½ cup hazelnuts, coarsely chopped
½ cup coarse whole wheat breadcrumbs

Preheat the oven to 350°F. In a saucepan; cook the apple slices in 2 cups of water until soft, but still retaining their shape. Drain and place in a greased casserole dish. Drizzle with the honey. Cover with the nuts and breadcrumbs. Bake for 30 minutes, or until the top is crunchy.

Serves 6

*   *   *

Anne of Bohemia

1366-1394, Wife of Richard the II and Queen of England

The love of my life, King Richard the II of England, was only ten when he assumed the British throne. Pressure to establish intercontinental trade routes led him to petition for my hand in marriage, as an important union between the monarchies of Britain and Bohemia. But our marriage at the age of fifteen did not come cheap. My half-brother, Holy Roman Emperor Wenceslas, demanded a huge dowry of 10,000 marks in addition to paying for my trip to England. When Richard accepted, I traveled on a perilous sea journey in which several accompanying ships were lost. But when I finally landed on the shores of England and met the King, it was love at first sight. I was married in London, in 1382 at St. Stephen's Chapel. In the beginning, the English people had great resistance to my status as a foreign born Bohemian Queen, but I soon won the hearts of the populace with my constant intercessions on the peasant's behalf. This earned me the title, "Good Queen Anne"

Richard and I lived a charmed life, filled with extravagant food and drink at the Palace of Sheen. It is said that our annual expenditures for food and drink alone were 18,000 pounds, an astronomical sum in those days. Breakfast was an early meal taken alone in the bedroom, and dinner, which had generally been at 12 noon, evolved into a later affair during the time of my reign. The great banquets Richard and I gave started in the afternoon and lasted all night long. At one banquet Richard and I gave for 2000 guests, people ate 120 sheep's heads, 12 boars, 144 partridges, 720 hens, 11,000 eggs, and 200 rabbits. The cooks prepared 250 mortrewes (meat paste containing ale, spices, bread and eggs). People ate from trenchers, made of large slabs of stale bread, cut 4 inches thick. On these trenchers were piled various meats, fishes and vegetables. There were no individual drinking vessels, unless only a select few were dining. When a guest wanted a drink, the cupbearer was signaled. They arrived with cup-in-hand, waited until the guest was satisfied and then took the cup away, washing and drying it, then returning it to the cupboard. But these banquets also required security. A food taster sampled the food eaten by Richard and I, ensuring it was free of poison before we could indulge.

Richard and I always sat at a separate table, on an elevated dais. Those of lesser rank sat below us, in descending order, with the lowest required to be seated on the other side of the elaborate salt containers in the middle of the table. Soup was served in a bowl to be jointly shared between two people, who ate it with a common spoon. Hands were wiped on the tablecloth, of which there were at least four on each table. When one became soiled, it was removed and the table reset. By the 13th century, women had been allowed to sit at the same tables as their husbands, and Richard and I ate from the same bowl and drank from the same cup. Entertainment consisted of minstrels and court musicians who played and sang for us while we ate.

A regular dinner consisted of many courses, with the best food reserved for the king and his entourage. During this time, the first cookbook of England was created by the scribes of my husband, called *The Forme of Cury,* which described the very expensive dishes created for our enjoyment.

The most important ingredients for our meals were spices, which were pounded mashed and incorporated into exotic sauces, pies and sweetmeats. Spices imported from eastern countries included cardamon, cinnamon, cloves, coriander, ginger, mace, nutmeg and saffron. They were valued for both their medicinal and culinary purposes. Since we observed fasting days according to the calendar of the church, our cooks could devise as many as 20 different fish courses on those days. Birds such as peacock, heron and swan were added to the various fowl we ate. Vegetables were seldom eaten on their own, but were added to soups and stews for flavor. By the time our reign, the French habit of eating vegetables, combined with spices and herbs, had become more accepted. When the knights returned from the Fourth Crusade, in the early part of the 14th century, they hastened the spread of Arabic food products, such as sugar, and rice, as well as new types of fruit such as the lemon and the Damson plum from Damascus. Large sugar constructions of ships, churches, palaces, and people, often formed large centerpieces on the table. It was truly a time of intricate meals for the wealthy, while the poor survived on bread, cabbage, and an occasional piece of meat. Still, they fared better than their predecessors, for more fields were being plowed instead of lying fallow, new bread laws were instituted, and the use of medicinal herbs by the Monks and Apothecaries all added to a longer life span.

*   *   *

Dinner at the Palace of Sheen

Borage Potage
Brie Tart
Eggs in Red Wine
Mussels Stewed with Saffron
Hashed Leeks
Cabbage with Fennel and Apple
Roast Beef with Egerdouce Sauce
Haricot of Lamb
Chicken and Almond Mold
Frumenty of Wheat Berries
Pears in Spiced Wine
Blackberry Pudding
Caudle

Note: Some recipes in the previous sections dealing with the Medieval period, based on *"Two Fifteenth Century Cookbooks, and Meals through the Ages.*

*   *   *

Borage Potage

This soup of borage, spinach, and chard or dandelion greens would have appeared on our table during springtime or Lent. Borage was considered by our physicians to be an herb of exhilarating qualities. So when our senses had been dulled and our spirits depressed by the long winters, we would have this soup to brighten and refresh ourselves.

    2 cups chopped borage leaves
    2 cups chopped spinach leaves
    1 cup chopped dandelion leaves
    1 cup minced scallions
    4 cups water
    1 teaspoon black pepper
    ½ teaspoon salt
    3 tablespoons vinegar
    4 slices peasant bread, toasted

Heat the water and add the greens and scallions. Simmer for 30 minutes. Then add the black pepper, salt and vinegar and simmer for another ten minutes. Add the bread. Simmer until the mixture is thickened. Serve in soup bowls.

Serves 4

Brie Tart

Cheese tarts such as this one of Brie were favorites during medieval times, because while the Church forbade the eating of meat on fast days, dairy products were not included in the list of banned foods. Spices were a very rare commodity and appeared only in the tarts and pies that were prepared for us.

    1 recipe, Flaky Whole Wheat Flour Pastry, page 389
    2 cups half and half

1 teaspoon saffron

1 cup Brie without the rind, diced

1 teaspoon sugar

½ teaspoon ground cinnamon

1 teaspoon ground ginger

3 eggs, and 2 egg yolks

Preheat the oven to 350°F. Line a 9-inch pastry shell with the flaky pastry and trim. Prick all over and bake for 10 minutes and remove from the oven. While the pastry is cooking, in a double boiler, heat the milk and saffron together then add the cheese, sugar, the cinnamon and the ginger. Cook until the cheese is melted. Remove the pan from the heat. Beat the eggs in a bowl until foamy. Add the cheese mixture to the eggs, a third at a time, beating after each addition. Pour into the pie shell and bake until puffed and golden.

Serves 8

Eggs in Red Wine Sauce

A common type of egg dish that we ate was stewed eggs in a wine sauce.

4 extra large eggs

2 medium onions, peeled and cut into ½ inch slices

2 cups dry red wine

1 tablespoon red wine vinegar

3 tablespoons verjuice or lemon juice*

---

*Note: Verjuice is the sour juice made from grapes. It can be sometimes found in Arab or Gourmet food stores.

2 tablespoons water

1 teaspoon salt

4 tablespoon olive oil

2 tablespoons minced chervil

1 tablespoon minced parsley

Steam the onions for 8 minutes. Drain well. Heat 2 tablespoons of the olive oil in a small frying pan. Add the onions saute until golden. Then add the wine, vinegar, and lemon juice. Bring to a boil and simmer for 20 minutes. In another frying pan, add the remaining two tablespoons of oil. Fry the eggs gently and then transfer to the sauce. Simmer for 5 minutes. Place one fried egg on each serving plate, and cover with some of the sauce. Sprinkle with the chervil and the parsley.

Serves 4.

Mussel and Onion Stew

Mussels were one of Richard's favorite foods. Cooked in a rich sauce comprised of saffron, ginger and onion, they would have been elegantly presented in bowls strewn with herbs.

4 pounds mussels, cleaned and the beards removed

6 cups chicken broth

2 cups onion, minced

½ teaspoon saffron

1 teaspoon ground ginger

1 teaspoon salt

1 teaspoon black pepper

½ cup flour

2 cups warm milk

½ cup minced parsley

5 sage leaves, minced

2 tablespoons minced sorrel

In a large pot, combine the chicken broth, onion, saffron, ginger and the salt and pepper. Bring to a boil, then reduce the heat and simmer for 30 minutes. Add the mussels, and cover tightly with a lid. Cook until the mussels have opened. Remove from the broth, and discard all unopened mussels. Remove the opened mussels from the shells, and set aside. Strain the broth and return 4 cups of it to the pan. Melt the butter in a saucepan and add the flour. Cook for 5 minutes. Add the milk slowly, whisking continuously. Pour this sauce into the mussel broth, and stir. Then add the mussel meat. Reheat. Ladle into the soup bowls. Decorate with the herbs.

Serves 6

Hashed Leeks

Vegetables began to be cooked on their own at the end of the 14th century, due to culinary influences from France. We still only ate them sporadically, preferring to have them in soups and stews.

2 ½ pounds leeks

½ pound bacon or pancetta, diced

2 large slices peasant bread, soaked in water

3 large eggs, beaten

1/8 teaspoon saffron, dissolved in water

¼ teaspoon ground cinnamon

¼ teaspoon ground ginger

1 teaspoon salt

Toast Snippets (pieces of toasted bread, cut in little triangles)

Bring a pot of salted water to a boil. Trim the leeks, and place in the water. Cook until tender. Remove from the heat and chop. In a frying pan, cook the pancetta until slightly crisp and add the leeks. Add the soaked bread, the beaten eggs and the spices and salt. Heat until the egg is cooked through. Serve in a bowl with the toast snippets.

Serves 4

Cabbage with Fennel and Apple

An exception to our habitual exclusion of vegetables was the Cabbage. Cabbage was a root vegetable grown in abundance. Since Roman times, it was believed to have restorative properties. Many times it was cooked with fennel, a vegetable the Monks at St. Gall in France extolled for its excellent digestive qualities.

¼ of a head Savoy cabbage, diced

1 small onion, diced

1 bulb fennel, diced

3 tablespoons olive oil

1 teaspoon salt

1 teaspoon pepper

1 apple, cored, peeled and diced

1 teaspoon ground ginger

1 cup chicken broth

In a pot of boiling water, cook the cabbage until tender. Drain. In a frying pan, heat the olive oil and add the onion and fennel. Sauté until tender. Then add the cabbage, apple, salt, pepper, ginger and chicken broth. Cook 15 minutes on low heat. Transfer to a serving bowl.

Serves 4

Roast Beef with Egerdouce Sauce

Egerdouce Sauce was a popular sauce that we ate with roasted meats. It combined breadcrumbs, wine, vinegar, honey and spices, to make a savory sauce.

1 (4 pound) Beef Tenderloin

Sauce:

2 tablespoons olive oil

1 large onion, minced

¼ cup raisins

¼ cup currants

½ teaspoon ground ginger

½ teasoon ground mace

½ teaspoon saffron dissolved in boiling water

½ cup white wine

1/3 cup red wine vinegar

3 tablespoons honey

½ cup water

½ cup coarse white breadcrumbs

In a large skillet cook the onions in the olive oil until soft. Add the fruits and spices and cook for several more minutes. Add the rest of the ingredients and cook for 15 minutes on low heat. Sauce should be thick. Serve with the meat.

Preheat the oven to 375°F. In a large roasting pan, place the tenderloin of beef. Place a meat thermometer in the tenderloin. Bake for 1 hour or until the thermometer registers 140°F. Remove from the roasting pan, and carve. Serve the meat with the sauce.

Serves 8

Haricot of Lamb

Lamb was not a large favorite of the masses, who preferred pigs, or the occasional joint of beef. However, Richard and I loved a good dish of lamb, especially at the end of spring, when they had spent a season feasting on fresh grasses.

1 ½ pounds lamb stew meat, cubed

3 large onions, diced

1 tablespoon lard

3 tablespoons minced parsley

1 tablespoon minced mint

1 teaspoon salt

½ teaspoon pepper

1 teaspoon ground ginger

3 cups beef broth

In a large cooking pot, heat the lard and add the lamb stew meat. Sauté until brown. Remove from the fat with a slotted spoon and add the onions to the pot. Sauté until the onions are limp. Return the lamb to the pot and then add the parsley, mint, salt, pepper and ginger. Sauté for several minutes. Then add the beef broth. Bring to a boil. Reduce the heat and simmer for 1-½ hours or until the lamb is tender. Transfer to a serving bowl and garish with additional minced parsley and mint.

Serves 6

Chicken and Almond Mold

Elaborate molds like this one, containing chicken and almond milk, were an everyday occurrence at royal dining tables. Almond milk was used in cooking, as a substitute for cow's milk. It had a rich, luxurious taste, which appealed to the palate of the wealthy class. The modern-day gelatin used in this recipe had to be obtained from the hooves of calves.

½ cup rice
1 cup Almond Milk, page 386
1 cup jellied stock, melted
¼ teaspoon saffron
½ cup diced chicken breast
2 tablespoons butter
1 teaspoon salt
½ teaspoon pepper
1 strip gelatin
1 cup slivered almonds
½ teaspoon paprika page 386

Boil the rice in the almond milk, until tender but firm. Drain and leave to cool. Mince the diced chicken breast, then puree in the blender. Remove from the blender and sauté for several minutes, in butter, saffron, salt and pepper, until tender and colored by the saffron. Remove from the heat and cool. Add just enough gelatin, softened and melted in hot chicken stock, to allow the chicken mixture to set slightly. Put this gelatin mixture in the bottom of a buttered mold. Add the layer of rice and the slivered almonds. Cover with the jellied stock. Chill in the refrigerator until ready to serve. Remove from the mold, and decorate with paprika, and more sliced almonds.
Serves 6

Frumenty

In lieu of potatoes, which hadn't been discovered yet, and rice, which was very expensive and had to be imported, wheat berries cooked in chicken broth were a form of grain served at almost every meal.

1 cup wheat berries

4 cups Chicken broth

1 teaspoon salt

½ teaspoon pepper

2 eggs, beaten

In a large pot, bring 3 cups of salted water to a boil. Add the wheat berries and cook until they burst open, (about 1 hour). Drain the wheat berries and place in a bowl. Cover with a cloth. Place in a warm place. On the next day, heat the chicken broth and add the wheat berries, salt and pepper. Cook until the wheat is thick like porridge. Then ladle a cup of the hot porridge into the eggs, and the pour the egg mixture back into the wheat berries. Stir. Serve in bowls.

Serves 6

Blackberry Pudding

Enhanced by wine and using expensive cloves, these puddings would have been destined only for our table. Trade with the Arabs introduced granulated sugar, which started to appear in recipes for desserts, although it was still reserved for the very well to do. Any food leftover was thrown outside for the poor. You can imagine how they waited in anticipation for the end of a feast; scraps of food, left over trenchers and perhaps even a taste of this delectable pudding could be salvaged.

1 ½ pounds blackberries, washed and drained

2 slices whole wheat bread, the crusts removed and toasted

2 tablespoons butter

¾ cup cabernet sauvignon

½ cup granulated sugar

5 cloves

Puree the blackberries in a food processor. Strain through a sieve. Remove the crusts from the bread and dice. In a heavy saucepan, heat the bread, blackberry juice, sugar, butter and wine. Bring to a boil and simmer for 10-15 minutes. Put into a serving bowl and chill well. Just before serving, stud with the cloves and sprinkle with sugar.
Serves 6

Pears in Spiced Wine

By medieval times, we were growing over 50 varieties of pears. Pears were used in stews with meat, puddings and tarts.
2 pounds pears, peeled cored and sliced in half

2 cups red wine
¾ cup granulated sugar
1 teaspoon ground ginger
¼ teaspoon pepper

In a saucepan, place the pears cut side down. Cover with the red wine. Poach for 25 minutes. Remove the pears from the red wine and place on a plate. Add the sugar, ginger and pepper to the red wine. Cook until reduced to thick syrup. Pour over the pears. Let them sit for several hours.
Serves 4-6

Caudle

One recipe appearing in *The Forme of Cury*, composed by Richard II's steward, was for caudle. A caudle was a drink that sustained medieval travelers while on the road. It was also offered at the end of a royal meal, fortifying those who did not have a place to stay for the night in the palace, on their journey to their alternate lodgings.

4 cups boiling water

¼ cup oatmeal, either quick or instant

Pinch of salt

½ teaspoon mace

¼ teaspoon powdered ginger

2 tablespoons honey

4 cups ale or stout

Cook all the ingredients except for the ale, until the oatmeal is tender. Heat the ale and mix with the oatmeal mixture. Serve in mugs.

Serves 6-8

*   *   *

Women of The Harem

14th-15th Century, The Arab Levant

We are the women of the Harem. Our place in history is timeless. Some of us were Arabic women born into poverty and sold into slavery. Others were European women, captured by the Persians and brought to the harems of their wealthy leaders. But all of us had one thing in common, our beauty made us a prized commodity for the sexual desires of our wealthy Arab captors. If we were lucky enough to be sold into the palaces of the kings and princes of the land, we lived a life of luxury, surrounded by flowing fountains, exotic flowers, and exquisite food. Food became an important aspect of harem life. Fresh herbs, fruits, lamb and cool refreshing soups played a large part in the meals of our day. Because most inhabitants of the Harem were from foreign places, the cuisine could reflect the tastes of their native country, but the majority of food, prepared by the palace chefs, was so extraordinary that the women soon forgot their native cuisine.

The food of Arabia contributed greatly to the cuisine of the west. Citrus fruits and sugar were imported from Arab countries. It was the Moors who first established the lemon groves in the Spanish cities they conquered. Other foods such as eggplants, spinach, rice and rosewater made their way to the Mediterranean kitchens of Italy and Spain, and to a lesser extent the kitchens of the English. The time-honored combination of nuts, such as walnuts with chicken dishes or almonds in stews, came to be used in many other types of medieval cuisine. Sorbet was first introduced to the West when Saladin presented a peace offering of ice flavored with fruit to Richard the Lion-hearted, during the Third Crusade. Spices were grown in abundance in the Middle East and were commonly used for cooking in the region. Saffron graced many of our rice dishes and in our puddings and desserts made of semolina, while cinnamon and cardamon figured in our meat dishes and sweetmeats. Lovely melons, oranges, plums and apricots often appeared on our dinner tables, sometimes fresh and some times in spiced syrup or pureed. During the 13th Century, an important cookbook was written by Muhammad ibn Hasen al-Baghadadi, who articulated the court cuisine of that time. Yet he leaves out many common dishes that would later become widespread favorites in the Middle East, such as Bamia (okra) and dried beans. These foods were staples of the common people and therefore not fit for the court.

Follow us into the enchanted palace, where eunuchs served us meals, flowers floated in ponds, gardens were filled with very kind of flower and silk pillows lined our seats of honor.

*   *   *

A Harem Dinner

Pomegranate Soup
Onions stuffed with Lentils and
Steamed Saffron Rice
Lamb Koresh with Peaches
Eggplant Iman Bayidi
Pickled Turnips
Almond Semolina Cake
Dates filled with Coconut
Rose Sherbet

*   *   *

Pomegranate Soup

We loved the taste of pomegranate juice, a legacy of our ancestors from Babylon and Assyria who used it to flavor many of their dishes. This lamb soup, with its flavors of spinach, onions, mint, and pomegranate juice is the same today was it was in the 14th century when we lived.

½ pound ground lamb

1 small onion, minced

¼ teaspoon cinnamon

¼ teaspoon pepper

8 cups water

2 teaspoons salt

½ cup rice

1 cup chopped spinach,

1 cup chopped parsley

½ cup green onions, chopped

1 cup pomegranate juice

1 tablespoon sugar

1 tablespoon lemon juice

1 tablespoon dried mint

Put the ground meat in a food processor and add the onion, cinnamon, pepper. Blend until a paste is formed. Heat the water in a large soup pot and add the salt, rice, spinach, parsley and green onions. Shape the ground lamb into small balls. Add these meatballs to the soup. Cook for 20 minutes. Then add the rest of the ingredients except for the dried mint. Cook for another 15 minutes. Ladle into soup bowls, and rub the dried mint between two fingers then sprinkle it over each bowl.

Serves 6

Onions Stuffed with Lentils and Fruits

Onions, beans and nuts were common staples of Persia. Combined with yogurt, they made delicate stuffed vegetables and one of the mainstays of our cooking.

4 large onions, peeled
½ cup red lentils, cooked
¾ cup yogurt, plain
2 tablespoons raisins, chopped
2 tablespoons walnuts, chopped
2 tablespoons bread crumbs
1 bunch parsley, chopped
Salt and pepper to taste
Olive oil

Place the onions in a large pot of boiling water. Reduce the heat and let simmer for 10 minutes. Remove the onions with a large soup ladle, and let cool. Remove the middle of each onion. Finely chop the middle section and combine in a bowl with rest of the ingredients. Stuff each of the onions with some of the mixture. Preheat the oven to 350°F. Place the onions in a large baking dish. Drizzle with olive oil. Bake for 20 minutes.

Serves 4

Steamed Saffron Rice

While rice was an expensive commodity in Europe, by the late Middle Ages we were using it everyday in our cooking. First imported from the Far East and then cultivated by us, the art of growing rice was then passed on to the Venetian's, who used it extensively in their cooking and traded it to other parts of Europe.

6 cups water
2 cups Iranian or long grained rice
½ teaspoon saffron threads
1 pinch sugar
5 tablespoons butter
¼ teaspoon dried sumac

In a heavy saucepot, bring the water to a boil. Pour in the rice, in a steady slow stream. Add the saffron threads and sugar. Bring to a boil. Cover with a dishcloth and then with a lid. Steam for ½ hour and do not remove lid. Remove the rice from the pot when done. Place in a large serving bowl in a conical shape. Pack the rice down. Unmold on a serving platter. Place the pats of butter on top of the rice. Sprinkle with the sumac.

Serves 6

Lamb Koreshe

A Koreshe is a meat stew sometimes combined with fruit and nuts, dating back to ancient times. It provided the sweet and sour taste we so enjoyed.

2 pounds lamb stew meat, diced
Salt and pepper
½ cup butter
1 onion, chopped
1 teaspoon turmeric
2 cups water
1 one inch cinnamon stick
3 large peaches, peeled, pitted and sliced
¼ cup lemon juice
2 tablespoons brown sugar

Heat the butter in a large Dutch oven. Add the lamb and the salt and pepper. Cook until browned. Then add the onion, turmeric, water and cinnamon stick. Bring to a boil and reduce the heat. Cover tightly with a lid and simmer for 2 more hours. Then add the peaches, lemon juice and the brown sugar. Cook for ½ hour more.

Serves 6

Eggplant Iman Bayildi

This is a very ancient Persian recipe dating back to medieval Arabia and combines eggplants, onions and tomatoes for a savory dish. There is a history accompanying this dish claiming that an Iman or Turkish priest fainted from the sheer pleasure of being served this dish. Hence its name: *The Iman Fainted*.

2 medium eggplants
1 cup olive oil
2 medium onions, minced
1 large tomato, chopped
Salt and pepper to taste
¼ teaspoon allspice
1 tablespoon parsley, chopped
¼ cup currants, soaked in water and chopped
1 bay leaf

Cut the stems off the eggplants, but do not peel. Cut several lengthwise slits into the eggplants, but do not slice through. Heat 2 tablespoons of the olive oil in a small skillet and sauté the onion until slightly brown. Add the tomato, salt and pepper, allspice, parsley and bay leaf. Cook for ten minutes. Add the currants and cook for another 10 minutes. Grease a large baking dish and preheat the oven to 350°F. Place the cooked mixture inside the eggplant slits and place the eggplant in the baking dish. Drizzle with the rest of the olive oil. Bake in the oven for 30 minutes. Remove from the oven and cool.
Serves 6-8

Pickled Turnips

Recipes for pickled vegetables can be found as far back as the cookbook of al-Baghadadi, dating back to the 13th century. Turnips were pickled with honey, vinegar, saffron and herbs.

2 pounds baby turnips
4 cloves of garlic
3 tablespoons honey
1 ¾ cups vinegar
3 cups water
1/8 teaspoon saffron
6 tablespoons salt
1 teaspoon coriander seeds

Wash and peel the turnips. Cut them in quarters. Place in a large clean jar with the garlic. In a saucepan, bring the rest of the ingredients to a boil, dissolving the salt and honey. Pour this mixture over the turnips, making sure that they are completely immersed. Cover the jar tightly with a lid. Place in a warm place and let sit for 10 days. Then store in the refrigerator.

Serves 6

Almond Semolina Cake

Delicacies like this almond semolina cake were indicative of the sweets of the medieval Persia. Semolina and farina are substitutes for flour in most Persian sweets.

3 large eggs

1 cup granulated sugar
½ cup water
½ cup semolina
1 cup farina
2 cups almonds, toasted and ground
Syrup:
1cup sugar
1½ cups water

¼ cup lemon juice

2 tablespoons rose water

The syrup: Combine the sugar, water and lemon juice and bring to a boil. Reduce the heat and boil gently for 15 minutes, or until the syrup has thickened. Remove from the heat and add the rosewater.

The cake: In a large bowl, beat the eggs with the sugar, until light. Add the water and mix well. Then add the ground almonds and the farina and semolina. Mix again. Pour into a well-greased pan. Bake at 350°F. for 40 minutes. Cut into diamonds while leaving the cake in the pan. Pour 1 cup boiling water over the top and then pour the syrup over the cake. Let the cake stand in the pan for 2 hours.

Serves 6

Dates with Coconut

Having a multitude of spices at our command, sweetmeats like this date with coconut were a lovely finale to the meal.

1 package dates, pitted

½ teaspoon cardamom, ground

1/3 cup toasted coconut

½ cup slivered almonds

With oiled hands, knead the dates with the cardamom, until a paste is formed. Shape the date dough around a small sliver of almond. Roll in the toasted coconut.

Serves 16 dates

Rose Sherbet

Sherbet was a favorite Persian dessert. Originally a drink, it developed into an ice served in small pear wood bowls with slender handled spoons.

3 cups fresh rose petals

2 ½ cups granulated sugar

¼ cup lemon juice

3 cups shredded fresh pineapple

1 tablespoon rose water

Soak the rose petals in 1 quart cold water in the refrigerator. Drain the water into a saucepan and discard the rose petals. Boil the sugar and the water for 7minutes. Cool. Add the rose water and the shredded pineapple. Freeze in ice cube trays until slushy. Remove from the freezer and beat. Refreeze. Serve in small scoops.

Serves 6

Lucretia Borgia

1480-1519,Daughter of Pope Alexander VI

I was the daughter of Pope Alexander VI and the sister of Cesare Borgia, who arranged all my marriages for his own political gains. I had three marriages. While the first is insignificant, the second to Alfonso of Aragon is notable only because my brother Cesare had him murdered. The third was the love of my life, Alfonso d'Este, the Duke of Ferrara. The many stories of my crimes, vices and murders have been translated as the subjects of dramas and plays, but they are totally unfounded. In reality, my husband Alfonso and I had a brilliant marriage, establishing a court filled with elegant and cultured people. To the people of Ferrara, I was known as a kind and beautiful person, which brought me much esteem.

While other European Aristocrats were smacking their lips over joints of meat and throwing the bones to their slobbering hounds, Renaissance Italians were setting down their knifes and forks and daintily wiping their lips on napkins. A regular meal would have included thirty-five dishes with exotic additions, such as dormouse pie, boiled calf head with herbs and a savory of wild cherries. The Arabs reintroduced vegetables such as asparagus and the artichoke, formerly cultivated by the Romans and rendered obsolete during the early Middle Ages. Roasts of veal began to appear on the tables of the wealthy, instead of the large haunches of meat common beforehand. Sauces of fruit accompanying meat dishes and chickens were cooked with rosewater, another inheritance of the Arabs. The first cookbook created in Italy was in 1475, by the Vatican librarian Platina, in the service of Pope Sixtus IV. One of the most elaborate recipes is for cooking a peacock, which according to Platina should always be eaten first at a banquet, because its aroma and taste whet the appetite for later courses.

Weddings were events lasting for days, with hundreds of dishes, elaborate table settings glittering with gold, crystal tableware, and a new invention in those days: the fork. Napkins were changed regularly during the meal, water was provided to wash the hands and toothpicks were distributed afterward. A typical wedding banquet included dishes of capons, pigeons, wild boar, sausages, hams, partridges, pheasants, figpeckers and whole sides of roasted meat. They were followed by fruit cooked with sugar and honey, asparagus cooked with saffron, pastries with pine nuts and sugar, cakes with dried fruit, potages and perhaps preserves of candied fruit and squash. Another important ending to the meal was the distribution of comfits, or sugared seeds, that could only be made by special apothecaries licensed for the job. The banquet below has only a few dishes in comparison to one held in Milan in 1488, but it provides a sample of the fantastic cuisine of Italy, as it made its way through the Renaissance years.

*   *   *

Banquet in Ferrara

Sausages Cooked in Red Wine
Fingers of Fresh Pecorino Cheese
Dishes of Fresh Radishes
Spinach Soup from Modena
Olives Cured in Olive Oil and Herbs
Dover Sole in Bitter Orange Juice
Orange Salad
Fresh Fruit, including Apricots, Strawberries, Peaches and Melon
Asparagus with Saffron
Grilled Mushrooms with Pancetta and Garlic
Rice with Raisins
Braised beef with Carrots and Proscuitto
Lamb with Rosemary
Puffed Pastry with Custard
Panoforte
Savory of Wild Cherries,

Marzipan
Toothpicks in Rose water

*   *   *

Sausages Cooked in Red Wine

A Renaissance banquet started with at least 10 dishes comparable to the appetizers of today. Sausages cooked in red wine were considered an enhancement to one's appetite.

2 pounds Italian garlic sausage
3 cups red wine
The juice of one orange

Brown sausages in a frying pan. Prick all over to allow fat to escape. Add the wine and simmer until sausages are tender. Remove from the pan and cut into slices. Skim the fat off the pan juices and serve spooned over the sausages, with a squeeze of orange.
Serves 6

Spinach Soup from Modena

This soup dates back to the 1400's in Modena. It is thickened by the inclusion of toasted bread at the bottom of the soup bowls.

4 pounds spinach washed and shredded
6 cups chicken broth
1 teaspoon salt
½ teaspoon pepper
4 tablespoons Parmesan cheese, grated
2 tablespoons minced parsley
4 slices peasant bread, toasted and cut in squares

Place the spinach and the chicken broth in a soup kettle. Season with the salt and pepper. Bring to a boil. Reduce the heat and simmer for ½ hour. Remove from the heat and cool. Puree in batches in the food processor. Return to the pot. Add the Parmesan cheese and the parsley. Place 4 of the toast squares in each bowl. Ladle the soup over them. Serve immediately.

Serves 6

Dover Sole with Bitter Orange Juice

Bitter oranges were often used in the culinary arts of Renaissance Italy and were imported from Arab countries. Orange juice mixed with lemon may be substituted for a similar taste.

4 large Dover sole fillets
3 tablespoons olive oil
1 teaspoon salt
½ teaspoon pepper
½ cup orange juice
½ cup lemon juice
1 tablespoon minced parsley

In a large frying pan, heat the olive oil. Add the Dover sole fillets. Sauté for 3 minutes on each side. Add the salt, pepper, orange and lemon juice. Cook for 3 minutes. Remove the fillets to a serving dish. Spoon some sauce on top of each. Garnish with minced parsley.

Serves 6

Orange Salad

We consumed many oranges ate our banquets. They were thought to cleanse the palate and to refresh the senses.

6 large blood oranges, peeled, sliced with pith removed
1 tablespoon minced parsley
2 tablespoons red wine vinegar
1 tablespoon olive oil

Lay the orange slices on a platter in a circular formation. Sprinkle with the parsley. Drizzle with the vinegar and oil.
Serves 6

Mushrooms grilled with Pancetta and garlic

Savory dishes combining garlic with bacon or pancetta was the epitome of cooking in 15th century Italy. These types of dishes were a drastic departure from the heavy sauced and spiced dishes of England.

1 pound mushrooms
4 oz pancetta
6 cloves garlic
1 tablespoon rosemary
1 tablespoon minced parsley
Olive oil

Wipe the mushrooms clean. Trim the stems. Chop the pancetta and garlic. Mix the two with the rosemary and the parsley. Distribute this mixture on top of the mushrooms. Drizzle with olive oil and grill for about 5 to 6 minutes.
Serves 6

Asparagus with Saffron

The Arabs reintroduced asparagus, which had disappeared from the tables of Renaissance Italy during medieval times. Saffron was both grown in Southern Italy and imported from the Middle East. It was used to flavor delicate vegetable dishes, custards, breads and cakes on both sides of the continent.

  1 large bunch asparagus, trimmed
  1 medium onion, minced
  2 tablespoons olive oil
  1/8 teaspoon saffron
  ½ cup chicken broth
  1 teaspoon salt
  ½ teaspoon pepper
  1 tablespoon minced parsley
  2 blood oranges, thinly sliced

Steam the asparagus until almost tender. In a saucepan, heat the olive oil and add the onion. Sauté until onion is limp. Then add the saffron, chicken broth, salt and pepper. Simmer for five minutes. Add the asparagus. Simmer until tender. Remove to a serving platter, sprinkle with the minced parsley and garnish with the sliced blood oranges.
  Serves 6

Venetian Rice with Raisins

The Venetians started an extensive rice trade during the Italian Renaissance. Aborino rice cultivated in the area around Venice became a staple of Italian meals. This rice dish combines savory rice with the sweetness of raisins to make a dish timelessly adored by the Venetians.

  1½ cups long grain rice
  3 tablespoons olive oil
  2 teaspoons garlic, minced
  1 medium onion, minced
  1 teaspoon salt
  ½ teaspoon pepper
  1 cup raisins

6 cups chicken broth

2 tablespoons minced parsley

In a saucepan, heat the olive oil. Add the onion and saute until golden. Then add the garlic and sauté for five minutes. Then add the rice, salt and pepper. Sauté for 5 minutes. Add the raisins. Sauté for two minutes. Then add the chicken broth, one-cup at a time, adding the next cup when the first is absorbed. When the last cup has been absorbed, add the parsley. Remove to a serving bowl and serve immediately.

Serves 6

Braised Beef with Carrots and Proscuitto

In Renaissance Italy, beef was braised for long periods of time, until it melted in the mouth. This dish is said to have originated in Italy, a long time before Italian Queen, Catherine De Medici brought it to France when she married Henri the II in the mid 1500's, to become the Italian Queen of France.

1 (4 pound) rump roast

½ pound proscuitto, thinly sliced

2 large carrots, peeled and cut into sticks

3 tablespoons butter

2 medium sized onions, sliced

2 small leeks, trimmed and sliced

2 cups Madeira

1 cup beef broth

3 tablespoons minced parsley

Salt and pepper

Additional minced parsley

Rosemary Sprigs

Preheat the oven to 350°F. Make slices in the rump roast and place the proscuitto and the carrot sticks in between the slices. Tie the roast up with twine. Heat the butter with the roast in a large casserole pan on medium high heat, until the roast is browned. Add the sliced onions and the leeks to the casserole pan. Pour in the Madeira and the beef broth. Add the parsley and season with the salt and pepper. Cover and bake for 2½ to 3 hours. Remove from the sauce and slice. Skim the fat off the sauce. Puree the sauce in a food processor. Reheat until just hot in a small saucepan. Spoon the sauce over the meat. Sprinkle with the minced parsley. Garnish with fresh rosemary sprigs.

Serves 6

Lamb with Rosemary

By the middle of the 15th Century there was a sizeable Jewish population in Italy and they introduced delectable lamb dishes like this one.

1 leg of lamb (approximately 5 pounds)

6 cloves of garlic

1 tablespoon salt

2 tablespoons dried rosemary

1 teaspoon black pepper

¾ cup olive oil

Preheat the oven to 375° F. Sliver three of the garlic cloves. Make several slits in the lamb and insert the slivered garlic. Crush the remaining garlic cloves with the salt, pepper and rosemary. Add ½ cup of the olive oil. Spread on the top of the lamb. Place the lamb in a large roasting pan. Pour the remaining ¼ cup of olive oil over the lamb. Bake for 1 to 1½ hours. Baste frequently. Slice and serve with the skimmed pan juices.

Serves 6-8

Puff Pastry Filled with Custard

Renaissance chefs became adept at creating large and elaborate cakes and pastries. Our chefs created puff pastry, a fragile buttery pastry of many layers, and this recipe was later brought to France by Catherine De Medici.

1 box (16oz) frozen puff pastry, defrosted
1 recipe-Pastry Cream, page 155
1 sheet gelatin
1 cup whipping cream
½ cup hazelnuts finely chopped

Preheat the oven to 400°F. Roll out the puff pastry to form three, 9-inch oblongs. Place on a cookie sheet and bake for 10 minutes. Then reduce the heat to 350°F. and bake for an additional 30 minutes. Make the pastry cream. Dissolve the gelatin in ¼ cup hot water. Add to the pastry cream. When the pastry cream is cool, whip the whipping cream until stiff peaks form. Fold into the pastry cream, then add the hazelnuts. Spread the pastry cream on one of the oblongs of pastry, then top with another oblong, and continue until all three are spread with cream, ending with a layer of pastry. Sprinkle the top with granulated sugar. Chill until ready to serve. Slice into pieces.
Serves 6

Panforte

This is a rich, traditional cake created during the winter when dried fruits were available. Cakes like this originated in the north of Italy, in Siena, Bologna, Padua, Verona and Milan. They were especially popular during the winter months, when we could make use of our excellent dried and preserved fruits.

2 cups blanched almonds

2 cups hazelnuts

1 cup minced orange peel

1 cup chopped dried figs

2 cups chopped dried apricots

1½ cups flour

2 teaspoons ground cinnamon

½ teaspoon ground coriander

½ teaspoon nutmeg, grated

1 teaspoon ground cloves

3 cups confectioners sugar

1¼ cup honey

¾ cup butter

Preheat the oven to 500°F. Spread out the hazelnuts and almonds on a baking sheet. Toast for 15 minutes. Remove from the heat and cool. Reduce the heat in the oven to 350°F. Roughly chop up the nuts. Mix the dried fruit and spices together. Prepare two 9-inch spring form pans. Grease the pans and then line them with parchment paper. In a saucepan, put the sugar, butter and honey. Heat to the softball stage of 240°F. If you don't have a candy thermometer, keep cooking until the mixture is smooth and bubbling fiercely. Mix the nuts with the dried fruit. Then quickly stir the sugar mixture into the nut and fruit mixture. Divide the mixture into two sections and spoon into the pans. Press down with a wet spoon. Cover each pan with a circle of parchment paper, pressing it down. Bake for 30 minutes and then remove from the oven. Cool. Unmold and remove the paper. Cut into squares and place in an airtight container.

Makes 48-64 squares

Savory of Wild Cherries

The cherry was introduced to Italy during Roman times. It became one of our most valuable fruits. This savory made of cherries uses sugar as its sole sweetener, so as to preserve the pristine flavor of the cherries.

   2 pounds ripe Bing cherries
   3 cups granulated sugar

Wash the cherries and remove the pits. Cut the cherries in half. Wrap 10 of the pits in a double thickness of cheesecloth and hit with a hammer to crack the pits. Combine the kernels of the pits, with the cherries and the sugar in a large pot. Cook slowly until the mixture is thick and syrupy. Serve as a dessert.
   Serves 10-12

*   *   *

Anne Bolyen

1507-1536, Queen of England, Wife of Henry VIII

Although I have been portrayed as a villainess, in truth I was but a political pawn. I was related to the powerful Howard family and my mother was the sister of the Duke of Norfolk, also a member of the Howards. To enhance their position, they placed my sister and I at the court of King Henry VIII. It was my sister Mary who first caught the King's eye and she became his lover for two years. By that time, I had also drawn the Kings attention and he became obsessed with me. Knowing what had happened to his other mistresses, whom he discarded upon tiring of them, I held out for marriage or nothing. This drove Henry mad. Finally I did yield to his advances, becoming pregnant. This forced Henry to make his final break with the Catholic Church, so he could divorce Catherine and marry me. I was married secretly by Archbishop Cranmer in January of 1533. In September of 1533, I gave birth to a daughter, Elizabeth, much to Henry's disgust.

With my inability to provide Henry with an heir, the slow descent to my downfall and death began.

But what times I had before this misfortune came upon me, for both Henry and I loved a good time. Sharing his passion for dancing, hunting and hawking, we traveled the realm, staying at various great houses. Meals at that time were grand affairs. Our cuisine was undergoing a transition from Medieval fare to Tudor dishes, which had less ingredients and flavors of a more subtle character. Our changing eating habits brought the consumption of more vegetables than ever before. Turnips, parsnips, onion, carrots, leeks, garlic and radishes all made their way to the Tudor table. In addition to the fruits grown in England for the many centuries previous, new ones were being imported from other countries. They included apricots, quinces, pomegranates, oranges, lemons and melons. Beef still remained the meat of choice, while chickens and capons replaced the herons and swans of the medieval period. Potages of vegetable and meat, later becoming the soups of the 17th century, remained popular with all levels of society.

The fledgling middle class of England fared better than they had during the Middle Ages, especially those who lived in the countryside, where they could preserve the bounty of the land. At our Manor houses, we had large pantries attached to our kitchens where we could preserve fruits, dry herbs and prepare medicinal concoctions. The Tudor housewife began to collect recipes, which would be handed down from generation to generation, in hand written books.

Dinners were held in the great halls of the manor houses. The time of dinner was changed, with a dinner at eleven in the morning and supper at six in the evening. Elaborate breakfasts provided another new addition to the meal and were held before the royal hunt.

Henry loved to eat. He was known to devour large haunches of meat, washed down with beer, several pies, salads and elaborate sweetmeats, all at one sitting. Henry was also a messy eater, spewing food all over the table, belching and spitting. Some times this was too much for me and feigning a slight malaise, I would retire to the solitude of my room to eat in peace. The gigantic meals Henry ate only served to contribute to his ill health, for he became very obese and suffered from gout.

It is best that I forget about the sadness and treachery of my death at Henry's command. I remember those days as lasting forever, with the soft perfume of flowers and trees, drifting in the windows at Hampton Court and madrigals playing softly in the background. After a good meal, Henry and I would often retire for some bed sport.

*   *   *

Dinner with Henry the VIII

Potage of Cabbage and Bacon
Savory Beef Pie
Venison in Broth
Stewed Chicken with Herbs
Costmary (Spiced Pork Loin)
Sorrel Applesauce
Eggs in Pastry Cases
Mushrooms Stewed with Onions
Quinces Stewed in Wine
Maids of Honour,
Spiced Plum Pastry
Ale

*   *   *

Potage of Cabbage and Bacon

Soup, also known as Potage, was a thick concoction served in bowls of wood or silver-gilt and gold. Cabbage was still a favorite vegetable during the time of Henry the VIII.

1 small head cabbage, diced

½ pound salt pork, diced

2 large onions, minced

8 cups of chicken broth

1 teaspoon ground ginger

1/8 teaspoon saffron threads

1 teaspoon salt

1 teaspoon pepper

4 slices peasant bread, toasted and the crusts removed

In a soup pot, sauté the salt pork and onion together until the salt pork renders most of its fat. Add the cabbage sauté for 10 minutes. Then add the chicken broth, ginger, saffron threads and the salt and pepper. Bring to a boil. Cook for 25 minutes or until the cabbage is tender. Place one slice of toast in the bottom of each soup bowl. Ladle the soup on top.

Serves 6-8

Savory Beef Pie

There would have been as many as three or four different kinds of meat presented at one meal in Tudor England. They would have included some sort of beef dish, such as this savory beef pie, or a roasted beef haunch. Mutton and venison were also common meats of the time. Pastry was now made with bolted white flour instead of the wheat flour of medieval times.

1 recipe—Short Crust Pastry, page 391

2 pounds beef stew meat diced in one inch cubes

2 teaspoons salt

1 teaspoon pepper

1 teaspoon cinnamon

1 teaspoon ground ginger

1 small onion, minced

2 tablespoons butter

½ cup currants

2 cups beef broth

In a large saucepan, heat the butter and brown the meat. Then add the onion, and cook for several minutes. Add the rest of the ingredients and bring to a boil. Reduce the heat and simmer covered for 2 hours. Remove from the pan and place in a casserole dish. Preheat the oven to 350°F. Roll out the pastry. Cover the top of the casserole with it. Decorate the top with scraps. Make several slits in the top. Bake until the pastry is golden brown.

Serves 8

VENISON IN BROTH

This dish of venison cooked with wine and spices dates back to the medieval era and was still a popular dish at our dining tables. We would have added blood at the very end of the preparations to enhance the taste.

2 pounds of venison, cut into chunks

¼ cup flour

2 tablespoons oil

½ teaspoon ground ginger

½ teaspoon ground cinnamon

¼ teaspoon mace

½ teaspoon pepper

1 teaspoon salt

1 cup dry red wine

1 cup chicken stock

2 tablespoons red wine vinegar
½ cup currants

Roll the venison in flour. Heat the oil in a large skillet. Brown the venison in the oil. Add the spices and cook for 2 more minutes. Then add the salt and pepper, red wine, and the chicken stock. Reduce the heat and cover. Simmer until the meat is tender. Then add the red wine vinegar and the currants and cook for 10 more minutes. Transfer to a large serving dish.

Serves 6

Stewed Chicken with Pot Herbs

Chicken was eaten at almost every meal during Tudor times. One common method of preparation was to stew the chicken with vegetables and potherbs. Barley was still used as a thickener for most of our stews.

1 (3 pound) chicken, disjointed
3 large leeks, trimmed and sliced
½ cup butter
3 cups water
¾ cup barley
3 tablespoons red wine vinegar
1 teaspoon salt
1 teaspoon pepper
¼ cup minced parsley
3 tablespoons minced sage

In a large Dutch oven, heat the butter. Add the chicken and the leeks. Sauté until the chicken is browned. Then add the water, barley, red wine vinegar, salt and pepper. Bring to a boil, then reduce the heat. Cover and simmer for 1½ hours, or until the chicken is very tender.

Add the herbs and cook for an additional ten minutes. Ladle into soup bowls and serve.

Serves 6

Costmary (Spiced Pork loin)

Pork meat favored by the lower and middle class now began to appear on the dining tables of the wealthy. We especially liked it cooked with wines and sweet spices such as cinnamon and cloves.

1 (3 pound) pork loin
3 cups dry red wine
4 garlic cloves, slivered
1 teaspoon cinnamon
1 teaspoon caraway seed
1 teaspoon ground ginger
½ teaspoon nutmeg
1 teaspoon salt

Mix the red wine with the spices. Place the pork loin in a large bowl and marinate it overnight in the refrigerator. Preheat the oven to 350°F. Remove the pork loin from the marinade and dry. Make cuts in the pork loin and place the slivered garlic in the cuts. Place the pork loin in a greased roasting pan. Roast for 2 hours. While the pork loin is roasting in the oven, prepare the sauce. In a saucepan, bring the marinade to a boil until reduced by half. Remove the pork loin from the oven and slice. Serve on a platter with the sauce spooned on top.

Serves 6-8

Sorrel Applesauce

Sorrel is an herb used a great deal in Tudor cooking as it provided a good source of Vitamin C. While many Tudor physicians recommended eating apples raw, this was an exception to the rule. Most uncooked fruits were looked upon with suspicion, as they were thought to be poisonous.

1 cup sorrel leaves4 red delicious apples, peeled, cored and sliced
1 cup water
1/3 cup red wine vinegar
½ cup granulated sugar
5 tablespoons butter

In a saucepan, heat the sorrel leaves and apples with the water. Cook until soft. Then add the red wine vinegar and sugar. Cook for 10 minutes. Add the butter. Cook until the butter is melted. Transfer to a serving dish.

Serves 4-6

Eggs in Pastry Cases

By the 16th century eggs in some form or another appeared at almost very meal. They were baked, stewed in wine, or encased in pastry such as the following recipe.

4 tablespoons water
1/8 teaspoon saffron
1 cup flour
2 tablespoons sugar
½ teaspoon salt
1 egg yolk
6 tablespoons butter
1 teaspoon ground ginger
1 teaspoon granulated sugar
4 large egg yolks

Bring the water to a boil, and add the saffron. Remove from the heat and cool. Chill the saffron water. Sift the flour with the salt and sugar. Cut the butter in with a pastry blender. Work in the egg yolk and the saffron-water as well. When the mixture is well blended, roll out on a floured board. Line four pastry shells with the pastry. Bake for 10 minutes at 400°F and remove the pastries. Add one egg yolk to each pastry and sprinkle with the ginger and the sugar. Bake until the eggs are set. Serve hot or cold.

Serves 4

Mushrooms Stewed with Onions

During the time of Henry the VIII, some vegetables such as mushrooms began to appear on the British dining table as separate dishes. They were braised and combined with other vegetables such as onions.

1 pound button mushrooms

2 medium sized onions, minced

¼ cup butter

¼ cup minced parsley

1 teaspoon thyme dried

1 tablespoon red wine vinegar

In a saucepan, heat the butter. Add the onions and sauté until soft. Then add the mushrooms. Reduce the heat and cook gently until the mushrooms are soft. Add the parsley, thyme, and red wine vinegar. Cook for 2 minutes. Transfer to a serving bowl.

Serves 4

Quinces Cooked in Wine

Quinces came from their place of origin in the Middle East. It soon became a favorite fruit for stewing with wine and sugar. Another popular method was to preserve them in jams and jellies.

1 ½ cups dry red wine
1 ½ cups granulated sugar
10 whole cloves
1 teaspoon ground cinnamon
2 large quinces

In a saucepan, heat the wine, sugar, cloves and cinnamon together. Cook until a thin syrup forms. In the meantime, prepare the quinces. Scrub the quinces under running water to remove the down. Then with a very sharp knife cut the quinces in half. Be very careful, as the quinces are very hard. Do not remove the seeds or the skin. Place the cut sides down in the pan with the syrup. Add enough water to cover them. Simmer for 1 hour, or until the quinces are soft. Remove the quinces from the syrup and scoop out the seeds. The syrup should be quite thick. Place the quinces on a platter and pour the syrup over the top.

Serves 6

Maids of Honour

Legend has it that I invented these tiny tarts to win Henry's heart, succeeding in elevating myself from maid of honor to Queen.

1 recipe Short Crust Pastry, page 391
1/3 cup soft white bread crumbs
Pinch of salt
1¼ cups milk, scalded

½ cup sugar

2 tablespoons butter

2 tablespoons grated lemon rind

2 eggs well beaten

¾ cup ground, blanched almonds

Add the breadcrumbs and salt to the hot milk. Stir and let stand for 10 minutes. Add the butter, sugar, lemon rind and eggs, mixing everything together thoroughly. Fold the almonds into the milk and bread crumb mixture. Roll out the pastry 1/8 inch thick and line16 large or 24 small buttered tart tins, leaving a rim of pastry above the edge of the tin. Prick well with a fork and line with wax paper. Fill the wax paper with rice to retain its shape. Bake at 450° for 6 minutes. Remove from the oven and cool. Remove the wax paper and rice. Then remove the pastry from the tins and fill with the custard. Place on a baking sheet, and bake at 300°F. for 20 minutes.

Makes 16-24 tarts

Spiced Plum Pastry

Pastries containing fruit began to be very popular during Tudor times. Damson plums, which had been introduced to our dining tables during medieval times, became a beloved Tudor fruit. Every housewife had a recipe for preserving them. Sometimes they were combined with rosewater, distilled from the Damask rose, a favorite flower of our time.

1 recipe—Short Crust Pastry, page 391

2 pounds plums, pitted

1 teaspoon ground cinnamon

1 teaspoon ground ginger

¼ teaspoon ground nutmeg

1 cup granulated sugar

2 tablespoons butter

1 teaspoon rosewater

Preheat the oven to 350°F. Roll out the pastry to fit a 9-inch tart pan. Place the plums in a circle, starting at the outside edge and working inward, until pastry is filled. Crimp the pastry. Sprinkle with the spices, and the sugar. Dot with the butter. Sprinkle with the rosewater. Bake for 45 minutes or until the pastry is golden.

Serves 6-8

*   *   *

Elizabeth the First

1533 –1603, Queen of England

I was the daughter of Ann Bolyen, who was put to death by my father Henry VIII. I suffered an emotionally tense childhood, with constant threat of banishment or even death, only to rise to victory after my sister Queen Mary died. I was an educated woman for my time, speaking five languages, trained in the art of conversation, dancing, hunting and hawking. I was known as the royal tease by the amount of men I kept hanging on my every word, some with promises of marriage and some not. When asked why I never married, I said, "I am already married to a husband, the people of England."

I certainly enjoyed my life and in between skirmishes with the Spanish and other foreign countries trying to subdue my power, I found time to travel around the country, staying at various great homes, while eating, dancing and hunting the time away.

Cooking in England had reached new heights by the time I became Queen. We ceased to rely on heavy spiced dishes and with the increasing influence of French cooking more delicate dishes appeared on the table. Meat always remained a major part of any meal. It was served boiled or roasted, both in pies and stews. Like my father, I enjoyed a good haunch of beef. Of the new vegetables to grace the English table, spinach and peas became common. My explorers and those of Spain and Italy discovered the tomato and the potato. However, because they belonged to the Nightshade family and were considered poisonous, it would be years before they would become a staple at the dining table. This era also saw the beginning of the pudding as a bag of food tied in cloth and boiled in water. Each region had their specialties, such as Gloucestershire bag pudding.

In 1577, a London clergyman named William Harrison, would describe the eating habits of the population of London at this time. He stated that nobleman, gentry and students ate their main meal at 11o'clock, the tradesmen at 12 noon, and all other members of society consumed a simple supper at 6pm. The poor fended for themselves, eating any time of day, trying simply to survive.

One of the new features of food in Britain was the advent of the separate banqueting hall. It was usually a structure adjacent the existing house. I had one constructed at Greenwich Park to host a reception for the French Embassy. These structures were sometimes made completely of tents, or could be a more solid structure of wood and brick. A large table, sometimes seating 100 people would be set up in this hall, with chairs replacing the benches of medieval times. Flags hung from the ceiling and there was an area where musicians would play. My father Henry replaced the bread trencher with a thin wooden plate, complete with recesses in which to place food. By the time of my reign, the first pottery bowls and cups were being produced. In the late 1500's, Jacomo Verzelini would produce the first Venetian glass in London. The fork was beginning to assume a place of importance at the table. On New Years Day, I would receive a fork of gold and crystal to eat the sweetmeats I so adored.

Hunting parties were elaborate affairs with special constructed bowers for my enjoyment. One such event, required that the steward of the house navigate his way to my place of encampment. All manners of food and drink were transported there by a multitude of horse-drawn wagons. Roasts of beef, lamb, mutton, pork, goose, pigeon pies, sausages, eggs, sweetmeats and fruit were the standard hunting party fare. While the food was being set out on specially constructed tables set with linen, the steward placed the wine and barrels of beer in the stream to cool.

Until the day I died in 1603, I dressed in my best, colored my hair, whitened my skin and danced as a young girl. Due to the consumption of many sweets, I unfortunately had blackened teeth. Even so, with advancing age I was still able to eat a good many of the things I loved. I was a hearty woman who enjoyed food, verbal banter and intrigue until the day I died.

*   *   *

A House Party for the Queen

Split Pea Soup with Onions
Herb and Flower Salad
Grilled Trout with Herbs
Pork with Oranges and Lemons
Roasted Neat's Tongues
Fennel with Ginger
Cheese and Sage Tart
Hippocras
Lemon Posset
Whole Pear Tart
Gingerbread

*   *   *

Split Pea Soup with Onions

Pea soup appeared on our tables as a regular addition. It was cooked in various different ways, sometimes with bacon, but more then likely as a delicate potage with herbs.

1 cup split peas
5 cups water
1 teaspoon salt
½ teaspoon pepper
¼ teaspoon ground nutmeg
3 large onions, peeled and sliced in rings
2 tablespoons olive oil
2 tablespoons minced chervil

In a soup pot, bring the split peas to a boil with the water. Reduce the heat. Simmer until the peas are done. In a frying pan, heat the olive oil and add the onions. Sauté until the onions are caramelized, about 15 minutes. Add the salt, pepper and nutmeg to the soup. Ladle the soup into bowls, and top with the fried onions and minced chervil.
6-8 servings

Herb and Flower Salad

Salads were largely frowned upon in Elizabethan England, because they contained raw vegetables. But in the springtime, salads composed of various greens were considered to be a tonic for cleansing the system. My physicians considered the dandelion to be especially advantageous for cleansing the dark humors of the blood.

1 bunch watercress, washed and torn
1 bunch mustard greens, washed and shredded
1 bunch dandelion greens, washed and torn

1 head butter lettuce, washed and torn
1 bunch sorrel leaves, washed
1 bunch parsley, chopped roughly
2 sprigs of rosemary, leaves stripped
1 sprig of thyme, chopped
1 bunch of mint, chopped
Assorted edible flowers
¼ cup garlic vinegar
6 tablespoons olive oil
1 teaspoon salt
½ teaspoon pepper

Place all the greens in a large salad bowl. Whisk together the garlic vinegar, olive oil, salt and pepper. Pour over the greens and toss. Garnish with the edible flowers.

Serves 6

Grilled Trout with Herbs

Trout was a preferred food during Elizabethan times. We especially liked it grilled with herbs, whose perfume permeated its delicate, succulent meat.

4 large trout, filleted
1 bunch parsley
1 bunch sage
4 tablespoons chopped chervil
Salt and pepper
Olive oil

Place the trout in a broiler pan and stuff the insides with the parsley, sage, and chervil. Sprinkle with the salt and pepper and brush with the olive oil. Broil 4 to 5 minutes, until the fish is cooked.
Serves 6

Pork with Oranges and Lemons

When oranges and lemons began to be imported from the Middle Eastern countries, my chefs discovered their compatibility with meat dishes. They were so expensive that only the very wealthy could afford to have them at their tables.

    4 pound pork tenderloin,
    2 tablespoons olive oil
    1 teaspoon salt
    1 teaspoon pepper
    4 cups red wine
    3 oranges, peeled and sliced
    2 lemon, peeled and sliced
    1 teaspoon ground ginger
    ½ teaspoon cinnamon
    4 tablespoons minced parsley

Preheat the oven to 350°F. Brown the pork tenderloin with the olive oil in a large casserole dish. Sprinkle with the salt and pepper and pour the red wine over the tenderloin. Lay the orange and lemon slices on top of the tenderloin. Sprinkle with the ginger and cinnamon. Bake for ½ hour. Remove the tenderloin to a serving platter. Place the fruit around it. Reduce the cooking liquid to ½ heat and stir in the parsley. Season to taste with additional salt and pepper. Spoon the sauce over the meat.
Serves 4-6

Roasted Neat's Tongue

The tongue of the calf or Neat was especially esteemed in Elizabethan England. Soaked in water and then boiled, or larded and roasted, it was served with a variety of sauces, like the garlic sauce of this recipe.

> 4 pound beef or calf tongue
> 3-4 oz salt pork cut into thin strips
> **Garlic Sauce:**
> 20 cloves of garlic, peeled and minced
> ½ cup fine white bread crumbs
> 3 tablespoons butter
> 1 teaspoon ground ginger
> ½ cup beef broth
> 1 tablespoon parsley

Soak the beef tongue in cold water for 1 hour. Place the tongue into a large pan and cover with water. Add 2 teaspoons of salt per quart of water. Bring to a boil and then skim the foam that accumulates on the top. Reduce the heat and simmer for 1½ hours, although not completely cooking the tongue. Remove the tongue from the water and cool. With a larding needle, pierce the tongue all over and lard it with the salt pork. Place the tongue in a roasting pan. Bake at 475°F. for 20 minutes. While the tongue is roasting, make the sauce. In a food processor, combine all the ingredients for the sauce and process until smooth. Pour into a saucepan and slowly heat. Remove the tongue from the roasting pan and slice. Place the sauce in a sauceboat to accompany the tongue.

Serves 6-8

Fennel with Ginger

Ginger remained a much-loved spice, still used lavishly in meat dishes, as well as with soups and vegetables, as during medieval times.

    2 pounds fennel cut into matchsticks
    4 large onions, thickly sliced
    1 teaspoon salt
    1 heaping teaspoon, ground ginger
    ½ teaspoon saffron, dissolved in water
    2 tablespoons olive oil
    2 cups water
    2 cups dry white wine

Preheat the oven to 350°F. Grease a large casserole dish. Layer the fennel and the onion, alternating each layer. Mix the saffron and ginger with l cup of the white wine. Pour over the fennel and the onions. Then sprinkle with the salt and olive oil. Then add the rest of the water and wine. Bake for one hour, or until the fennel is tender.

Serves 6-8

Cheese Tart with Sage

Tarts of cheese remained an integral part of the royal menu, even after my father, Henry the VIII dispensed with the fast days required by the Catholic Church. This savory tart replaced those prevailing in medieval times, containing sugar, heavy spices and raisins or dates.

    1 recipe Short Crust Pastry; see page 391
    2 large onions, sliced
    3 tablespoons olive oil
    1 tablespoon fresh sage, minced
    1 cup cheddar cheese, shredded

½ cup milk

3 eggs, beaten

1 teaspoon salt

½ teaspoon ground ginger

2 tablespoons minced parsley

Preheat the oven to 350°F. In a frying pan, heat the olive oil and sauté the onions until tender. Then add the sage leaves and sauté for 2 more minutes. Remove from the heat and set aside. Divide the pastry into two discs. Roll one out to fit a 9-inch pie tin. Freeze the other disc for further use. Then layer the onions on the bottom. Cover with the shredded cheese. Beat the milk with the eggs, salt and the ginger. Pour over the onion-cheese mixture. Sprinkle with the parsley. Bake for 45 minutes, or until the pastry is puffed and golden.

Serves 6-8

Hippocras

Sweet wines such as this Hippocras were second only to ale and mead at the dining table.

2 tablespoons coriander seeds, crushed

1 cinnamon stick

2 tablespoons gingerroot, sliced

½ nutmeg, grated

1 cup brandy

2 cups honey

2 bottles claret

Thinly sliced lemon

Combine all the ingredients in a saucepan and bring to a boil. Reduce the heat and simmer for 2 hours. Strain, then reheat. Serve in punch glasses. Garnish each glass with a slice of lemon.

Serves 6-8

Lemon Posset

Delicate possets of cream, egg whites and sometimes spirits, evolved from the cauldes served during the Middle Ages. These desserts were to stay in fashion, all the way through the 16th and 17th century.

1 cup whipping cream
1 cup half and half
3 tablespoons lemon juice
½ cup sweet white wine
½ cup granulated sugar
2 egg whites beaten until stiff
1 tablespoon, lemon zest

Beat the two creams together. Add the white wine and lemon juice. Beat well. Then add the granulated sugar. Mix well. Fold in the egg whites. Spoon into dessert dishes and chill. Serve sprinkled with lemon zest.

Serves 6-8

Whole Pear Tart

Tarts like this were sometimes also made with apples. Our pastries and cakes tended to be heavy. A cake for example, with all its additions of butter, eggs, cream, flour and fruits, could weigh as much as 20 pounds.

1 recipe Short Crust Pastry; page 391

6 Bosc pears, peeled and cored with the stems left on

¾ cup granulated sugar

1 teaspoon ground cinnamon

1 egg yolk beaten

Preheat the oven to 350°F. Divide the dough into two discs. Roll one disc out to fit a 9-inch pie pan. Place the pears on the pastry in the pie pan. Sprinkle with the sugar and the cinnamon. Roll out the other disc to cover the pears, making a hole where each pear stem is, so that the stems poke through. Press the ends of the dough together and crimp. Brush with the beaten egg yolk. Bake for 45 to 55 minutes or until golden brown. Serve each person slice of the tart containing a pear.

Serves 6

Gingerbread

Ginger cakes had been made since the Middle Ages. Originally, they were composed of bread, toasted and then crumbled and combined with honey, wine and spices. During my reign, my chefs created a more cake-like gingerbread, which they formed into shapes like men. These gingerbread men were molded after my favorite lords of the time. You can imagine how surprised Sir Walter Raleigh was to find a effigy of himself at the dining table, especially when it was required of him to bite off its head.

½ cup molasses

6 tablespoons butter

½ cup brown sugar

½ teaspoon baking soda

1 egg, beaten

2 cups all-purpose flour, sifted

1 teaspoon baking powder
½ teaspoon salt
2 teaspoons powdered ginger
½ teaspoon ground mace
¾ cup sour cream
1 teaspoon grated lemon rind

Preheat the oven to 350°F. Heat the molasses. Add the butter, sugar and baking soda. Cool. Beat in the egg. Resift the flour with the baking powder, salt, ginger and mace into a large bowl. Make a well and pour in the molasses and sour cream. Beat until smooth. Fold in the lemon rind. Butter and flour an 11-inch spring form pan and pour in the batter. Bake for 20 minutes or until the cake springs back when touched. Remove from the oven and cool.

Serves 12-24

*   *   *

Chapter 3

Queen Christina

1626-1689, Queen of Sweden

My father was Gustav II of Sweden, who died when I was six years old. I succeeded my father as the Queen of Sweden, with Axel Oxenstierna acting as regent until I assumed full royal power at the age of 18. When I came to the throne, the nobility of Sweden exercised a great deal of power. I spent the first years of my reign fighting to increase the authority of the Crown. I sometimes dressed like a man while joining my troops in battle. Sweden had been led to economic ruin by the Thirty Years war and I was unable to resolve this crisis. I was a highly educated woman, who was greatly influenced by the great French philosopher Rene Descartes. I decided not to marry, as I did not want to be the pawn of some man's quest for power. Tired of the constant infighting and disheartened by the lack of popular support, I abdicated my throne to my cousin Charles. Having become interested in the Roman Catholic religion, I converted and decided to move to Rome, where I lived for the rest of my life, in pursuit of my religious inclinations.

Swedish food at the time of my reign was geared towards surviving the cold winters we had to endure. We developed a taste for hearty food, especially meats cooked with root vegetables, thick pea soups and hearty rye and wheat breads. In the midlands of Sweden the food was plentiful, but in the remote parts of the north, food was sometimes scarce in the winter and meat was rarely eaten.. Holidays such as St. Martins Day, or Martinmas, where we celebrated the life of Saint Martin of Tours, renowned for his charity to the poor were very important. This meal turned into a celebration, countering the dark sunless days of November. I invited many distinguished officials to celebrate this day with me at the palace, providing them with excellent food and drink, including the traditional goose, always served on St. Martins Day. Other foods that became associated with our cuisine are the herring, salmon, trout, cabbage, sauerkraut, beets, cucumbers, rhubarb, Swedish meatballs, dill, cloud berries and the lingonberry. The Swedish Court was a very lonely place for me for I had few friends. The days of boredom were punctuated only by special feast days like these, brightening even my most dark of moods.

*　　　　　*　　　　　*

St. Martins Day Feast

Swedish Liver Paste
Herring Salad
Salmon Pudding
Limpa
Cinnamon Apples
Roast Goose
Red Cabbage with Currants
Swedish Pancakes
Red Fruit Jelly

*　　　　　*　　　　　*

Swedish Liver Paste

After the Romans conquered Sweden, one of the legacies they left included the making of soft pates of meat. These savory pates would sometimes start off a meal, or actually be the main course with a side of bread and fruit.

1 pound calf's liver
1 pound bacon
2 medium onions chopped
1 teaspoon pepper
1 tablespoon salt
1 teaspoon allspice
½ teaspoon ground cloves
¼ teaspoon dried mustard
1 recipe Béchamel Sauce, page 387
3 eggs separated
1 egg white

Preheat the oven to 350°F.Remove the membranes and tubing from the calf's liver. Grind liver 3 or 4 times in a food chopper with the bacon and onions. Add the pepper, salt and spices to the meat and mix well. Then add the béchamel sauce. Add the egg yolks, beating well after each addition. Then whip the egg whites until stiff. Fold into the meat mixture. Spoon into a buttered, 8-cup loaf pan. Place in a pan of boiling water. Bake for 1½ hours. Remove from the oven and cool in a pan. Remove from the pan, and serve with thinly sliced black bread.

Serves 6-8

Herring Salad

Salads in Sweden during the 16-century were substantial dishes, occasionally served as the main course of a meal. We fished for herring in the Baltic Sea, which became a major industry as a result of the formation of the Hanseatic League, a group of Baltic countries banded together for trading in 1241.

1½ pound salted herrings, washed, boned and skinned
2 cups cooked beets, diced
2 tart apples, cored, peeled and diced
1 pickled cucumber, diced
4 tablespoons vinegar
½ teaspoon granulated sugar
3 hardboiled eggs, chopped
1 cup half and half

Combine all the ingredients except for the half and half in a large bowl. Toss till coated. Refrigerate until ready to serve. Before serving, pour the cream on top of the salad and toss again.

Serves 6

Salmon Pudding

This pudding would have originally been made with breadcrumbs, as the potato had not yet reached Sweden.

We fished for salmon in the rivers and lakes of Northern Europe and thus salmon began to appear as a major fish course on the menus of our day.

1 pound smoked salmon
1 cup fine white breadcrumbs
8 eggs separated
2 cups milk
3 tablespoons butter
Salt and pepper to taste
Sour cream
1 tablespoon minced dill

Preheat the oven to 350°F. Chop the smoked salmon finely. Place in a bowl with the breadcrumbs and toss. In a separate bowl, beat the egg yolks until pale and lemon colored and add the milk. Stir in well. Then add eggs to the salmon and mix. Add the salt and pepper. Then whip the egg whites until stiff. Fold into the salmon mixture. Pour into a buttered, 2-quart, soufflé dish. Bake until puffed and golden, about 35-45 minutes. Remove from the oven and serve immediately. Spoon on to serving plates. Place a dollop of sour cream on each serving and sprinkle with minced dill.

Serves 6-8

Limpa (Swedish Rye and Molasses Bread

This is wonderful bread that has almost a cake like constancy. It pairs very well with the liver paste and the herring salad.

16 oz of dark ale
4 cups of coarse rye flour
4 cups of milk
3 ½ oz of yeast
4 cups of white flour
2 cups of molasses
1 tablespoon of fennel seed
2 tablespoons of minced orange peel
½ cup butter (1 stick) softened

Warm the ale. Put the rye flour in a large bowl and add the ale. Mix for 15 minutes, with an electric beater. Dissolve the yeast in milk that has been heated to lukewarm. Then add the milk and yeast mixture to the rye flour mixture. Mix well. Then add the white flour and mix again. Mix until the dough is soft and velvety. Oil a large bowl, and place the dough in it. Cover the bowl with a clean cloth, and let sit in a warm place until the dough has doubled in bulk. Then punch down and work in the rest of the ingredients. Form into a ball again. Let rise once more. Shape into two oblong loaves, and place them on a baking sheet. Brush the tops with cold water and bake in a 375°F., for 40 minutes. Brush the bread twice more during baking with the water. Remove from the oven and cool.

Make two loaves

Cinnamon Apples

An apple roasted with cinnamon and honey was one of the traditional dishes eaten with our St. Martins Day goose.

    8 large apples, cored but not peeled
    2 teaspoons cinnamon
    3 tablespoons butter
    1 cup white wine
    1 cup honey

Preheat the oven to 350°F. Butter a large baking dish. Place the apples in the dish. Melt the butter and combine with the cinnamon, white wine and honey. Pour over the apples. Bake for 1 hour or until the apples are soft.

Serves 4

Roast Goose

Roman colonists are credited with bringing the goose to Sweden, where it became one of our favorite meats, appearing on holiday tables from Martinmas to Easter. Sometimes it was stuffed, but more often it was cooked on its own, with spices rubbed into the skin. Although the goose is very fat, the Swedish liked to stuff butter under the skin as well, to make it extra tender.

10 pound goose
½ cup butter
Salt and pepper
1 teaspoon allspice
½ teaspoon ground cloves
1 onion quartered
1 orange halved

Mix the butter with the salt, pepper and spices. With a paring knife, cut the membrane that connects the skin to the breast of the goose, creating a pocket. Stuff the butter and spices into this pocket, underneath the goose skin. Then place the onion and the orange in the cavity of the goose. Place the goose on a rack over a baking pan. Preheat the oven to 400°F. Roast the goose for 30 minutes at this temperature and then lower the heat to 350°F. Roast for an additional 1½ hours, while basting several times. Remove from the oven and carve. Serve the slices on a platter. Skim the fat off the surface of the pan juice and serve in a sauceboat with the goose.

Serves 6-8

Red Cabbage with Currants

One of the most common vegetables in the Swedish diet was the cabbage, because it grew so well in the cold climates of the northern countries. Every country had their own way of preserving the cabbage. We especially liked this cabbage dish when paired with spices and currants.

1 head red cabbage, cored and shredded
4 tablespoons butter
1 teaspoon salt
½ teaspoon pepper
¼ teaspoon allspice

2 cups beef broth

½ cup currants

Heat the butter in a saucepan and add the cabbage. Sauté for 5 minutes. Then add the salt, pepper, and allspice. Sauté for 1 minute. Add the beef broth and currants. Bring to a boil and reduce the heat. Cover and simmer for 20 minutes. Transfer to a serving dish.

Serves 6-8

Swedish Pancakes

Pancakes became an easy meal to fix, with the invention of a pan that was suspended from a hook in the middle of the fireplace. Pancakes were very filling and provided an easy meal when the larder was low on other foods. Sometimes they were eaten plain, with butter, as a dinner course, or spread with jam as a dessert.

2 ½ cups flour

2 eggs

1 quart of milk

4 tablespoons butter, melted

½ teaspoon salt

½ cup additional butter

1 cup lingonberry or raspberry jam

Mix the flour and salt together in a bowl. Beat the eggs with the milk and add to the flour mixture. Mix well until smooth. Then add the melted butter and mix again. Let the mixture stand for 1 hour. Beat again before using. Butter a griddle. When the griddle is very hot, ladle 2 tablespoons of batter on it for each pancake. Turn when bubbles form on the top. Remove from the griddle and keep warm in the oven. To serve, place 4 pancakes on each plate. Spread the additional butter and jam between each pancake.

Serves 6

Red Fruit Jelly

Red fruit jelly is a Scandinavian treat, commonly enjoyed by the Danes, Swedes and Norwegians. This dish was anticipated when the berries were in season, during the short summers of northern Europe.

1½ cups raspberries

1½ cups red currants

¾ cup granulated sugar

½ cup cornstarch

1 teaspoon vanilla

8 oz half and half

Wash the berries. Place in a saucepan and cover with cold water. Bring to a boil and simmer for 10 minutes. Strain through a sieve and then return to the saucepan. Add the sugar and boil for 1 minute. Dissolve the cornstarch in 1 tablespoon of water. Add to the juice in the pan. Simmer, but do not boil. Stir until thickened. Add the vanilla. Pour into a serving bowl. Refrigerate until set. Spoon into individual dessert bowls and serve with half-and-half and a sprinkling of sugar.

Serves 6

*   *   *

Anne Bonny

1700-?, Pirates of the Caribbean

In compiling a list of famous women, none could forget me, for I was the most notorious female pirate of the 18th century. Born in Ireland, I was the illegitimate daughter of a prominent lawyer and his wife's maid. I will say this for my father; his courage led him to give up his life of wealth and he left Ireland for a new life in the Carolinas, with my mother and I. While living there, he made quite a fortune on his plantation. When I was sixteen, I had the misfortune to fall in love with James

Bonny, who turned out to be nothing short of a scoundrel with designs to steal my father's plantation. My father tried to dissuade me from marrying him by threatening me with disinheritance, but I would not listen. This left my father no choice but to disown me and I was forced to go with my erstwhile husband to the Bahamas, where I began to live a life of crime. While living there, I began to befriend the Pirate elite, as I soon became bored with the less than pleasant nature of my husband. So I left him and took up with one of the richest men in the Caribbean, Chidey Bayard. After this relationship fizzled out, I joined ranks of Calico Jack Rackham and together we went to sea, in search of ships. I was a liberated woman, wearing pants and becoming an expert with a pistol and rapier. Many battles and scandals ensued and by the time I was 20, Calico Jack and I were sentenced to hang, but I received a stay of execution because I was pregnant. Here ends the known story of my life, as any further information regarding my whereabouts disappeared at this time. But I escaped the hangman's rope and found a new life as rich in adventure as the one I led previously. Some even say I was rescued by my father and brought back to his plantation. This is a secret I will forever keep to myself.

Ever since the discovery of the West Indies by the Spanish and the English, European countries were provided with Caribbean foodstuffs that were superb additions to their formerly dull diet. While American colonists were surviving on bacon, corn, and whatever they could forage from the woods, Caribbean settlers, were enjoying pineapples, coconuts, sweet potatoes, plantains, mango, guava, papaya, and of course, lavishly used spices. One new food that would revolutionize English cuisine was the turkey, which by the time of the 16th century, had replaced swan and peacock as a principle source of meat.

Back in New Providence, the food was excellent. Meals were a combination of native and English fare and plenty of rum of course. Salt pork appeared in soups, cooked with native vegetables such as plantains, yams and collard greens. We were also blessed with an abundance of seafood, lobster, crabmeat, shrimp, sea bream, mullet, grouper and snapper. Yet these were just some of the seafood available on the islands.

Many unusual fruits grew in abundance as well, such as cherimoya, coconut, guavas, mangos, jackfruit, passion fruit, soursops and pineapples. Besides the black pepper that had graced dinner tables since the Middle Ages, the discovery of chili peppers by Columbus added a new spice range to cooking. Likewise, cinnamon, ginger and allspice all added a variety of tastes to our meals. The dinner banquet would have been served at the Governor of Jamaica's house, where even pirates like us were welcome.

*   *   *

The Governor's Dinner

Callaloo Soup
Pork Pie
Salt Cod Fritters
Beef with Pickled Walnuts
Spiced Turkey with lime
Plantain's with Salt Pork
Saffron Wigs
Pineapple Soaked in Rum
17th Century Cheesecakes

*   *   *

Callaloo Soup

Callaloo is a green leaf vegetable resembling spinach. It was often combined with salt pork, the most common seasoning meat available on the islands during the 17th and 18th century.

4 oz salt pork, diced into 1 inch squares
4 cups water
4 cups callaloo leaves, washed, stemmed and chopped
1 small onion, minced
2 whole cloves
½ cup coconut milk
1 cup cooked crabmeat

In a large saucepot, cover the salt pork with the water. Bring to a boil. Simmer for 1 hour or until the meat is tender. Add the callaloo, onion, and the cloves. Simmer for 1 hour. Then add the coconut milk and the crabmeat. Season with salt and pepper. Simmer for 6 minutes. Serve in soup bowls.
Serves 6

Pork Pie

Savory pies of all types, including beef, pork and fish, were a common item in the cuisine of the Caribbean in the 17th, century as it was highly influenced by the existence of a substantial British migrant population, especially on the islands of Jamaica and the Bahamas.

1 recipe Short Crust Pastry, page 391
2 (1pound)-pork tenderloins cut into 1 inch cubes
1 tablespoon butter
1 pound apples, peeled, cored and chopped
1 teaspoon salt

¼ teaspoon ground nutmeg
¼ teaspoon ground white pepper
¼ cup sugar
2 cups apple cider
1 egg, beaten

Preheat the oven to 350°F. Butter a pie dish and arrange the pork cubes and apples in it. Sprinkle with the salt, pepper, nutmeg and the sugar. Pour the apple cider on top and dot with the butter. Roll out the pastry to form a lid. Brush with the beaten egg. Bake for 1 1/2 hours or until the pastry is golden brown.

Serves 6

Salt Cod Fritters

Salt cod was imported to the islands by the Spanish, and became a staple of the islands of Jamaica and the Bahamas. We ate quite a lot of salt cod, as it was the one fish we could take on our ships without fear of spoilage.

1 pound salt cod
3 cups of milk

Batter:

1 cup flour
1 cup milk
2 eggs, beaten
Pepper
Vegetable oil

Soak the cod in the milk overnight in the refrigerator. Rinse and dry. In a saucepan, heat 3 cups of water, add the cod and cook until tender.

Then remove from the water and mince. Make the batter by mixing the flour, milk and eggs together. Let the batter sit for 30 minutes. Stir in the salt cod and add a generous amount of pepper. Pour two inches of vegetable oil into a large frying pan and heat until smoking. Drop heaping tablespoons of the fritter mixture into the oil. Cook until golden brown. Drain on paper towels and serve.

Serves 4

Beef with Pickled Walnuts

A favorite recipe since Tudor times, this meal would have been considered a real treat. Beef was rare and usually served in the jerked form on the islands. This beef recipe, with its pickled walnut sauce, would have been served at a special occasion, such as a dinner at the Governor's house.

3 pound brisket of beef
2 tablespoons allspice berries
2 onions, minced

Sauce:

3 tablespoons chopped parsley
1 onion, minced
2 ½ cups beef broth
¼ teaspoon pepper
1 teaspoon salt
1 tablespoon butter, rolled in flour
3 pickled walnuts, chopped*

*Note: Pickled Walnuts can be found in Gourmet shops or supermarkets in the condiment section.

Tie up the brisket with strong thread. Cover with water in a large saucepan. Add the onion and the allspice berries, and bring to a boil. Then skim. Salt the water. Simmer for 3 hours while covered or until tender.

To make the sauce: In a saucepan, add two cups of the beef broth from the cooked meat. Add the onion and parsley and simmer for 10 minutes. Then add the salt, pepper and butter. Simmer for 5 more minutes and add the pickled walnuts. Slice the meat into thick slices and drizzle with the sauce.

Serves 6

Spiced Turkey with Lime

Wild turkeys were prized in the Caribbean by the native peoples and we soon adapted their way of cooking them for our own dinner tables.

10 pound turkey

Marinade:

1 teaspoon ground allspice

1 teaspoon ground ginger

1 teaspoon ground cumin

1 teaspoon ground cinnamon

½ cup lime juice

½ minced Scotch Bonnet Chili Pepper*

¼ cup olive oil

---

* Scotch Bonnet Chili Peppers are native to the Caribbean. They are one of the hottest chili peppers, and must be handled with care. When removing the seeds from any chili pepper, wear plastic cloves, and do not touch your face.

Combine all the ingredients for the marinade in a small bowl. Whisk together. Wipe down the turkey and truss its legs together. With a pastry brush, spread the marinade all over the turkey. Refrigerate overnight. The next day, place the turkey in a large roasting pan. Preheat the oven to 350°F. Roast the turkey for 3 ½ hours, basting frequently with the marinade. Remove from the pan and let the turkey sit for 10 minutes. Carve and place on a serving platter.

8 servings

Plantains with Salt Pork

Plantains are a species related to the banana and were very plentiful on the Caribbean islands. We cooked it with salt pork and sometimes added chili peppers for taste.

2 pounds plantains peeled and diced*
¼ pound salt pork, diced
1 onion, minced

Cover the plantains with water and cook until soft. Drain and mash them. In a frying pan, sauté the salt pork until crisp and the fat is rendered. Add the onion, and sauté for 5 minutes. Then add the plantains and cook until hot. Transfer to a serving bowl.

Serves 6

---

*Note: Plantains can be found in Asian or Mexican Markets.

Saffron Wigs

Saffron continued to be a favorite spice of the British, but by the 18th Century it had been relegated to an addition for breads and cakes only. Gone were the elaborate sauces of the medieval and Tudor eras, where saffron appeared in every sauce, as well as cakes and tarts.

4 cups flour

2 teaspoons salt

2 tablespoons yeast, soaked in ¼ cup warm water

2/3 cup granulated sugar

2/3 cup butter

¼ teaspoon saffron, soaked in ½ cup water

2 eggs

1 tablespoon caraway seeds

1 egg, beaten

Sift together the flour, salt and sugar. Warm the butter until melted. In a large bowl, combine the butter, saffron water, and yeast and flour mixture. Stir well. Then add the two eggs and the caraway seeds. Mix well until smooth. Oil a bowl and add the dough. Leave to rise while covered in a warm place for 2 hours, or until doubled in size. Punch the dough down and shape into buns. Leave on a greased cookie sheet until doubled in size. Brush with the melted butter and egg and bake for 15 minutes at 425°F.

Makes 12-15 rolls

Pineapple Soaked in Rum

By the 18th century, sugar cane had been introduced to the islands. Rum was also being produced and became a major industry for export.

1 large pineapple, peeled, cored and sliced
½ cup granulated sugar
1 cup dark rum

Place the pineapple in a large bowl. Heat the rum and the sugar together until the sugar is dissolved. Pour over the pineapple. Let marinate until ready to serve.
Serves 4

17th century Cheesecakes

Interestingly enough, many tarts containing eggs and fruits were called cheesecakes during the 17th century, although they contained no cheese.

1 recipe Short Crust Pastry, page 391
2 cups half and half
4 large eggs, lightly beaten
½ cup butter
½ cup granulated sugar
½ cup currants
1 pinch nutmeg
¼ teaspoon ground cinnamon
2 tablespoons brandy or rum

Line 16 pastry tins with the short crust pastry. Boil the cream and eggs, until the mixture has curdled. Strain the curds in cheesecloth until all the liquid has drained away. Soften the butter and beat with the sugar, currants, spices and the brandy. Fold in the curds and spoon the mixture into tins. Bake at 350°F. for 25 to 30 minutes. Remove from the oven and cool.
Serves 16 small tarts

*   *   *

Catherine the Great

1729-1796, Empress of Russia

It was unfortunate that I was married to one of the craziest rulers of Russia, at a time when Russia was in desperate need of strong leadership. The Empress Elizabeth was childless and needed to have a strong heir, so she searched through the minor German Royalty for a candidate and found me. I was actually a cousin to her nephew Peter, whom I was to marry. The marriage was a sham, for Peter actually preferred to play with toys in bed, rather than pay attention to me. For ten years I endured a childless marriage, and finally gave birth to my son Paul, who was the son of my lover, Sergei Saltykov. In 1762, when Peter was absent from court, planning one of his senseless battles against Denmark, I decided to act. I had watched Peter become crazier and crazier by the day. Donning a lieutenant's uniform, I rode into St. Petersburg with a regiment of imperial guards and took over the throne. Then I had Peter arrested and murdered. Some historians say I was ruthless, but I had to be, for Russia was in dire straits. While I reigned, the power of the clergy waned and I put down several major rebellions, while organizing a civil service and adding to the territory of Russia. It was I who made Russia a European power to be reckoned with.

In a country as large as my Russia, cooking was affected by the climatic conditions and varied in the different parts of the country. The origins of Russian cookery are obscure. We did not have a long, documented culinary history like England, France and Spain. Because I was a well-educated woman who read the works of Montesquieu and various other writers, I was determined to bring the civilized world to Russia. I patronized foreign cooks who adapted our rather plain cuisine into international fare.

Dinners were affairs of grandeur at my Court. Starting with Zakuski, or Russian hors d'oeuvres, of smoked fish, pickles, Russian blini and caviar, before moving on to meat dishes, salads, and grains.

Then the dinners were finished with many desserts. Russian Easter was a particulary festive event. After church, the Lenten fast would be broken, and course upon course of food would be presented, ending with the two traditional Russian Easter desserts, Paskha and Kulich. All this food was washed down with various wines, and of course Vodka, of which there were many different varieties. Beets, Morello cherries, cranberries, apples, cabbage, kasha or buckwheat groats, mushrooms, sour cream, farmers cheese, turbot, carp, herring, carp and caviar, were just some of the foods that constituted the Russian diet during my reign. But the majority of these foods would have appeared only on the tables of the aristocracy, for the peasant contented himself with rye bread, or some cabbage and onions, kasha and the occasional dish of meat or fish.

So come let us eat and be merry. For it is Russian Easter and we sing praises to the resurrection of the Lord.

*   *   *

The Russian Easter Dinner
Smoked Sturgeon

Black Bread
Smoked Sausages
Pickled Cucumbers
Fish Soup
Russian Cheese Fritters
Kasha and Mushrooms
Turbot with Wine and Cherries
Veal Roast with Caviar Sauce
Loin of Pork with a Sweet Sauce
Paskha
Kulich
Dried Fruit Compote
Vodka

*   *   *

Pickled Cucumbers

The Russian people relished pickled vegetables, especially beets and cucumbers. Even the peasant would have a small plot of land in which to grow them. Soups made of beets were especially popular among all the social classes of Russia.

3 large cucumbers, peeled and sliced
1 large onion, sliced
2 teaspoons salt
2 tablespoons fresh minced dill
2 cups white wine vinegar

In a large bowl, combine the cucumbers and the onion. Heat the salt dill and vinegar together until just hot. Pour over the cucumbers. Cool. Chill for at least 24 hours.
Makes 4 cups

Fish Soup

During the 18th century, fish soup became very popular. With many courses of heavier food to follow, this type of soup was thought to be a refreshing start to the meal.

1 pound of sea bass
2 ½ pound fish trimmings
1 ¾ cups white wine
3 medium onions, chopped
1 parsley root, scraped
2 stalks of celery, chopped
1 cup mushrooms, chopped
4 tablespoons minced dill weed
1 bay leaf
5 peppercorns
2 quarts water
2 teaspoons salt
¼ teaspoon pepper
¼ cup butter
2 scallions, chopped

Wipe the fish and set it aside. Put the fish trimmings, wine, onion, parsley root, mushrooms, three tablespoons of the dill, the bay leaf and peppercorns in to a soup pot with the water, salt and pepper. Simmer for 1 hour. Then strain and return the broth to the pot. Cut the fish into 2-inch pieces. Melt the butter, sauté the fish in a skillet with the scallions, for 5 minutes. Add to the broth and simmer for 10 minutes. Serve in soup bowls sprinkled with the extra dill.
Serves 6-8

Russian Cheese Fritters

We Russians have always loved cheese. We especially liked farmer's cheese and cottage cheese, using them for a variety of fillings. Sour cream usually accompanied fritters such as these. Today, these fritters would be considered a dessert, but during my lifetime they were a main course.

> 4 cups farmer's cheese or pot cheese
> 2/3 cup sifted flour
> 4 egg yolks
> ¼ teaspoon salt
> 2 tablespoons sugar
> Sour cream

Squeeze the moisture from the cheese. Rub through a sieve. Mix the flour; egg yolks, salt and sugar together. Add to the cheese. Mix well. Form into 4-inch thick sausages. Chill for 1 hour. Cut into 1-inch cakes and fry in melted butter until golden brown on both sides. Serve hot with sour cream.

Makes 20 fritters

Kasha with Mushrooms

The staple grain in Russia was buckwheat groats or kasha, forming a filling meal for the Russian peasant. Usually cooked with boiling water or stock and combined with mushrooms, it made for a very savory addition to the menu.

> ½ cup butter
> 1 ½ cups kasha (Buckwheat)
> 1 teaspoon salt
> 1 pound mushrooms diced and sautéed in butter

Heat the butter in a large pan. Add the kasha, the salt and pepper. Stir over medium heat for 10 minutes. Put into a 2 quart buttered casserole dish. Add boiling water to cover the kasha. Preheat the oven to 350°F. Bake for 1 hour. Add more water if necessary. Let stand for 15 minutes. Then add the mushrooms and stir. Reheat on medium heat for 10 minutes. Serve with additional butter.

Serves 6

Turbot with Wine and Cherries

We liked the combination of sweet and sour, creating many recipes for fish such as turbot, pike, or carp with the combination of fruit and wine.

    3 pounds turbot fillets
    ½ pint white wine
    1 tablespoon pickle juice
    1 leek, chopped finely
    1 stalk celery, chopped finely
    2 medium onions, chopped finely
    1 bay leaf
    1 teaspoon peppercorns
    1 teaspoon salt
    1 cup cherry syrup
    2 tablespoons light brown sugar
    1 tablespoon gerkins chopped finely
    ¼ teaspoon ground cinnamon
    ¼ teaspoon ground cloves
    ¼ cup butter
    1 cup Madeira
    1 ½ cups cherries, pitted

Stock: In a large pot combine the wine, pickle juice, onions, celery, bay leaf, peppercorns and salt. Bring to a boil. Reduce the heat and simmer for 20 minutes. Then add the fish and simmer until the fish is opaque.

Sauce: In a saucepan, heat the cherry juice and add the rest of the ingredients except for the cherries. Whisk until smooth and thick. Add the cherries. Place the Turbot on a serving plate and spoon the sauce over the top.

Serves 6

Veal Roast with Caviar Sauce

Veal was the preferred meat of the time among the aristocratic classes. Beef was used mainly to make soup stocks, or in large roasted hunches of meat. Caviar was eaten plain with bread, combined with sour cream in blini, and used in sauces.

    2 pounds veal fillet or tenderloin
    1 cup white wine
    4 tablespoons caviar
    2 tablespoons lemon juice
    1bay leaf
    2 whole cloves
    1 teaspoon salt
    1 teaspoon pepper
    Additional lemon juice
    2 tablespoons butter

Lard the veal roast. Preheat the oven to 350°F. Brown in a large Dutch oven. Then add the rest of the ingredients, except for the caviar. Bake for 1 hour. Remove the roast from the pan and keep warm in the oven. Strain the cooking juices. Place in a saucepan; add caviar and additional lemon juice if necessary. Reheat. Right before the sauce is done, add the butter and whisk to incorporate. Slice the veal fillet and serve on a platter napped with the sauce.

Serves 6

Loin of Pork in a Sweet Sauce

We loved to serve a teaspoon of our exquisite jams in our tea. This love of sweets carried over into our sauces made with jam that accompanied our pork dishes.

1 (2-pound) Loin of Pork, cut into 2 inch slices
1 cup fine white breadcrumbs
2 eggs beaten
¼ cup butter
Flour

Sauce

2 tablespoons of apple or plum jam
3 tablespoon of honey
2 cups of beef stock
3 tablespoons of port wine
1 teaspoon grated lemon rind
1 teaspoon ground cinnamon
5 whole cloves

Preheat the oven to 350°F. Butter a large casserole dish and set aside. In a frying pan, heat the butter. Wipe the tenderloin slices dry. Dredge in flour, then dip in the beaten egg, and finally dredge in the breadcrumbs. Fry until golden brown on both sides. Remove the slices from the frying pan, and place in the casserole. In a saucepan, heat the beef stock and add the rest of the ingredients. Bring to a boil. Reduce the heat and simmer for 10 minutes. Then pour over the tenderloin slices. Bake in the oven for 20 minutes. Remove from the oven and place the tenderloin slices on a platter. Cover with the sauce..

Serves 4-6

Paskha

Paskha is a conical mold of cheese, filled with fruit and decorated with icing with the Russian lettering for Christ. It is one of our traditional Easter foods. It is always served with Kulich, the Russian Easter bread.

2 pounds cottage cheese
1 cup granulated sugar
4 eggs
1 teaspoon vanilla
2 containers (7oz) of farmer's cheese or pot cheese
1 cup raspberry jam seedless
¾ cup butter, softened
2 teaspoons lemon rind
¼ cup golden raisins
1/3 cup candied orange peel, chopped
¼ cup ground almonds
Candied cherries for garnish
Sliced almonds for garnish

Line a paskha mold or an unglazed flour pot containing a drainage hole, with 3 double thicknesses of cheesecloth. Place the paskha mold on a wire rack set, over a cake pan. Place 1container (7oz) of the farmer's cheese, the sugar and the eggs in a food processor and puree. Remove to a pan and cook over medium heat, stirring constantly for 6 minutes. Stir in the vanilla and pour into a large bowl to cool. Puree the remaining farmer's cheese, the jam, and butter and lemon rind.

Pour into the bowl containing the cooked cheese mixture. Then fold in the raisins, orange peel and almonds. Mix well.

Pour into the mold, folding the excess cheesecloth over the top. Cover with plastic wrap. Place a flat-bottomed weight, slightly smaller then the mold inside, to weight it down. Refrigerate over the cake pan for 3 days. Weight again with two 23-oz cans, for 2 more days. Unmold and remove the cheesecloth. Decorate the mold with candied fruits and almonds. Slice into wedges.

Serves 12

Kulich

2 envelopes active dry yeast
¼ cup warm milk
1 teaspoon sugar
1 ½ sticks butter
½ cup granulated sugar
1 tablespoon grated lemon peel
1 teaspoon salt
2/3 cup scalded milk
2 whole eggs and 4 egg yolk
3 cups flour
½ cup sultanas
½ cup raisins
¼ cup dark rum
½ cup almonds sliced
2 cups flour

Glaze:

½ cup confectioners sugar
2 teaspoons milk

Soak the raisins and sultanas in the rum In a small bowl, combine the yeast with the warm milk and sugar. Let it rest for 10 minutes. Combine the butter, sugar, grated lemon peel and salt in another bowl. Add 1 cup of the flour, and the yeast mixture. Mix well. Then add the eggs, the rest of the milk, the rest of the flour and mix well. Drain the raisins then add them to the dough. Then add the almonds to the dough. Mix well. Remove the dough to a floured surface. Knead for 10 minutes, incorporating the rest of the flour. Form the dough to a ball and place in a buttered bowl. Cover with a cloth and let rise, until doubled in volume.

Punch the dough down after it has risen. Butter a large 2-pound coffee can. Fold a double sheet of foil around the outside of the top of the can. Shape the dough into a ball and drop it into the can. Cover with a cloth and then let rise until it almost reaches the top of the tin. Bake at 350°F. for 60 minutes, or until a skewer inserted in the middle comes out clean. Cool and then remove from the can. Make a glaze with the powdered sugar and the milk. Spread on top of the bread. Let it drizzle down the sides. Serve with the Paskha.

Serves 10

Dried Fruit Compote

Because we had a relatively short summer, we dried many fruits for use all year long. Some of our favorites were prunes, pears and apples. By preserving them, we would be assured of a supply of fruit to last us all through the winter months.

½ cup dried prunes, pitted
½ cup raisins
1cup dried apple slices
1 cup dried pear quarters
1 cup honey
1 cinnamon stick

6 whole cloves

2 quarts apple cider

2 tablespoons lemon juice

1 tablespoon lemon rind

Combine the fruit in a large pot. Fill with the apple cider. Add the cloves and the lemon peel. Simmer until the large pieces are cooked but not falling apart. Pour off the liquid into a pan, and cook it until reduced by 1/3rd. Add the honey, cinnamon, lemon juice and fruit. Reheat, stirring several times. Place the fruit in a large glass-serving bowl. Pour the syrup over the top. Chill until ready to serve.

Serves 10

*   *   *

Charlotte of Mecklenberg-Strelitz

1744-1818 Queen of England, Consort of George III

I was born in Mecklenberg-Strelitz, a minor German principality, over which my father ruled. I led a rather secluded life as a child and a young girl, only allowed to go out on Sundays for church and a carriage ride. The first time I heard of my proposed marriage with George the III, occurred when I was told to come to the drawing room to meet the British Ambassador. I was asked to lay down on the sofa. The Ambassador put his foot on my dress, claiming me for George the III.

I had my first glimpse of English demeanor when the ladies designated to escort me to London viewed me with horror, because of my less than sophisticated dress. They wanted to fix me up for the King, but I would have none of it. George would have to like me for what I was. I am delighted to say he did and I was able to satisfy his strong physical needs, while at the same time producing an unheard of amount of royal children. George and I were very compatible. We both liked the home, loved music and languages. Peace was insured until 1765, when George had his first breakdown. I knew that I must become a buffer between George and his ministers, for George would be at their mercy.

I moved George to Windsor, so as to keep him away from the stress of the Court It was hard work keeping George out of the public eye for periods of time, until the fits of madness passed. George never recovered from these bouts of madness, they went on until the end of his life. It was more of a struggle after my son, the Prince of Wales, whom I disliked intensely, came for a visit. George tried to strangle him. The Prince set out to spread the rumor of his father's illness, in order to become the Regent himself. Thank god George had a period of lucidity and we were safe again.

Allow me to describe the food that was available during my lifetime. Due to our colonies we had established in America, we had an abundance of new foods like squash, corn and turkeys. Coffeehouses started to spring up around London and tea, which was introduced to the country by Catherine of Braganza, was destined to become an English passion.

Dinner started later in the evening at 7 or 8:pm. Dinner consisted of three courses, but each course had a multitude of dishes. For example, the first course might start with soup, progress to fish dishes and end with the meat course, followed by a second round of lighter dishes of meat. Savory pies, tarts and fish puddings would follow. Then on to the third course of jellies, sweetmeats, fruits, nuts and cheese.

Butter as an ingredient was used generously in almost every dish, replacing the elaborate sauces of the Tudor Age. Shellfish replaced the more muddy water fish such as carp or pike. Oysters were all the rage in Georgian England, since they could be transported easily from the coastal regions. Green vegetables began to assert themselves, but it was still a slow process. Usually they were boiled and served with a simple butter sauce. Some of the favorite fruit of the time included rhubarb, which was introduced from Italy, as well as gooseberries, damson plums and oranges, which came from the Middle East. Trade with exotic places brought rare new foods, which of course could only be afforded by the very wealthy. Sago, macaroni, curries, pineapples, spices from the Caribbean and sugar began to appear on our tables. Beverages included beer, wine, brandy and of course gin, which was plentiful and cheap.

Come join George and I as we eat, surrounded by our multitude of children, dining on gold plates and served by liveried footmen.

*　　　　　*　　　　　*

The Madness of King George Dinner

Tomato Soup with Fennel
Veal with Lemon
Madeira Ham with Cinnamon
Beef Birds
Spinach in Cream
Pickled Eggs
Whipped Syllabub
Cherries and Figs in Port
St. Catherine's Cakes
Pineapple Pie

*Note: Recipes composed from ingredients available during the 18th century in England, and adapted from Hannah Glasse and Robert May's cookbooks.

*　　　　　*　　　　　*

Tomato and Fennel Soup

Tomatoes were imported from the Americas during the 18th Century. My cooks looked upon them with suspicion, as they were part of the Nightshade family, They would only serve them cooked, like in this recipe for tomato soup.

2 tablespoons olive oil

1 small onion, minced

2 fennel bulbs, minced

1 can (32-oz) whole tomatoes

8 cups chicken broth

Salt and pepper to taste

1 tablespoon minced chervil

Heat the olive oil in a soup pot. Add the onion and sauté until limp. Then add the fennel and sauté for 5 minutes. Drain the liquid from the tomatoes and chop them. Add the tomatoes and the chicken broth to the pot. Bring to a boil. Simmer for 30 minutes. Add salt and pepper to taste. Then add the chervil. Simmer for 10 more minutes. Ladle into soup bowls.

Serves 4

Veal Cutlets with Lemon

As in Russia, veal was a favorite source of meat among the gentry of the 17th century. More delicate than beef, its flavor was especially pleasing. It could be combined with many different herbs, spices and of course the lemon. I especially liked the delicate taste of the meat, enhanced by the sharpness of the lemon juice.

8 veal scallops

1/3 cup flour

1 teaspoon salt

½ teaspoon pepper

¼ teaspoon grated nutmeg

1 egg, beaten

½ cup fine white breadcrumbs

¼ cup butter

1 tablespoon lemon rind, grated

2 cups beef broth

¼ cup flour

2 tablespoons lemon juice

Heat the butter in a skillet. Pat the veal scallops with paper towels to dry them. In a plate, combine the flour, salt, pepper and nutmeg. Dip the veal scallops first in the flour, then in the egg and finally in the breadcrumbs. Fry the scallops until golden brown on both sides. Remove from the skillet and keep warm in the oven. Stir the flour into the pan juices. Add the beef broth, stirring continuously. Add the lemon juice. Arrange the cutlets on dinner plates and spoon the sauce over the top.

Serves 8

Madeira Ham with Cinnamon

Ham, rather than just being boiled or roasted, was now combined with spices, tomatoes, olives, capers or fruit, for a more interesting recipe.

2 pounds of ham steaks, 2 inches thick

1½ cups Madeira

2 cloves

10 peppercorns

1 teaspoon marjoram leaves

1 teaspoon ground cinnamon

2 tablespoons olive oil

1 large onion, thinly sliced

2 medium tomatoes, diced

2 large turnips, diced

1 apple peeled and sliced.

1 tablespoon capers

In a bowl, combine the Madeira, cloves, peppercorns, marjoram and cinnamon. Place the meat in the bowl with the marinade. Marinate in the refrigerator for several hours. Spread the olive oil on the bottom of a roasting pan. Preheat the oven to 350°F. Arrange the diced vegetables, apple and capers on the bottom of the pan. Place the ham steaks on top. Pour the marinade over the top of the ham steaks. Bake for 1½ hours.

Remove the ham steaks from the pan. Place on a serving platter and spoon the vegetables and sauce over the top.

Serves 6-8

Beef Birds

Beef birds date back to the time in England when chicken and capon meat was very expensive. Robert May, who wrote the *Accomplisht Cook* in 1660, proclaimed that this was an inexpensive way of stretching meat. Especially for those whose pocketbooks could not afford the more expensive cuts. Although this was a dish reserved for the middle class, George and I liked it well enough to have it on our table.

8 slices top round beef steaks, pounded thin
1 onion, minced
6 tablespoons of butter
4 slices bacon, fried crisp and crumbled
1 teaspoon dried thyme
1 tablespoon minced parsley
¼ teaspoon mace
8 olives, minced
3 tablespoons flour
Salt and pepper
½ cup dry red wine
1 cup beef broth

Pound the beef between sheets of waxed paper until very thin. Brown the onion in 2 tablespoons of the butter. Add the bacon, herbs, mace and olives to the onion mixture. Season with pepper. Spread the mixture on each of the beef slices and roll up. Tie each roll with kitchen twine. Mix the flour with the salt and pepper and spread on a plate. Then dredge the beef rolls in it. Heat the remaining 4 tablespoons of butter in a large skillet and brown the rolls. Add the red wine and beef broth. Simmer uncovered for 10 minutes. Transfer the rolls to a serving platter and spoon the pan juices over the meat.

Serves 4

Spinach with Cream

Spinach, which had made its debut in Tudor England, was now firmly entrenched in 18th century cuisine. One favorite way of cooking spinach was to combine it with nutmeg and cream. Nutmeg was a spice used a great deal in the 18th century. In fact, the wealthy class carried around elaborate nutmeg graters in their pockets.

2 pounds spinach
3 tablespoons butter
1 onion, minced
1 tablespoon flour
1 cup peas, cooked and pureed
1 cup heavy cream
¼ teaspoon grated nutmeg
Salt and pepper to taste
Fried bread triangles

Wash the spinach and place in a large skillet. Steam in its own moisture for 3 minutes until it wilts. Press out the water and chop fine. Melt the butter and sauté the onion. Add the flour and cook for 3 minutes. Then add the spinach, pureed peas, cream and nutmeg.

Simmer for 4 minutes. Transfer to a serving bowl and garnish with the fried bread triangles.

Serves 6-8

Pickled Eggs

Pickled eggs, a standard of pub fare today, first made the scene in 17th century England. For the journey by carriage between London and Windsor, there was nothing like a good pickled egg to stave off hunger, served with cheese and fruit.

8 large eggs
1 pint white vinegar
2 tablespoons black peppercorns
2 tablespoons allspice berries
2 tablespoons ginger root, peeled and sliced

Boil the eggs for 10 minutes. Cool in cold water and then remove the shells. In a saucepan, simmer the vinegar and spices together for 5 minutes. Place the eggs in a warmed, sterilized jar and then pour the hot vinegar mixture over the top, leaving in the spices. Cover with a lid. Store in the refrigerator for 2 weeks to allow the pickled eggs to mature and mellow.

Makes 8 pickled eggs

Whipped Syllabub

Like the posset of the Tudor Age, Syllabubs combined cream and sherry and were some of the most delightful desserts of Georgian England.

1 cup whipping cream
2 tablespoons granulated sugar

¼ cup sherry, sweet
1 egg white

Whip the cream until soft peaks have formed and add the sugar. Whip again for 1 minute. Stir the sherry into the whipped cream. Beat the egg white until stiff peaks have formed. Fold into the whipped cream. Spoon small amounts of syllabub into cordial glasses. Chill 2 hours before serving.

Serves 4

Cherries and Figs in Port

Fruits were often cooked in wine, sherry, or port, a practice developed in the Middle Ages. Cherries were particulary well liked in my lifetime. We brandied and candied them, as well as using them in pies and cakes.

2 cups Bing cherries, pitted
2 cups fresh figs, diced
1 tablespoon granulated sugar
2 teaspoons grated lemon zest
2 teaspoons grated orange zest
1 cinnamon stick, one inch long
2 tablespoons blackcurrant jelly
2 cups ruby port

In a saucepan, combine the sugar, lemon zest, orange zest, cinnamon stick, blackcurrant jelly and ruby port. Bring to a boil, then reduce the heat and simmer for 5 minutes. Remove from the heat and cool. Place the cherries and figs in a serving dish. Pour the port over the fruit and chill in the refrigerator until ready to serve.

Serves 4

St. Catherine's cakes

Seed cakes, which originated in the nunneries of the Middle Ages, had become a secular treat by the time of my reign. They appeared on the table at breakfast, teatime and dinner. Originally, St. Catherine's cakes containing caraway seeds were served at the end of a meal to aid with digestion.

> 4 cups flour
> 2 teaspoons salt
> ½ cup butter
> 1 tablespoon yeast
> ¼ cup granulated sugar
> 2 eggs, beaten
> 2 tablespoons caraway seeds

Sift the flour and the salt together. Melt the butter and add the sugar. Dissolve the yeast in 1/3 cup of warm water. In a bowl, place the flour and make a well. Add the melted butter mixture, the yeast and the eggs. Mix well. Then add the caraway seeds. Mix again. On a floured board, knead the dough until elastic. Then place in an oiled bowl. Cover and let rise in a warm place. Punch the dough down. Place in a greased spring form pan. Let rise again. Bake for 1 hour at 350°F.,or until the cake sounds hollow when tapped.

Makes 1 large cake

Ananas or Pineapple Pie

The pineapple imported from British holdings in the West Indies was more than just a novelty during the 18th century. Just like when the Quince was imported during Tudor times; there appeared a multitude of recipes for the pineapple. Its sweet, yet acidic taste was very pleasing to the 18th century palate.

1 recipe Short Crust Pastry; page 391

1 large fresh pineapple, peeled, cored and sliced

½ cup Madeira

4 tablespoons granulated sugar

Mix the Madeira and the sugar. Add the pineapple slices. Marinate for 3 hours. Place the pineapple slices and the marinade in a saucepan. Cook covered for 30 minutes. Preheat the oven to 350°F. Roll out the pastry to fit a 9-inch tart pan. Prick all over and cover with a circle of parchment paper. Fill with beans or pie weights. Bake for 15 minutes. Remove the piecrust from the oven. Then remove the beans, and paper. Place the pineapple slices in overlapping circles in the tart pan. Boil down the Madeira and the sugar until thick syrup forms. Paint the pineapple with the glaze. Bake for another 20 minutes. Remove from the oven and cool

Serves 6-8

*   *   *

Marie Antoinette

1755-1793 Queen of France

I was the youngest daughter of Francis I, the German Emperor and the Empress Maria Theresa. I was spoiled horribly by my family and was married off at a very early age to the Dauphin of France. I would like to be vindicated, as I am always portrayed as a frivolous, selfish woman who didn't give a damm about anyone. The truth is that while I was adept at entertaining myself with balls, sleigh racing, hunting in the Bois de Boulogne and parties at Le Petit Trianon, I was married to the most uninteresting, dull man in the world. Needless to say, my marriage to the Dauphin was not a happy one for me. Nor was it particulary pleasing from a political standpoint. For the French people resented a Franco-Austrian alliance. I indulged in a great deal of amusing parties, dances and other entertainment's because I was so unhappy. To compound problems further, I was unable to have a child. Finally, the Dauphin was convinced to have surgery to correct an anatomical problem and I was able to fulfill my dreams of a family through my son and daughter. Life was filled with wonderful pleasures now that I had my family. The French people however, were unhappy. Poverty was rampant among the poor classes. Finally taking the law into their hands, they overturned the government and abolished the throne, hastening Louie and I to an early death.

But before this event, there was a vast amount of food at the French Court and always elegantly prepared. Tables were set with imported china and crystal. Dinner was sometimes staged to invite trysts later on. The entertainment consisted of love poems, singing and dancing of an inflammatory nature. Potatoes became the rage at court when the army pharmacist, Monsieur Parmentier, presented a bouquet of its purple flowers to Louie on his birthday. Catherine De Medici, who also brought pasta for the first time to the dinner table, had introduced asparagus and artichokes to the French Court. Peas had become a very popular food in Paris, during the time of Louie XIV, the Sun King. His mistresses ate copious quantities of them because they were thought to be aphrodisiacs. Speaking of aphrodisiacs, by the time of my reign oysters, truffles and special concoctions of herbs had been added to the list of sexual enhancements. It suffices to say that I too ate large amounts of these foods, in the hope that they would stimulate the Dauphin to give me a child. Dinner might include, stewed pheasant, crayfish, a delicate soup, vegetables and fish presented in elaborate aspics. Followed by pates, puff pastries, cakes filled with almond paste, chocolate confections and strawberries in cherry syrup. Rich sauces and complex dishes of many ingredients were standard fare of the day. Coffee and chocolate were consumed at almost every meal.

I personally hated to eat with others watching me, so I tried to escape from state banquets and dine alone. Even while we were in jail during the French Revolution, we were treated fairly and dined on sliced roast beef, joints of fowl, pies, asparagus, mushrooms and truffles, complimented by cakes, biscuits and fruits, wine and coffee. One fact that remains true is that the French people developed a love of good food over the 18th century that was to produce the great gastronomic meals of the 19th.

*   *   *

Dinner at Versailles
Vol-Au-Vent-of Oysters
Trout Cordon Bleu
Squab with Duxelles
Shoulder of Lamb with Cucumbers
Potatoes Parmentier
Petit Peas in Cream
Parsley of Macedonia
Tart Aux Fruits
Petit Pots de Crème Au Chocolat
Strawberries in Cherry Syrup

*   *   *

Vol-Au-Vent-of Oysters

Louis XIV's second wife, Madame de Maineton, founded the cooking school St. Cyr, which was later to become the Cordon Bleu, was the creator of this recipe.

1 quart of shucked oysters
½ cup butter
Salt and pepper
¼ teaspoon nutmeg
1 tablespoon lemon juice
1 large truffle minced
½ pound mushrooms, sliced and sautéed in butter
3 cups Veloute sauce, page 391
6 Puff pastry patty shells
2 tablespoons minced parsley

Drain the oysters, conserving any liquid for later. Melt the butter in a sauce pan and add the oysters. Gently stew the oysters until the edges curl. Add the salt, pepper and lemon juice. Sauté for 1 minute. Then add the Veloute sauce and oyster liquor previously conserved. Preheat the oven to 400°F. Place the patty shells on a non-greased cookie sheet. Bake in the oven until the patty shells are golden brown, about 10-12 minutes. Remove from the oven and place on individual serving plates. Fill with the oyster mixture. Spoon the remaining oyster mixture around the shells. Sprinkle with the minced parsley. Serve immediately.

Serves 6

Trout Cordon Bleu

Fish was served both with rich sauces and more simple methods like this trout, cooked with vinegar and peppercorns.

6, 10 oz trout

4 quarts of water
1½ cup white wine vinegar
2 bay leaves
15 peppercorns
Salt
Melted butter

Remove the fins from the fish. Combine the water with the rest of the ingredients except for the melted butter in a large Dutch oven. Bring to a boil over medium heat. Add the fish and simmer for 10 minutes. Remove the trout from the Dutch oven. Serve immediately on individual plates with melted butter.

Serves 6

Squab with Duxelles

Created in the 17th century by the French chef La Varenne, chef to the Marquis d'Uxelles, this squab dish was representative of the intricate dishes that Louie liked to eat.

4 slices bacon, minced
6 squabs
8 tablespoons butter
4 green onions, minced
3 shallots, minced
½ pound mushrooms, minced
Salt and pepper
½ teaspoon dried thyme
½ teaspoon dried basil
3 teaspoons minced parsley
¾ cup dry white wine

1 cup beef broth

6 slices ham

6 slices peasant bread, crusts removed

Fry the bacon until crisp in a Dutch oven. Remove the bacon and reserve. Brown the squabs in the bacon fat, breast sides down. Turn them and add 2 tablespoons of the butter, the scallions, shallots and mushrooms. Sprinkle with salt and pepper. Cook for 5 minutes. Then add the herbs, white wine and broth. Simmer for 5 minutes. Preheat the oven to 350°F. Bake the squabs, covered for 40 minutes. In the remaining butter, fry the ham and then the bread. Place the ham on the fried bread, on a heated platter. Place a bird on each piece of the ham. Add the bacon pieces to the juices in the pan, and pour over the squabs.

Serves 6

Shoulder of Lamb with Cucumbers

While we French were not lovers of mutton like our English neighbors, a delicate cut of spring lamb served with a savory stuffing of bacon and mushrooms with sautéed cucumbers, was a dish fit to set before the King.

Five pounds shoulder of lamb, boned

Salt and pepper

1 teaspoon mace

¼ pound lean bacon, minced

½ pound mushrooms, minced

4 shallots, minced

2 onions, minced

1 cup bread crumbs

½ teaspoon thyme, marjoram, and tarragon

2 tablespoons parsley, chopped

1 egg
½ cup butter
1½ cups beef broth
8 cucumbers
3 tablespoons flour
2 tablespoons lemon juice

Season the lamb with salt, pepper and mace. In a large casserole dish, place the bacon and cook until slightly browned, then add the mushrooms, shallots and half of the onions. Saute until the onions are translucent. Remove to a mixing bowl. Add the breadcrumbs, herbs, half the parsley and the egg. Spread the meat with this stuffing and tie neatly with kitchen twine. Add 3 tablespoons of the butter to the casserole. Brown the meat and the remaining onions. Add 1 cup of the broth and cover. Bake in a preheated oven at 350°F. for 2 hours for medium rare meat.

Peel the cucumber and cut into 2-inch sticks. Put in a bowl with salt. Let stand for 1 hour. Then press as much of the water out as possible. Roll the cucumber sticks in flour, seasoned with the salt and pepper. In a small skillet heat the remaining butter and fry the cucumber sticks to a golden color. Carefully lift the meat out of the casserole and add the remaining ½ cup of beef broth to the pan drippings. Whisk the sauce until the pan drippings are incorporated. Slice the meat. Pile the cucumbers to one side of the meat and then sprinkle with the parsley and drizzle with the sauce.

Serves 6-8

Potatoes Parmentier

After the introduction of the potato to the French Court, Louie demanded that his chefs create dish after dish of them. It would not do to just eat them plain, for they must be carefully sauced with cream, butter and spices.

2 pounds medium russet potatoes, peeled and sliced

3 cups Béchamel Sauce, page 387

1 teaspoon salt

½ teaspoon pepper

1 cup toasted buttered breadcrumbs

Preheat the oven to 350°F. Butter a large casserole dish. Layer the potatoes with a cup of sauce between each layer, ending with a layer of sauce on the top. Then sprinkle with salt, pepper and the toasted bread crumbs. Bake in the oven for 45 minutes. Remove from the oven and serve immediately.

Serves 6

Petit Peas in Cream

By the end of the 18th century petit peas were all the rage in France, having been made popular at the court of Louis XIV. Considered to be an aphrodisiac, their popularity ran rampant with the aristocrats, who were always looking for new foods to fuel their amorous natures.

2 pounds young green peas

Bouquet garni: 1 whole clove, 4 sprigs of parsley, 1 small onion, cut up and tied in cheesecloth

1 cup beef broth

½cup heavy cream

Salt and pepper

1 tablespoon butter

1 teaspoon flour

1 pinch sugar

¼cup orange juice

¼ cup of minced parsley

Place the peas with the Bouquet garni in a saucepan and simmer for 10 minutes or until the peas are tender. Add the cream and salt and pepper. In a small saucepan, melt the butter and add the flour. Whisk for 1 minute. Then add the orange juice and whisk again. Pour into the peas and stir until thickened. Serve in a bowl, with minced parsley sprinkled on top.

Serves 6

Parsley of Macedonia

In the 18th century, Macedoines of different vegetables were popular on both sides of the English Channel. A Macedoine was a salad of vegetables, fish or meat, jelled in aspic.

½ cup Aspic; page 386
½ cup finely chopped parsley
½ cup carrots, diced and cooked
½ cup green beans, cooked
½ cup green peas, cooked
½ cup lima beans, cooked
½ cup Vinaigrette; page 392
1 envelope gelatin
¼ cup water
2 cups mayonnaise
½ cup lobster meat, cooked
1 black truffle, minced
Sprigs of parsley, and chervil

Coat a 6-cup mold with the aspic. Chill and repeat 2 more times. Mix the parsley and the vegetables with the vinaigrette. Season to taste. Soak the gelatin in the cold water and melt over boiling water. Cool till tepid and mix with the mayonnaise. Then mix the vegetables, lobster and truffle with the mayonnaise. Pour into the chilled mold.

Chill until hardened. Unmold on a serving platter and garnish with parsley and chervil sprigs.

Serves 6

Tarte Aux Fruits

Sweet pastry was introduced to France by the chefs of Catherine De Medici. It quickly gained popularity because of its fragile gossamer quality and its buttery, rich taste. What a wonderful experience, to bite into a fragile sweet pastry, filled with a smooth cream and topped with glazed fruits. It quickly relieved some of the boredom that I felt while at court.

Sweet pastry:

1 cup unsalted butter, room temperature

½ cup granulated sugar

1 egg beaten

1 drop vanilla

2 cups all-purpose flour, sifted

1 pinch salt

Pastry Cream:

2 ½ cups milk

1 vanilla pod split lengthways

3 egg yolks

½cup granulated sugar

2 tablespoons flour

1/8 cup cornstarch

2 tablespoons kirsch or cognac

Fruit:

1 basket strawberries, hulled and halved

1 basket raspberries

3 figs, sliced

3 tablespoons apricot jam, melted

1 tablespoon water

Pastry: Cream the butter and sugar until light. Add the egg and the vanilla. Then add the flour and the salt and form into a rough ball. Wrap in plastic wrap. Chill for at least 20 minutes. Butter a 10-inch tart pan. Preheat the oven to 350°F. Roll out the pastry to fit the tart pan. Chill for a further 30 minutes. Prick all over and cover with a circle of parchment paper. Weight down with pie weights or rice. Bake for approximately 10 minutes. Then remove the pie weights and paper. Bake for 10 more minutes. Remove from the oven and cool completely before filling with the pastry cream.

Pastry Cream: Bring the milk and the vanilla pod slowly to a boil. In a bowl, whisk the yolks until pale. Mix in the cornstarch and the flour. Pour into the scalding milk slowly and then mix thoroughly. Simmer for 1-2 minutes. Pour into a bowl and cover with plastic wrap. Cool completely.

To Assemble: Spoon the pastry cream into the tart pan. Remove the tart from the pan. Decorate with the strawberries, raspberries and figs. Melt the apricot jam with the water and brush on top of the fruit.

Chill until ready to serve.

Serves 6

Petit Pots De Crème Au Chocolat

His Spanish bride, Anne of Austria, first introduced chocolate, to the French Court of Louis XIII. It is said that Anne consumed so much chocolate that by the time of her death, all her teeth had been rotted.

2 cups heavy cream

¼ cup granulated sugar

4 egg yolks

4 oz bittersweet chocolate

¼ cup strong coffee or water

1 teaspoon vanilla

Scald the cream and add the sugar. Remove to a mixing bowl. In a small saucepan, melt the chocolate in the coffee or water. Add the egg yolks to the melted chocolate one at a time, beating well after each addition. Then stir the chocolate mixture into the cream. Pour into 6 individual custard cups. Put the cups in a pan containing an inch of hot water and bake in a preheated oven at 350°F. for 15 minutes, or until a knife inserted in the middle comes out clean. Remove from the oven and cool. Then chill in the refrigerator.

Serves 6

Strawberries in Cherry Syrup

Fruits steeped in sweet syrups were another of my favorite foods. I would wait avidly for the first crops of strawberries to be brought to the palace. Sometimes they would not make it to the dinner table. I would have my maids bring them to me as they were brought in fresh from the fields.

2 baskets strawberries, hulled and halved

1 tablespoon lemon juice

1 cup white wine

½ cup cherry syrup

Place the strawberries in a large bowl and add the rest of the ingredients. Mix gently. Chill until ready to serve.

Serves 6

*   *   *

Mary Wollingstonecraft

1759-1797 Write, Feminist

My first taste of the inequality of the male dominated world occurred when I was a little girl. My father was a drunkard who beat my mother. I was forced to sleep on a mat outside of their bedroom. When my mother would start screaming, I would run in and beat my father off her with anything I could lay my hands on.

This experience was seared into my brain and was to make me a champion of women's rights as long as I lived. I was fortunate however to be given an education of sorts, far more than most women received during the time I lived. This enabled me to start a school with my sister and a friend Fanny Blood at Newington Green. While teaching there, I met the minister Richard Price who was to have a great effect on my thinking. I wrote articles condemning the way girls were taught and suggested new teaching methods and topics to be studied.

My *"A Vindication of the Right's of Man"* brought me the attention of some of the great thinkers of the time, such as William Godwin, and William Blake. Through their encouragement, I felt able to attack what I considered the worst crime of all, the crime against women. So I wrote my *"Vindication of the Rights of Woman,"* a revolutionary book that generated great controversy for its time.

In 1793, I moved to Italy with the American writer Gilbert Imlay. George the III had issued a proclamation against radical writers such as myself, threatening very serious consequences against many of us.

While in Italy, I gave birth to my daughter Fanny and when my relationship with Imay came to an end, I returned to England and married William Godwin in 1797. Shortly after being married, I gave birth to my famous daughter Mary Godwin Shelly. I died of childbed fever soon after giving birth to her.

As for food, we ate a great deal of meat, beef, mutton and pork. Some vegetable such as spinach, peas, carrots and turnips had now become popular. We ate many pies both savory and sweet, cakes, jams, jelly, conserves, sweetmeats and cheese. Some very serious health problems ensued due to the large consumption of meat, spirits and sweets. Much like the ancient Egyptians, we suffered from obesity and gout, not to mention liver disease from the consumption of demon gin and rum. The poor were especially vulnerable to the effects of liquor. During the Tudor era, ale and stout provided some kind of nutrition, while gin provided none. Hograth, a famous lithographer of the time, extols the virtues of beer in his picture entitled "Beer Street" and bemoans the effects of gin in "Gin Lane". Kitchens were also killers, whether from scalding by boiling water, noxious fumes, or the use of brass and copper pans with acidic foods, causing the poisonous condition of verdigris. Sometimes foods were deliberately cooked in these pots to keep their bright green color. Spoiled food, rancid butter, bad meat and stale fish were the lot for the unwary buyer. Many cookery books of the day, like those by Hannah Glasse, told how to save spoiled food and make it eatable. Botulism was prevalent, as preserved food was not bottled in sterilized conditions.

However, we did manage to survive and those living in the countryside had a better diet of fresher foods. The poor fared as the poor always do. Surviving on bread and cheese, a few potatoes and numerous cups of tea. The following meal is typical of the 18th century and would have been enjoyed by the wealthier middle class in England. I would have prepared it for my dear friend William Blake.

*   *   *

Dinner for William Blake

Stewed Prawns

Egg Sallet

Baked Hyssop Chicken

Veal Pie

Potato Pudding

Celery Fritters

Apple Tansy

Mincemeat Pie

Stewed Prawns

With the advent of better roads, shellfish from the coast appeared on dining tables in London and other inland cities, as a main course, replacing fish such as the carp that came from muddier waters. Even living in London, I would have found some fairly decent, fresh prawns.

36 large prawns
6 tablespoons sweet butter
1 teaspoon grated nutmeg
1 cup whipping cream
½teaspoon salt
Freshly ground pepper
1 tablespoon orange juice
Paprika

Place the prawns in lightly salted water and simmer for 3 minutes. Cool, shell and devein them. Melt the butter. Add the nutmeg, the prawns and the cream. Simmer until the sauce thickens slightly. Season with salt and pepper and sprinkle with orange juice. Serve in scallop shells. Sprinkle with paprika.

Serves 6

Egg Sallet

Salads were usually elaborate affairs, combining many ingredients and an abundance of fresh herbs.

1 head Boston lettuce
8 hardboiled eggs cut lengthwise
1 head of fennel, thinly sliced
8 anchovy fillets
2 teaspoons minced parsley
1 tablespoon minced chervil

1 teaspoon minced tarragon

1 tablespoon minced chives

2 tablespoons capers

½ cup Vinaigrette; page 392

Wash the lettuce and separate the leaves. Place the lettuce on four individual salad plates. Place two eggs on each plate. Then arrange the anchovy filets and the fennel slices on top of them. Add the herbs and the capers to the vinaigrette and drizzle over the salad.

Make 4 servings

Baked Hyssop Chicken

Herbs like Hyssop, which has a strong medicinal flavor, had been used in cooking as far back as medieval times and continued to figure in the recipes of the 18th century.

3 pounds of chicken, cut into serving pieces

3 tablespoons butter

1 large onion chopped

1 teaspoon salt

½ teaspoon pepper

4 large plums, pitted and quartered

1 cup port wine

1 tablespoon fresh minced hyssop

2 tablespoons minced parsley

Preheat the oven to 350°F. In a large ovenproof skillet, heat the butter and brown the chicken. Remove the chicken from the skillet and set aside. Then add the onions to the skillet and sauté until golden. Place the chicken back in the skillet and add the rest of the ingredients. Cover tightly with a lid and bake in the oven for 1 hour, or until the chicken is cooked.

Serves 6

Veal Pie

Savory pies, containing mutton, pork and veal, continued to be a major entrée for 18th century meals. Dinner during this time had always to include some type of pie. These pies were elaborately decorated, with scraps of pastry cut in for design. This presented a very attractive presentation on the dining table.

3 pounds boneless veal cut into 1-inch pieces

1 onion, stuck with cloves

1 carrot, quartered

4 slices lemon

1 bay leaf

1 teaspoon dried thyme

Salt and pepper

3 tablespoons butter

3 tablespoons flour

¼ teaspoon mace

2 egg yolks

½ cup whipping cream

2 tablespoons capers

1 recipe Short Crust Pastry, page 391

Cover the veal with cold water in a large saucepot and bring to a boil. Simmer for 5 minutes. Then drain the meat and rinse the pot. Replace the meat in the pot and add 5 cups of cold water, the onion, carrot, lemon slices, bay leaf, thyme, salt and pepper. Bring to a boil. Simmer gently covered for 1 hour. Remove the onion, carrot and lemon. Remove the meat and strain the broth. In a separate saucepan, melt the butter and add the flour. Cook for 2 minutes.

Add 3½ cups of the strained broth and season to taste with salt and pepper. Add the mace. Beat the egg yolks with the cream and pour a little of the broth mixture into the egg yolks. Whisk. Pour back into the broth, a little at a time, whisking all the time. Remove from the heat, add the meat and the capers. Pour into a round deep-dish pie tin and cover with the short crust pastry. Make slits in the top of the pastry and bake for 20-25 minutes in a preheated oven at 425°F.

Serves 6

Potato Pudding

Potatoes introduced during the Tudor era began to assert themselves in menus of the 18th century. By the time of the industrial revolution of the 19th century, potatoes had a firm hold on the English population. Oranges having become more available during this time and were a seasoning I would have used, even in a potato dish like this one.

3 pounds potatoes, scrubbed
2 large carrots, finely grated
½ cup orange juice
¼ cup butter
2 eggs
1 teaspoon sugar
Salt and pepper

Steam the potatoes in their jackets and then cool. Peel them. Puree with a masher or ricer and add the rest of the ingredients, beating them into the potato thoroughly. Adjust the seasoning to taste. Spoon into a baking dish and bake at 350°F. for 20 minutes. Serve at once.

Makes 4 servings

Celery Fritters

Fritters of vegetables became a popular way to add a vegetable dish as a main course.

1 bunch of celery, cut into 2-inch pieces
2 eggs separated
¼ cup milk
Salt and pepper
1 cup flour
Vegetable shortening for frying
1 ½ cups Sauce Espagnole; page 390

Cook the celery in boiling salted water, until tender but still firm. Drain. Beat the egg yolks with the milk and season with the salt and pepper. Whisk into the flour. Beat the egg whites until stiff and fold into the flour mixture. Dip the celery in the batter. Heat the oil until smoking. Fry a few pieces at a time, and then drain on paper towels. Serve on a platter with the sauce.

Serves 4

Apple Tansy

Sweet omelets like this apple tansy began to replace the heavier cakes and desserts of the Tudor Era.

2 tablespoons butter
2 large apples, peeled and sliced
4 large eggs
2 tablespoons milk
1 tablespoon rosewater
1 tablespoon granulated sugar
1 small lemon
Confectioners sugar

In a large omelet pan, heat the butter and cook the apple slices, until soft but firm. In a large bowl, beat the eggs, milk, rosewater and sugar. Pour the egg mixture over the apples. Preheat the oven to 350°F. Bake the omelet in the oven for 20 minutes, until soft and browned. Remove from the oven and cool. Sprinkle with lemon juice and confectioners sugar. Cut into wedges.

Serves 4

Mincemeat Pie

The original mincemeat pie, was more of a main course during Tudor times. But with the addition of dried and candied fruits made the pie a dessert.

1 pound boiled beef

¼ pound suet

2 cups Beef broth

1 teaspoon salt

1 pound apples, peeled, cored and chopped

1 ½ cups brown sugar, tightly packed

1 cup raisins

1 cup currants

1 teaspoon powdered cinnamon

½ teaspoon ground mace

½ teaspoon ground cloves

½ teaspoon grated nutmeg

1 cup finely chopped candied fruits

½ cup finely chopped lemon peel

½ cup finely chopped orange peel

½ cup cider

½ cup cognac

½ cup dark rum

2 recipes of Short Crust Pastry; page 391

Grind the meat with the suet. Combine with the broth and all the ingredients except the rum and short crust pastry. Simmer over low heat for 3 hours, stirring frequently. Cool. Add the cognac and rum. Preheat the oven to 400°F. Roll out the pastry to fit two nine inch pie pans, then add the filling to the pans. Roll out the rest of the pastry to fit the top. Trim and crimp. Make slits in the top of each pie. Bake for 30-35 minutes. Remove from the oven and cool.

Makes 2 large pies

*   *   *

Chapter 4

Elizabeth Barrett Browning

1806-1861 Poetess

My father, Edward Moulton Barrett, was a very wealthy man and also very possessive. Up until I was twenty-two, when my mother died, I was a healthy young girl, riding my horses and arranging all kinds of outings for my brothers and sisters. I was also well educated for a girl, learning Shakespeare, Dante, and studying both Greek and Latin. During the thirties, when my father lost a great deal of his money, we moved to Wimpole Street and I became virtually a recluse, having contracted some vague illness that confined me to my room. In 1838, I managed to publish my first volume of poetry, called " *The Seraphim"* and other poems as well. As more of my work began to be published, I became one of the more famous poetesses of the day, which is how I met Robert Browning.

I could not believe my lucky stars that such a worldly and sophisticated man could love me in this way. Over the next two years, Robert Browning and I met and read our poetry to one another, even though my father was against any kind of relationship. We were married secretly in 1846. A week later we both left for Italy, knowing full well that my father would disinherit me. We lived in Italy for the rest of my life and I gave birth to my son, Robert Wiedeman Barrett Browning.

The food in Italy was hard for my English taste to tolerate. It took me many years to teach my Italian cooks to make decent English dinners. What an experience that was, with my Italian cook screaming and yelling while I tried to teach her how to make a Christmas pudding. The Christmas Goose was unheard of and she was always trying to cut it up in pieces, rather than cooking it whole. However, the vegetables and fruits, were so much fresher in Italy. We could count on beautifully ripe, red tomatoes, pristine lettuce and wild greens, luscious oranges and lemons. I could write a sonnet about their beauty. I also began to enjoy a small breakfast of coffee with milk, with a roll as a substitute for the heavier English breakfast of the day. What desserts there were to be had, especially the ice cream and granitas that were the pride of Italian chefs. I would sometimes marvel at the beauty of it all, laying back on a sofa with a dish of perfect pistachio ice cream on a warm Italian night, the wind gently blowing through the cypresses, listening to the soft patter of the servants.

*   *   *

Casa Guidi Dinner

Lobster Bisque
Pork Roast Cooked in Milk
Baked Polenta
Fennel Baked with Cheese
Green Pea Puree with Peppercorns

Tomato, Basil and Onion Salad
Pine Nut Cake
Walnut and Chocolate Soufflé

Lobster Bisque

Rich, creamy soups were a welcome start to most dinners of the wealthy class during the 19th century. Silky lobster bisque could be found on almost any menu, from the beginnings of the 1900's to the end.

1 pound ripe tomatoes

2 slices bacon

2 tablespoons butter

2 cups milk

4 tablespoons butter

4 cups vegetable stock

1 onion, minced

1 garlic clove, minced

2 cups Lobster meat, finely diced

1 cup half and half

Salt and pepper to taste.

Cut up the bacon and tomatoes into small pieces. Place in a soup pot with the onion. Cook gently with the garlic and a little of the butter. Add the stock and simmer for 35 minutes. In another saucepot, melt the rest of the butter and add the flour. Cook for 1 minute. Then add the milk, making a thin sauce, whisking constantly. Strain the tomato soup, into the sauce and whisk in a small stream. Then add the lobster meat and heat. Add the cream and the salt and pepper and cook only until just hot.

Serves 6

Pork Roast Cooked in Milk

Pork cooked in milk with garlic and sage was a preparation method that started with the Romans and continued down through the centuries to the Italy of today.

1, 4 pound pork tenderloin
2 cups milk
½ cup olive oil
2 large bay leaves
2 large garlic cloves, minced

Preheat the oven to 350°F. Sliver the garlic cloves and place them in slits in the pork tenderloin. Heat the olive oil and brown the meat. Add the bay leaves and the milk. Bake covered for 1 ½ hours or until the meat is done.
Serves 6-8

Baked Polenta

Yellow cornmeal was very popular as a accompaniment to meat in the area of Italy that we lived in.

¼ pound of fine yellow cornmeal
2 ¼ cups of water
1 teaspoon salt
½ teaspoon pepper
3 tablespoons of butter
1 ½ cup of Parmesan Cheese

Preheat the oven to 350°F. Butter a large 2-quart casserole dish. In a large cooking pot bring the water to a boil and add the salt. Add the polenta in a steady stream, stirring constantly. It will take approximately

20 minutes to thicken, and you need to stir it constantly, to avoid it burning and sticking to the bottom of the pan. Then the polenta is thick, remove it from the heat and stir in the butter and the pepper. Pour the polenta into the casserole, and smooth the top. Sprinkle with the Parmesan cheese. Bake for 30 minutes, or until the cheese has melted. Remove from the oven and serve immediately.

6 servings

Fennel Baked with Cheese

Fennel continued to be a popular vegetable in the 19th century. While in England, we used fennel in salads, soups and creamed dishes. In Italy, I was introduced to an entirely different way of cooking it, baked in a savory dish with cheese.

4 ½ pounds fennel bulbs
1 teaspoon salt
¼ teaspoon pepper
¼ cup grated Parmesan cheese
½ cup olive oil

Preheat the oven to 400°F. Oil a large baking dish. Wash and trim the fennel bulbs, cutting away the stalks and the outer leaves. Quarter the bulbs. Blanch the fennel in boiling salted water, for about 8 minutes. Remove the fennel from the water and layer in the baking dish. Drizzle with the olive oil and sprinkle with the salt, pepper and Parmesan cheese. Bake for about 20 minutes, or until the cheese is bubbling.

Makes 4 6 servings

Pea Puree with Green Peppercorns

To the English, who now made their homes in a foreign country such as Italy, a puree of peas like this one with peppercorns would have brought fond memories of the pease puddings of home.

1 pound green peas, fresh shelled
1 medium onion, minced
1 carrot, minced
1 teaspoon dried thyme
1 teaspoon salt
1 teaspoon pepper
2 tablespoons green peppercorns, brined
2 tablespoons butter

In a saucepan, heat 2 cups of salted water and cook the peas, onion and carrots until tender. Drain and place in a food processor. Puree and then add the rest of the ingredients and puree again. Serve in a bowl with a pat of butter on top.

Make 6 servings

Tomatoes, Basil and Onion Salad

Vegetables were so much better in Italy than what was being sold in London at the time. I was very fortunate to have a profusion of fresh vegetables with which to create salads.

1 pound ripe tomatoes, sliced
1 large red onion, sliced
2 tablespoons basil, minced
¼ cup olive oil
¼ cup red wine vinegar
Salt and pepper to taste

In a salad bowl, combine the tomatoes, red onion and basil. In a small bowl, whisk together the olive oil, red wine vinegar and the salt and pepper. Add to the salad and toss.

Serves 6-8

Pine Nut Cake

Cakes in Italy during the 19th century were made with a sweet dough that usually incorporated nuts or fruit. They were certainly different then the rich cakes of my native England.

1 ½ cups flour

1 teaspoon baking powder

1 pinch salt

½ cup butter

½ cup granulated sugar

3 large eggs

½ cup pine nuts

Preheat the oven to 350°F. Sift the flour, baking powder and salt in a bowl. Using a food processor, cream together the butter and sugar until fluffy. Add the eggs, one at a time and process after each addition. Add the flour mixture. The dough should be quite soft. Butter and flour a loaf pan. Pour the dough into the pan and sprinkle with pine nuts. Bake for 40 minutes. Cool completely before removing from the pan.

Serves 8

Walnut Soufflés

Delicate soufflés, like this one of walnut and chocolate, often graced the Italian dessert table.

1 cup walnuts
1 cup granulated sugar
½ cup unsweetened chocolate
4 large eggs

Preheat the oven to 350°F. Butter a large soufflé dish. Grind the nuts with the sugar in the food processor. Then add the egg yolks and the chocolate. Process again until smooth. Pour into a mixing bowl. In another bowl, beat the egg whites until stiff. Fold the egg whites into the yolk mixture a third at a time. Spoon into the soufflé dish. Bake for 30 minutes or until puffed.

Makes 4 servings

*   *   *

Cosmia Von Bulow Wagner

1813 TO 1883, Daughter of Franz Liszt, Wife of Richard Wagner

As you can imagine, being married to the great composer Richard Wagner was a gigantic endeavor. It wasn't that I was unaccustomed to composers, for my father was the Hungarian composer, Franz Liszt. When I first met Wagner I was still married to his dearest friend, Hans von Bulow. But because of Wagner's illustrious intellectual reputation, my husband offered me to Wagner on our honeymoon. Fortunately there was no problem with Hans, who would gladly share his wife with his famous friend. But I began to be torn and eventually left Hans for Wagner, taking my two children with me. After Wagner's wife Minna died and Hans sued for divorce, I was free to marry Wagner. He only required that I be able to devote myself to his entire well being, running his household, creating meals with his favorite foods and keeping all kinds of dead beats away from the door. This I did and when Wagner died, I was bereft to the point of cutting my hair and placing it in his coffin.

Wagner had a hearty appetite and loved the heavy German food of the day. A typical meal might start with a soup and include fish, such as pike, trout, or carp. Not to mention boiled ham with a sauce, huge dishes of vegetables, such as carrots and potatoes, or rich desserts of cakes and pastries. We have a fondness for the sour sweet flavoring of food and a liking for sugar in the dressings of our salads. Cabbage is one of the pillars of our diet, appearing in many different dishes including sauerkraut. The main meal might last as long as three hours, with drinking and lively conversation. German food was considered to be heavy and monotonous, but by the 19th century it had become more varied then just rye, cabbage, potatoes and pork. We had delicate veal dishes, beautiful cakes like the Black Forest Cake, strudels, piquant salads and wonderful wursts.

Wagner lived a life of luxury, and he had friends who gladly provided the money for this lifestyle, considering it an honor to provide for such a genius. So we lived in beautiful surroundings and ate excellent food with premium wines, while Wagner composed music for the Gods.

*   *   *

The Flying Dutchman Dinner
White Asparagus in White Sauce
Fresh Herring with Bavarian Mustard Sauce
Veal Steaks with Lemon and Curry
Caraway noodles
Ham with Cream
Sauerkraut with wine
Wine Ice
Blitz Torte
Cold Duck

*   *   *

White Asparagus in Ham Sauce

With springtime came the season of the white asparagus. The white asparagus has a more delicate taste than the green variety and so we served it in salads with a simple vinegar dressing or covered in white sauces.

2 cans (14oz) of white asparagus
1 recipe Basic White Sauce, page 392
4 oz cooked ham, cut into julienne strips
1/8 teaspoon grated nutmeg
¼ teaspoon salt

Drain the asparagus spears, reserving ½ cup of the liquid. Place the asparagus spears in a buttered casserole dish. Mix the white sauce with the ham strips the reserved asparagus liquid, the nutmeg and the salt. Pour over the asparagus. Bake at 350°F. for 30 minutes. Transfer to a serving platter and spoon the sauce over the top.

Serves 4

Fresh Herring with Bavarian Mustard Sauce

Since the start of the Middle Ages, herring remained an important part of revenue for the northern European countries.

6 fresh herring, cleaned and the heads removed
1 teaspoon salt
1 tablespoon flour
2 tablespoons vegetable oil
Sauce:
2 tablespoons butter
2 tablespoons onion, minced
2 tablespoons flour
½ cup white wine
½ cup fish stock
½ teaspoon salt
¼ teaspoon pepper
1/8 teaspoon cayenne pepper
2 tablespoons lemon juice
2 teaspoons sharp German mustard
½ teaspoon granulated sugar
½ small dill pickle, minced

Remove the center bone from the fish while leaving the fish intact in one piece. Sprinkle lightly with salt and dredge in flour. Heat the oil in a large frying pan and add the fish. Fry slowly, until the fish is golden brown.

Sauce: Melt the butter in a saucepan. Sauté the onion until golden brown. Sprinkle the flour on the butter, and stir. Cook until the flour turns a medium brown. Pour the liquids in and whisk until smooth. Add the salt, pepper, cayenne and lemon juice. Simmer 10 minutes. Then add the mustard, sugar and pickle and simmer for another 6 minutes. Serve the fish on serving plates and drizzle with the sauce.

Serves 6-8

Veal Steaks with Lemon and Curry

Veal was eaten by the more affluent classes of Germany during the 19th century. Meat dishes were served with either noodles or potatoes on the side.

1 pound veal cutlets, sliced thin
½ teaspoon salt
¼ teaspoon pepper
1 teaspoon curry powder
3 tablespoons butter
1 large onion, minced
2 tablespoons half and half
2 tablespoons tomato paste
2 tablespoons lemon juice
¼ cup minced parsley
2 tablespoons cognac

Season the veal with the salt and pepper. Heat the butter and brown the veal slices on both sides. Remove the meat and reserve. Add the onion and sauté until softened. Then add the half-and-half and the tomato paste. Cook until bubbly. Then add the lemon juice, curry powder and the parsley. Return the veal slices to the pan. Add the cognac and heat through. Serve on a preheated platter with the caraway noodles in the center.

Serves 4

Caraway Noodles

1, 8-oz package egg noodles

4 tablespoons butter

2 tablespoon lemon juice

2 teaspoons caraway seed

¼ teaspoon salt

1 tablespoon minced parsley

Cook the egg noodles in a pot of boiling salted water until cooked. Drain and return to the pot. Add the rest of the ingredients and toss until the butter is melted. Transfer to a serving dish and sprinkle with the parsley.

Serves 4

Ham with Cream Sauce

No meal in 19th century Germany was complete without pork, either roasted, stewed, in sausages, or as ham, cooked in a savory sauce like the one below.

1 (10) pound precooked ham

2 stalks celery, chopped

2 medium onions, chopped

6 mushrooms, chopped

1 carrot, chopped

Bouquet Garni: (4 sprigs parsley, 8 peppercorns, 1 bay leaf, 1 sprig thyme) tied up in cheesecloth

½ cup port
1 cup beef broth
1 cup heavy cream
1 cup sour cream

Simmer the ham in water for 30 minutes. Cool slightly and remove the skin. Place in a roasting pan with the celery, onions, mushrooms, carrot, Bouquet Garni, the port and the beef broth. Bake at 325°F. for 1 hour, basting frequently. Remove the ham and keep warm in the oven. Remove the fat from the drippings and strain. Pour into a saucepan. Bring to a boil, and boil until liquid is reduced by one half. Then reduce the heat and add the heavy cream and the sour cream. Heat until just hot. Carve the ham, and place on a platter, serve with the sauce on the side.
Makes 8-10 servings

Sauerkraut with Wine

Almost every German dinner had Sauerkraut on the menu. Sometimes it was served cooked with meats as a main dish, or like this one baked with wine, was an addition to the meal.

1 jar (32oz) sauerkraut
6 tablespoons of butter
½ bottle dry white wine
½ teaspoon black pepper

Preheat the oven to 350°F. Grease a large baking dish. Place the sauerkraut in the baking dish. Dot with the butter. Pour the white wine over the top, and sprinkle with the pepper. Bake for 40 minutes. Then remove from the oven and transfer to a serving bowl.
6 servings

Wine Ice

The Germans were producing great wines as far back as the 13th century. The Italians introduced ice cream introduced ice cream making into Germany during the 18th century. A light ice became a palate cleanser before the heavy desserts that followed.

    1 cup water
    1 cup granulated sugar
    2 teaspoons grated lemon rind
    ½ cup lemon juice
    1 bottle rose wine

Combine the water and sugar in a saucepan. Bring to a boil and stir until the sugar dissolves. Let cool. Combine the sugar syrup and the remaining ingredients. Pour an ice cream maker and freeze.
    Serves 6-8

Blitz Torte

Lightening torte or Blitz torte was a typical 19th century dessert, made of nuts, custard and cakes. The Germans excelled at making rich cakes, filled with all kinds of syrups, macaroons, candied fruits, fruits in syrups, custards and whipped cream.

    1 cup flour
    1 teaspoon baking powder
    1 cup granulated sugar
    1 ½ cups granulated sugar
    1 teaspoon vanilla
    6 eggs separated
    3 tablespoons milk
    1 recipe pastry cream, Tart Aux Fruits, page 391

1 ½ cups slivered almonds
Confectioners sugar

Preheat the oven to 350 °F. Sift the flour with the baking powder. Butter and dust two 9 inch, round cake pans. In a bowl, combine the sugar and the butter and cream until fluffy. Then add the egg yolks, one at a time, beating after each addition. Add the vanilla. Add the flour and mix well, alternating with the milk. Beat the egg whites until stiff and fold in a third at a time into the flour mixture. Pour into the cake pans and bake for 35 minutes or until golden brown. Remove from the oven and cool. When cooled, remove from the pans and split each cake layer into two. Spread pastry cream on each one of the four layers, ending with the pastry cream. Sprinkle each layer with the almonds and when ready to serve, dust with powdered sugar.

Make 6 servings

Cold Duck

Cold Duck or *Kalte Ente*, is a German punch that relays on the bubbling quality of Moselle wine. It gets its name from the creative chefs who would carve their lemon peel decoration in the shape of a duck.

2 tablespoons lemon juice
5 tablespoons granulated sugar
1 large lemon
2 bottles Moselle wine, chilled
1 bottle champagne, chilled

Combine the lemon juice and sugar in a large glass punch bowl and stir until the sugar dissolves. Carve the lemon rind in a long spiral for the neck, ending with the top piece of lemon as a cap. Place the whole lemon in the bottom of the punch bowl and pour the wine into it. Chill for 1 hour. Then add the chilled champagne right before serving.

Makes 24 serving cups

*   *   *

Charlotte Bronte

1816 to 1854, Novelist, England

I was born in 1816, the third daughter of the Rev. Patrick Bronte and his wife Maria. The early part of my life was composed of schooling, although interrupted because of family crises. However, in 1842 my sister Emily and I went to Brussels to complete our studies. Emily was to return home for good, while I remained in Brussels until 1844. Upon returning home, I decided to publish some poems that my sisters and I had written, under the pseudonyms of Currer, Ellis and Acton Bell. Later, three novels were published as well, *Jane Erye* by me, *Wuthering Heights* by my sister Emily, and *Agnes Grey* by my other sister Anne. After their publication, we went to London and reveled that we were the secret writers of these books.

The year 1848 was terrible for me. My sister Emily died, as did my beloved brother Branwell, who by then was a hopeless opium addict. Anne died the next year. After these tragedies I felt I needed a change of scenery to recover from my grief, so I traveled to London to visit with the great literary geniuses of the day. In 1852 I married the Curate of Haworth, A.B. Nicholls, whom I admired but did not love. I was ready to leave my home because I could no longer stand the sadness occupying it. After I was married, it was my job to give dinners for the clergy that came to visit my husband.

Only the very wealthy and the more affluent middle classes were able to afford finer food. The poor in the cities existed on nothing but bread and strong tea. The strong social reforms spurred by the books of Charles Dickens had not yet arrived. Children of all ages toiled in the cotton mills, worked in the coalmines and died at a young age from malnutrition and premature aging. An example of a meal provided in the workhouse or poorhouse consisted of bread and weak turnip soup, served with salt pork and tea.

The country folk fared better, at least those who had been able to keep their farms. During the early 1800's, thousands of rural people lost their small homes because of land enclosures. The Vicarage where we lived had some land attached and we were able to culti-vate an extensive kitchen garden, even keeping a few chickens for personal use. My sisters and I had been taught the culinary arts of making butter, jams, jellies, pickles and preserves, which allowed us to supplement our dinner table. Foods such as game and fish were bought at the local purveyors, along with imported items such as tea, coffee and sugar. Dinners were a simple affair most days. When guests came by, we were always able to provide a more ample meal, though I must say, I was annoyed to have to stop my writing to supervise the help on such occasions.

*   *   *

The Clergyman Dinner
Turnip Soup
Vegetable Salad with Creamed Dressing
Broiled Flounder with Lemon Butter
Lamb and Apple Hot Pot
Blackberry Chutney
Kale in Cream
Old English Cider Cake

*   *   *

Turnip Soup

We had been growing turnips in Great Britain since the Middle Ages. They appeared in soups, stews and creamed or sauced as a side dish.

1 ½ pounds turnips, peeled and sliced
2 large onions, chopped

6 cups chicken stock

1 teaspoon salt

½ teaspoon pepper

1 teaspoon thyme

1 cup half and half

1 cup milk

2 tablespoons minced parsley

In a large soup pot, place the turnips, onions and chicken stock. Cook for 20 minutes, or until the turnips are soft. Remove from heat and cool. Puree in a blender. Return to the pot and add the rest of the ingredients. Heat but do not boil. Ladle into soup bowls. Garnish with minced parsley.

Serves 4-6

Vegetable Salad with Creamy Mustard Dressing

Salads with cooked vegetables became very popular during the early 19th century. Living in the country allowed for a much wider assortment of fresh foods. During the 18th century, mustard seeds were ground into powder or made into a paste, to be used as a condiment and in sauces.

2 cups cooked beets, diced

1 cup cooked celery, diced

1 cup green peas, cooked

2 cups cooked potatoes, diced

2 tablespoons vegetable oil

1 cup whipping cream

1 tablespoon strong mustard

2 tablespoons apple cider vinegar

½ teaspoon salt

¼ teaspoon pepper

In a bowl, combine all the vegetables. Whip the cream until soft peaks form. Fold the rest of the ingredients into the whipped cream and pour over the vegetables. Toss until the vegetables are coated. Chill until ready to serve.

Serves 6-8

Broiled Flounder with Lemon Butter

A fish such as the flounder had to be packed in ice. It was transported to remote areas of England, via the new railway system. The fishmonger provided me with a larger assortment of fish to choose from.

6 large flounder fillets
3 tablespoons flour
Salt and pepper to taste
¼ cup butter
2 tablespoon lemon juice
1 tablespoon minced parsley

Roll the flounder in the flour, seasoned with salt and pepper. Preheat the broiler. Broil the fish until cooked through, about 3 minutes on each side. Melt the butter in a small saucepan. Add the lemon juice and the parsley. Place each flounder fillet on a serving plate and drizzle with the lemon butter.

Serves 6-8

Lamb and Apple Casserole

In the North, where I lived, the weather was much colder than in London. So the cooking of the region consisted mostly of hot, one-pot dishes that put meat on the bones and kept one warm. It is interesting to note that the pairing of meat and fruit introduced in the Middle Ages, was still a strong part of the English meal.

2 pounds lamb stew meat
1 cup onion, minced
1 large cooking apple, peeled and diced
1 pound potatoes, peeled and diced
Salt and pepper to taste
½ cup seedless raisins
1 teaspoon thyme
½ teaspoon marjoram
2 cups beef broth
2 tablespoons butter

Preheat the oven to 350°F. and heat the butter in a large Dutch oven. Add the lamb and brown it on all sides. Then layer with the rest of the ingredients. Dot the top of the casserole with butter. Cover with a lid and place in the oven. Bake for 1-½ hours. Then remove the lid and bake for another 30 minutes.

Makes 4 servings

Kale with Cream

Green vegetables like kale, cabbage and Brussels sprouts, were the norm for country cooking during the 19th century.

1 large bunch, kale
1 cup half and half
Salt and pepper to taste
¼ teaspoon ground nutmeg

Shred the kale and cook it in a pot of boiling, salted water until quite tender. Remove from the pot and drain. Return the kale to the pot and add the half-and-half, salt, pepper and nutmeg. Stir until the cream is just hot. Transfer to a serving dish and place a pat of butter in the middle.

Serves 6-8

Blackberry Chutney

Chutneys began to grace the English table during the 18th century. Every middle class housewife had her own recipe for making it. Chutneys were a legacy of the English colonization of India. They were served with meat dishes such as the lamb and apple hot pot.

1 pound blackberries

2 large onions, chopped

2 tart apples, peeled, cored and chopped

1 teaspoon salt

1 cup brown sugar

2 teaspoons mustard seed

1 teaspoon ground ginger

½ teaspoon mace

½ teaspoon cayenne pepper

1 cup malt vinegar

Place all the ingredients in a saucepan and cook for 1 hour or until very thick. Remove from the heat and cool. Place in a sterilized jar and refrigerate. Will keep refrigerated for 2 weeks.

Makes 2 cups

Old English Cider Cake

Apples and apple cider were two popular products for cooking during the 19th century. Besides being drunk in its pristine form, many cakes and pies were made from the cider itself.

2 large eggs, beaten
½ cup butter
½ cup granulated sugar
2 cups flour
1 teaspoon baking powder
1 teaspoon ground nutmeg
½ teaspoon mace
1 cup apple cider
Sweetened whipping cream

Preheat the oven to 375°F. Cream the butter with the sugar until fluffy. Add the beaten eggs. Sift the flour, baking powder and nutmeg together. Fold into the egg mixture, alternating with the apple cider. Pour into a greased, 9-inch springform pan. Bake for 30 minutes. Remove from the oven and cool. Serve with whipping cream, if desired.
Serves 8-10

*   *   *

Queen Victoria

1819 to 1901 Queen of England

Life ceased to be enjoyable for me when my beloved consort, Prince Albert died. I was born in 1819, a product of the scramble by the sons of King George III to produce an heir, to follow King William. I became heir apparent at the age of 11, and Queen at 18. I chose to marry Albert of Saxe-Coburg because he was a gentile winning man, but soon he became more then just a husband, he became everything for me. We both detested London, preferring to bring up our children in the country surroundings of Windsor, Balmoral, and the Osborne house on the Isle of Wright. I always had a hearty appetite, so when Albert died, eating became one of my ways to assuage my grief. One of my favorite outings was to go on picnics with my manservant, John Brown. Sometimes we would surprise a crofter at his home, stopping by suddenly to take tea with them.

Dinners at Balmoral were very formal. We ate good Scotch salmon, vegetables grown on the estate, exquisite cakes, pastries and ices. Dinner had as many as 10 courses, followed by coffee and brandy, provided afterwards for the men in the library, while the women still took theirs separately in the drawing room. I was a great stickler for timeliness. It was so annoying to me when my daughter-in-law, Princess Alexandria, was always late to the dinner table. It was my wish that all my children eat at the dinner table with Albert and I. We wanted to introduce them to the etiquette of eating as soon as possible. After Albert died and my son Edward married, I preferred to leave most of the entertaining to he and Alexandria. He held lavish balls, fetes and dinners at Marlborough House, their London residence. In my later years, when freed from some irksome court function, I preferred to eat with just a few people, or by myself.

During my reign there were great changes in food production and importation. The railroad was a lifeline of food, connecting all the seaports, cities and even remote towns. The railway would contribute to the lowering of prices on foods, as more fresh, eggs, vegetables, fresh fish and meat became available. The 19th century saw the rise of social reformers. Those who abhorred the inhumane apparatus of industry strived to make changes in working conditions. This was accomplished by a series of Reform Acts starting in 1832. While the afternoon tea started in the 1800's, it was the Duchess of Bedford who contributed to making it a lasting British ritual. She served it every afternoon on her estate. The need for better food brought about changes in packaging, canning procedures, and marketing. Certain noxious substances used in pickling and canning, such as bole Armenian, and copper, were removed. There was a move towards government regulation of food-stuffs, finally coming to fruition in the 20th century. By the time I died in 1901, Britain was well on its way towards safer and healthier food production and consumption.

*   *   *

The Balmoral Dinner
Sorrel Soup
Salmon in Elderberry Sauce
Duck breasts with Cherries and Mint
Cucumbers Braised with Onions
Leek and Potato Gratin
Puff Pastries with Brandied Fruits
Cabinet Pudding
Hot Cheese Canapés

*   *   *

Sorrel Soup

In Victorian England, sorrel was used in cream soups, salads and in dressings. It was craved because of its piquant, lemony taste.

4 cups sorrel leaves, washed
¼ cup butter
8 cups chicken broth
2 cups potatoes, grated
1 teaspoon salt
1 cup whipping cream

½ teaspoon salt

½ teaspoon pepper

Chop some of the sorrel leaves and set aside. In a large soup pot, melt the butter and add the sorrel. Stew the leaves until wilted. Then add the stock, grated potatoes, salt and pepper. Simmer for 1 hour. Remove from the heat and cool. Then place in the food processor and puree in batches. Return to the soup pot and add the whipping cream. Heat until very hot, but do not boil. Ladle into soup bowls and garnish with the reserved, chopped sorrel leaves.

Serves 8

Salmon in Elderberry Sauce

Salmon teeming in the waters of Scotland started to grace the tables of 19th century England. Elderberries, had been part of the English diet since Tudor times, when they began to be used for wine, jams and in tarts.

1, 8 pound salmon, whole

1 cup butter

1 teaspoon salt

1 teaspoon pepper

3 tablespoons lemon juice

3 cups White Sauce, page 392

2 tablespoons minced parsley

2 tablespoons capers, drained

½ cup elderberry jam

Preheat the oven to 350°F. Clean the salmon and remove the bones, head and skin. Place in a large baking pan. Season with the salt, pepper and lemon juice. Melt the butter and drizzle on top. Bake for 30 minutes. While the fish is baking, heat the jam in a saucepan and melt.

Add one tablespoon of the lemon juice and the white sauce to the melted jam, whisking all the time. Then add the capers, the remaining lemon juice and parsley, then whisk again for five minutes. Remove the salmon from the oven and slice. Place several slices on each plate and drizzle with the sauce.

Serves 6-8

Duck Breast with Cherries and Mint

The sport of hunting birds gained immense popularity by the middle of the 19th century, when the aristocratic class held shooting parties on their large estates. As many as 300 birds might be shot in a single day. Poaching on estate grounds was a serious offense, yet indulged by the country folk, who needed to supplement their diet.

    4 duck breasts
    2 cups red wine
    1 cup chicken stock
    2 tablespoons cherry jam
    2 cups cherries, stems removed and pitted
    1/8 cup shredded mint leaves
    Salt and pepper to taste.

Preheat the oven to 400°F. Season the duck breasts with salt and pepper. Prick the skins all over with a fork. Place the duck breasts on a rack, with a roasting pan underneath. Roast until brown on the top, about 15 minutes. Remove the roasting pan and pour off most of the fat. Place on oven burner, set at medium high heat. Add the wine and de glaze. Let the wine boil until thick. Add the chicken stock and boil, until reduced by half. Add the jam and the cherries. Simmer for a few minutes. Stir in the shredded mint. Carve the duck breasts into serving portions and place on dinner plates. Spoon the cherry sauce on top.

Serves 6-8

Cucumbers Braised with Onions

Vegetables such as cucumbers were delicately cooked, sauced and sometimes braised with other vegetables.

    10 baby onions, peeled
    2 large cucumbers, peeled
    1 cup vegetable stock
    2 thyme sprigs
    ¼ cup butter
    Salt and pepper to taste

Pour the vegetable stock into a saucepan and bring to a boil. Add the onions to the stock. Simmer for 20 minutes. Then cut the cucumbers into slices, lengthwise, and add to the pot, with the thyme sprigs. Simmer for 10 more minutes. Remove the vegetables from the stock and place in a serving dish. Keep warm in the oven. Boil the stock until reduced by half, and then add the butter. Whisk. Season with salt and pepper to taste. Remove from the heat. Pour over the vegetables and serve.

Serves 6-8

Leek and Potato Gratin

During my lifetime, the potato was no longer just a starch eaten by the Irish. It appeared as a mainstay of most menus, for both the laboring classes and the wealthy. Some of the potato dishes made popular during this time were Bubble and Squeak, Champ, Stoved Taties and gratin's, such as this one containing leeks and potatoes.

    2 tablespoons butter
    3 leeks, cleaned, trimmed and diced
    4 large potatoes, cooked and sliced

1 cup bread crumbs, buttered
1 cup half and half
Salt and pepper to taste
1 tablespoon minced chives

Preheat the oven to 350°. In a frying pan, heat the butter and sauté the leeks until soft. Remove the leeks from the frying pan and place in a greased baking pan, layering them with the potato slices. Cover with the breadcrumbs and pour the half and half over the top. Sprinkle with the salt and pepper and the minced chives. Bake for 40minutes, or until the potatoes are tender.
Serves 4-6

Puff Pastries with Brandied Fruits

The desire for richer and more complex desserts reached the English shore from France during the 19th century. The wealthy class imported French chefs to preside over their kitchens, for the more extensive balls and dinners. A ball held on a country estate might have as many as ten different types of cakes, pastries and creams.

1 package puff pastry
1 large egg yolk
2 cups milk
1 teaspoon vanilla
½ teaspoon orange zest
2 additional egg yolks
½ cup granulated sugar
¼ cup all purpose flour
1 cup strawberries, hulled and halved
1 cup raspberries
1 cup peaches, peeled, pitted and diced

3 tablespoons brandy
Mint
Confectioners sugar

Preheat the oven to 375°F. Roll out the puff pastry and cut the sheet into quarters. Brush with the beaten egg yolk. Bake until golden brown and puffed. While the puff pastry is baking, boil the milk with the vanilla and orange zest in a saucepan. Mix the additional egg yolks with the sugar and flour. Pour into the milk gradually, whisking continuously. Boil for one minute until thickened. Remove the pastry cream from the heat. Cut the pastry quarters into half. Toss the fruit with the brandy. Place some of the custard on each pastry half, and cover with another one. Top with more custard, spooning some of the brandied fruit around the sides of the puff pastry. Sprinkle the pastry with confectioner's sugar and garnish with mint sprigs.
Serves 6-8

Cabinet Pudding

This dessert has been part of the English repertoire of sweets since the 17th century. Every cook has her own version of Cabinet Pudding, depending on what is in her larder. The angelica used in this recipe, a sweet root that was candied and used for decoration. There is an interesting legend connected with Angelica. It is said that St. Michael appeared to a Monk during the time of the Black Death, and told him that angelica would protect one from getting sick. Angelica became one of the herbs carried in a bag hung around the neck, during the times of the plague.

1 pound cake, sliced into fingers
½ cup glaceed whole cherries.
½ cup candied Angelica strips*
1 recipe Custard page 388

10 Ratafia biscuits or Amaretti
2 tablespoons Rum or Brandy
Sweetened whipped cream

Preheat the oven to 350°F. Butter a large baking mold. Alternate the pound cake stripes with the candied fruit to make a decorative design around the bottom of the mold. Line the sides with the rest of the pound cake. Place the biscuits on top of the pound cake that lines the bottom of the mold, sprinkle them with the brandy or rum. Then pour the custard on top Cover the mold with Aluminum foil. Set the mold in a pan filled half way with boiling water. Bake until the custard is set, about 45 minutes. Remove from the oven and cool. Unmold on a large platter. by carefully running a knife around the mold. Garnish with whipped cream rosettes.

Hot Cheese Canapés

Sweets, followed by a savory dish often appeared on the Victorian table, a custom still followed by the British today.

¼ pound Brie, rind removed
¼ cup butter
¼ cup almonds, chopped
1 teaspoon Garam Marsala
Salt and pepper to taste
Toast circles

---

*Note: Candied Angelica can be found in Gourmet food or baking stores.

In a small bowl, combine all the ingredients except for the toast circles. Place one tablespoon of the mixture on each toast circle. Place on a baking sheet and broil for 2 minutes, or until the cheese has melted.
    Serves 4-6

Emily Dickinson

1830-1886, Poetess, Massachusetts

Amherst Massachusetts was to be my home for all of my life. Born and raised there, I never ventured forth, except for the one year that I spent at Mt Holyoke Female Academy. I cannot tell you what made me a recluse, but perhaps it was a thwarted love affair, or perhaps I was over sensitive to life around me. I was quite content to live my life writing poetry, letters and notes to my dearly beloved friends and family. Sometimes I would send a special treat I made along with my notes.

Food on the American side of the ocean made use of many different ingredients, in contrast to England. Corn was a mainstay, showing up in breads, pones and pancakes. Squash was also a very important vegetable, one that was eaten especially at wintertime. Wild birds, turkeys, chicken, pork, lamb and beef all appeared on the dining table, in baked, stewed and roasted form. Bacon was a favorite flavoring for beans and dishes of greens. A great favorite for dessert was the Betty, made with whatever fruits were available, according to the seasons. Pie making was perfected, including such American classics as the sweet potato, shoofly and chess pies. Maple syrup was used in baking and on pancakes and in beans. The American Indians introduced blueberries and cranberries to us. Valleys all over the United States were to reap the benefit of seeds strewn by Johnny Appleseed. Molasses was used a great deal for sweetening, as was sorghum. Tea, chocolate and coffee were consumed in large amounts. The English custom of afternoon tea was observed in the larger cities.

Though my sister Lavinia and I lived together, we never had any dinner parties, as we preferred to dine alone. Sometimes, even her company was too much for me, so I ate in my room alone. We did have a cook, and sometimes I would assist in the kitchen, creating little dishes for an ailing friend, or cookies for a special advent. I wish I could tell you about the dinner parties, abounding in scintillating conversations, but alas, I am a recluse and cannot.

*   *   *

An Amherst Dinner

Bean and Bacon Soup
Old Fashioned Corn Bread
Pork Chops Baked in Cream
Baked Wild Rice,
Acorn Squash Rings with Cranberries and Apples
Peach Brown Betty

*   *   *

Bean and Bacon Soup

Beans, such as navy and kidney beans, were common staples in the United States, during this time period. This era saw the advent of Boston baked beans and this bean and bacon soup.

3 slices salt pork
1 cup celery, diced
2 medium carrots, chopped
1 medium onion, chopped
1 cup turnip, chopped
6 cups Beef broth
1 bay leaf

½ teaspoon thyme

1 can (19oz) navy beans, rinsed

Sliver the bacon and sauté in a large soup pot, for 5 minutes. Then add the vegetables and sauté for another 10 minutes. Add the beef broth, thyme and bay leaf and bring to a boil. Simmer for 20 minutes. Add the navy beans and simmer for another 20 minutes. Remove the bay leaf and season with salt and pepper to taste. Ladle into soup bowls.

Serves 6-8

Old Fashioned Cornbread

Cornbread was served at almost every dinner during the early 19th century in America. Easy to make, it traveled with the Pioneers, who could bake it over a fire in a Dutch oven.

1 cup sifted flour

3 teaspoons, baking powder

½ teaspoon salt

1 cup yellow cornmeal

1 cup milk

2 eggs, beaten

¼ cup honey

¼ cup melted butter

Preheat the oven to 425°F. Sift together the flour, baking powder, and salt. Add the cornmeal and stir until well mixed. In another bowl, combine the milk, eggs, honey and the butter. Add the liquids to the dry ingredients and stir, until all are moistened. Pour the batter into an oiled, 8-inch square-baking pan. Bake for 20 minutes or until done in the center and lightly browned.

Serves 10-12

Pork Chops Baked in Cream

Even though we lived in a large town, we always had a few chickens and pigs, raised and kept for meat in our large backyards.

4 large pork chops, 2 inches thick
2 tablespoons butter
½ pound mushrooms, finely chopped
1 tablespoon lemon juice
1 tablespoon flour
Salt and pepper to taste
1 teaspoon thyme
½ cup half and half
1 tablespoon minced parsley

Preheat the oven to 325°F. Sauté the pork chops in the butter, until golden brown on both sides. Remove from the heat and set aside. Spoon most of the fat off the pan. Add the mushrooms and sauté until limp. Then add the lemon, juice, flour, and thyme. Sauté for several more minutes. Add the salt and pepper. Lay the pork chops in a buttered casserole dish. Spread the mushrooms over the top. Add the cream and the parsley. Bake for 45 minutes. Remove from the oven and place one pork chop on each plate. Top with the mushroom mixture.

Serves 4

Baked Wild Rice

The American Indians showed us how to harvest wild rice and use it in soups, salads and vegetable dishes. We especially liked its nutty flavor.

1 ½ cups wild rice, rinsed in cold water
2 ½ cups water

2 ½ teaspoons salt
4 strips bacon cut into strips
1 onion, peeled and chopped
½ cup mushrooms, chopped
1 cup finely grated carrot
½ cup half and half
1 large egg, beaten
½ teaspoon black pepper

Place the wild rice, water and salt in a large saucepot. Bring to a boil. Cover the pot and boil vigorously for about 10 minutes. Turn off the heat and let sit, covered, for 20 minutes, or until all the water has been absorbed. Brown the bacon and remove from the drippings. Sauté the onion in the drippings until limp. Mix the bacon, the onions, mushrooms and grated carrots into the wild rice. Pour into a greased casserole dish. Mix the half and half with the egg and the black pepper. Pour over the rice. Bake at 325°F. for 30 minutes. Remove the cover, and stir. Bake for another 15 minutes.

Serves 6

Acorn Squash Rings with Cranberries and Apples

Another native food, the cranberry, made itself known to us, having figured in the cooking of the native Americans. It was assimilated into the food of the white settlers and remained there.

1 large acorn squash
¼ cup butter
½ cup cranberries
¼ cup brown sugar, packed
½ cup apple, chopped finely
1 teaspoon cornstarch
2 teaspoons water

Preheat the oven to 350°F. Butter a large baking dish. Cut the acorn squash into rings and discard the seeds. Place the acorn squash in the baking dish. In a skillet, heat the butter and add the brown sugar, cranberries, and apples. Sauté for several minutes. Then mix the cornstarch with the water. Stir into the fruit mixture. Cook until slightly thickened. Spread the fruit mixture on top of the acorn squash. Bake for 45 minutes, or until the squash is soft.

Serves 6-8

Peach Brown Betty

Desserts with crisp, rich crusts had become popular, because of their quick and easy preparation. This dessert could be hung over the fire, or in a Dutch oven just like cornbread, which made it a valuable recipe for the Pioneers.

1/3 cup butter, melted

2 cups soft bread crumbs

6 cups peaches, peeled, pitted and sliced

1 cup granulated sugar

½ teaspoon mace

1 teaspoon cinnamon

1 tablespoon lemon rind, grated

2 tablespoons lemon juice

¼ cup water

Preheat the oven to 375°F. Toss the bread crumbs with the butter. Combine the sugar and spices together. Arrange 1/3 of the breadcrumbs on the bottom of a greased, 1-quart casserole. Cover with ½ of the peach mixture and 1/3 of the sugar mixture. Repeat layering, ending with a breadcrumb layer. Mix the lemon rind, lemon juice and water together. Pour over the peaches. Bake in the oven for 1 hour.

Remove from the oven and spoon into dessert dishes. Serve with half and half, if desired.

Serves 6

*Note: Some recipes adapted from *The Original Fanny Farmer Cookbook 1896.*

*   *   *

Amelia Edwards

1831 to 1892, Egyptologist, Victorian England

I never wanted to marry, only to travel, and so I did. My father was an army officer turned banker and my beautiful mother educated me at home. I was a very precocious child, writing poetry at the age of 7 and having my short stories published at the age of 12. I loved to write and decided to write novels, which were very successful. When my parents died, I was free and not wanting for money, as they had left me a large inheritance. I was thus able to travel and write. Being a woman traveling alone during this time was largely frowned upon, so I found a woman friend who was very compatible. We traveled and lived together for 30 years.

In 1870, I discovered the other love of my life, Egypt. While traveling through Egypt, I fell in love with the history and the culture. Disturbed by the destruction of the tombs and the wanton black marketing of their goods, I decided to come home and promote the cause of Egyptian archeological conservation, advocating the use of scientific methods to study the remains. In 1880, I founded the Egyptological Society at the British Museum and formed lasting friendships with Gaston Maspero and Flinders Petrie, two great Egyptologists. I lectured all over the world, funding countless expeditions to Egypt and thus helping to finance the work of Flinders Petrie, the first truly scientific Archeologist.

Sometimes, while sitting in my house in the West Country in Britain, I would think of the wonderful world of Egypt, and of the culture and cuisine. I often longed for a dinner with the subtle spices of cumin and coriander, or the delicious meatballs and soups. Dinner would begin with a savory soup, containing either lamb or fava beans, or the national favorite, Melokhia leaves, a green that is much like spinach. We then moved to stuffed grape leaves, sliced cheese, hard-boiled eggs dipped in spices, as well as various meatballs and dips of beans and sesame seeds. The main course was grilled meat, with an onion sauce and an Egyptian dish called Rishta, made of lentils and noodles. Tea with mint would have been served and delicate sweet-meats with fruit.

I was never afraid to try the food of the common people, for through eating their food, one is able to uncover their soul.

*   *   *

A Dinner for an English Traveler in Egypt
Broad Bean Soup
Hard Cooked Eggs with Cumin and Coarse Salt
Stuffed Grape Leaves
Kofta

Onion Sauce
Lentils with Noodles
Honey Nut Candies
Peanut Macaroons
Melons
Mint Tea

*   *   *

Broad Bean Soup

The broad bean, or Fava bean, has been grown in Egypt since the time of the Pharaohs. During the time I traveled in Egypt, this type of soup would have been enjoyed by all classes of people.

2 cups large broad beans, soaked for 24 hours
8 cups water
1 tablespoon olive oil
2 tablespoons ginger root, grated
3 tablespoons, garlic, minced
1 teaspoons salt
1 teaspoon pepper
1 teaspoon ground cumin
¼ cup lemon juice
2 tablespoons, minced parsley

Drain the beans and remove the skins. Place the beans in a soup pot with the water and bring to a boil. Cover and cook over medium heat for 1½ hours. Remove from the heat and cool. Puree in batches in the food processor. Return to the soup pot and bring to a boil, adding more water if necessary. Stir in the remaining ingredients, except the parsley. Simmer for 5 minutes. Ladle into soup bowls and garnish with parsley.

Serves 8

Hard Cooked Eggs with Cumin and Salt

In Cairo, there were street vendors who provided many snacks, such as these hard-boiled eggs, sprinkled with spices.

1 tablespoon cumin seed

1 teaspoon coriander seed

8 large, hard boiled eggs

2 tablespoons sea salt

1 tablespoon cayenne pepper

In a skillet, toast the cumin seed and coriander seed until fragrant. Place in a grinder, with the salt and cayenne pepper. Add grind until fine. Sprinkle the eggs with the spice mixture and serve.

Serves 8

Stuffed Grape Leaves

Stuffed grape leaves were a common feature of Middle Eastern cuisine. I preferred eating these savory appetizers, followed by the European food provided in hotels, such as Mena House and Shepherd's.

1 Jar grape leaves

1 small onion, minced

1 pound ground beef

2 cloves garlic, minced

¼ cup butter

½ cup uncooked rice

2 cups chicken broth

Rinse and drain the grape leaves and remove the stems. In a bowl, combine the onion, ground beef, garlic cloves, butter and rice. Cover the bottom of a soup pot with a layer of grape leaves, to prevent burning. Place each grape leaf, smooth side down. Place a spoonful of filling on one end and roll up. Place in the pot, seam side down. Continue until all the grape leaves are used up. Then add the chicken broth. Weight down with a plate. Cover the pot with a lid. Bring to a boil and reduce the heat. Simmer for about 1½ hours.

Serves 6-8

Kofta

Ground beef was a more common meal than veal or lamb. Pork was not eaten, as the Muslims forbade it.

2 pounds ground beef
2 large onions, minced
3 garlic cloves, minced
1 teaspoon salt
1 teaspoon pepper
1 teaspoon ground cumin
1 slice soft bread
½ cup milk

In a bowl, combine all the ingredients and knead, until a smooth paste is formed. Shape into balls and thread on skewers. Broil until very brown and crisp.

Serves 6

Onion Sauce

This sauce, which is more like fried onion rings, would have been served with the Kofta.

2 large onions, peeled and sliced
4 large garlic cloves, minced
½ cup olive oil

In a large pan, sauté the onions in the olive oil for 5 minutes. Then add the garlic and sauté, until the onions are very brown and crisp, around 20 minutes-30 mintues..
Serves 6

Rishta (Noodles with Lentils)

Another common feature of Egyptian cooking is the combining of noodles with lentils, to make a meal out of a single dish.

1 pound egg noodles
1 cup lentils
3 cups water
Salt and pepper to taste
1 teaspoon ground coriander
1 teaspoon ground cumin
2 large onions, sliced and quartered
¼ cup olive oil

Bring the water to a boil and add the lentils. Cook for 10 minutes. Then add the rest of the ingredients and bring to a boil again. Reduce the heat and cook until the noodles are tender. Serve in bowls, with a sprinkling of cayenne pepper.
Serves 6

El Majoun (Honey Nut Candies)

The penchant for sweets which has existed in Egypt since ancient times is evidenced by this brittle candy, sold all over Egypt by street vendors and in stores.

½ pound whole almonds, toasted and ground
1 cup golden raisins, chopped fine
1/3 cup honey
3 tablespoons unsalted butter
2 tablespoons, crystallized ginger, minced
1 teaspoon allspice
1/8 teaspoon mace
1/8 teaspoon ground nutmeg
1/8 teaspoon, fennel seeds, ground fine
1 teaspoon ground cinnamon
1 pinch cayenne
1 pinch Saffron threads
½ cup toasted sesame seeds

In a small heavy saucepan, stir together all the ingredients, except for the sesame seeds. Cook over a very low heat, stirring occasionally for 20 minutes. Then cook for another 40 minutes, stirring frequently so the mixture does not burn, until very thick. Remove pan from heat and let mixture cool slightly. Form tablespoons of warm mixture into 1-inch balls and roll in sesame seeds to coat. Store in an airtight container.
Makes 56 candies

Peanut Macaroons

Delicate cookies like these peanut macaroons were served after dinner, with strong mint tea.

1 cup unsalted peanuts
2 egg whites
¾ cup granulated sugar
½ teaspoon vanilla

Preheat the oven to 350°F. Brown the peanuts in a pan, shaking them frequently. Then chop them coarsely. Whisk the egg white with a pinch of salt, until stiff. Add the sugar and vanilla and whisk until glossy. Fold in the peanuts. Put some parchment paper on a baking tray and grease it lightly. Using a teaspoon, form small heaps of the nut mixture onto the baking tray. Bake for 20 to 25 minutes, or until the macaroons are golden.

Turn off the oven and leave the macaroons to dry out for 1 hour. Remove from the oven. Store in an air tight container.

Makes 10 servings, or 48 cookies

Mint Tea

Mint tea is a standard Egyptian and Middle Eastern drink, served at the end of a meal. It is usually served very sweet.

4 black tea bags
1 quart of water
1/2-cup mint leaves, fresh
1 cup sugar

Bring the water to a boil and add the mint leaves and sugar. Cook until the sugar is dissolved. Add the tea bags and let steep for 1 hour. Strain the tea bags and mint leaves out of the tea. Reheat. Serve in small glasses, with additional sugar and garnished with whole mint leaves.

Serves 4

*   *   *

Adelina Patti

1843-1919, Opera singer, Italy

Guiseppe Verdi claimed I was the greatest singer of Opera to ever grace the stage in the 19th century. My voice moved even Queen Victoria to tears. Born to a musical family, my parents moved to New York where I made my debut at the Astor Place Opera House, when I was only eight. By the time I was eighteen, I was singing at the Covent Garden Opera house and then on to Milan, Monte Carlo, and all the great cities of Europe. I had a prodigious memory and could learn the libretto to an Opera rapidly. By the time I was forty, I had memorized 42 operas. One of my greatest roles was Rosina in the Barber of Seville. While lucky in my career, I did not receive a similar fortune with men. My first husband, a French Marquis, was not a passionate man and soon I turned elsewhere for love. I fell in love with my leading man, Ernesto Nicolini, who left his wife and five children for me. Finally, after eight years and lots of money, I was able to divorce the Marquis and marry Nicolini, who I lived with until he died. I married my third husband, a Swedish Baron, a year after my beloved Ernesto died. He was thirty years younger and the union was tranquil, lasting 19 years, until I died.

Food was my third favorite pursuit, after Opera and men. I was partial to the food of my childhood and the recipes my Sicilian mother prepared. A good dish of pasta always made me happy, after a night of strenuous singing, followed by a fish dish, vegetables and a dessert. Pasta with a good meat sauce and other sauces consisting of raisins, capers and breadcrumbs, all take me back to my southern Italian roots. I remember the wonderful seafood dishes made with garlic, parsley, and lemon. Or the salads of peppers, with shaved pecorino cheese, or lettuce glistening with fruity olive oil and lemon. I especially loved Cassata de Siciliana, a rich cake made of ricotta cheese, served with candied fruit, liqueur and chocolate. The Bomba de Crema were little cream puffs made for the feast of St. Joseph. Cannoli was prepared stuffed with ricotta cheese and candied fruits. Fruit poached in honey and liqueur and fresh melons and various cheeses were also some of my favorite desserts. I ate very little before a performance, preferring to save up my appetite for later on. When I traveled around the world singing, I always had a chef with me who would prepare for me my favorite foods. Bellismino!

*   *   *

The Barber of Seville Dinner

Spaghetti with Clam Sauce
Swordfish with Salmoriglio Sauce
Peas Braised in Tomato Sauce
Salad with Walnuts and Pecorino Cheese
Red Pepper Salad
Cassata de Siciliana
Coffee Granita

*   *   *

Spaghetti with Clam Sauce

Contrary to popular opinion, that Marco Polo brought pasta back from the orient. It has been discovered that pasta was being produced in Italy, as far back as ancient Rome.

1 pound spaghetti
¼ cup olive oil
2 garlic cloves, minced
1 large onion, peeled and minced
1, can (32 oz) whole Roma tomatoes
1 teaspoon oregano
½ teaspoon salt
2 cans (4oz) clams
¼ cup Romano cheese, grated

In a saucepan, heat the olive oil, add the garlic cloves and the onion. Sauté until the onion is golden, then add the tomatoes, oregano and salt. Break up the tomatoes and simmer on low for 20 minutes. Bring two quarts of salted water to a boil. Add the spaghetti. While the spaghetti is cooking, add the clams to the sauce and heat. When the spaghetti is ready, drain, and place in a large serving bowl. Spoon the sauce over the top, sprinkle with the grated cheese.
Serves 6-8

Swordfish with Salmoriglio Sauce

A recipe my mother always made was this swordfish dish, served with Salmoriglio sauce. It was a very popular recipe in Sicily, my mother's country of origin.

½ cup olive oil
2 garlic cloves, minced

3 tablespoons lemon juice

2 tablespoons minced parsley

4 swordfish steaks

In a double boiler, heat the olive oil until warm, then whisk in the lemon juice and the garlic cloves. Whisk until thick sauce forms. Add the parsley. Brush the swordfish with olive oil and broil until opaque, but still juicy. Swordfish can be easily over cooked and becomes dry. Serve on dinner plates and drizzle with the sauce.

Serves 4

Peas Braised in Tomato Sauce

This is a typical dish from Naples, as in most of Southern Italy, where vegetables are braised in a savory sauce, usually containing tomatoes.

1½ teaspoons tomato paste

½ cup water

2½ tablespoons olive oil

¼ cup onion, coarsely chopped

1 garlic clove, minced

1 teaspoon dried oregano

¼ teaspoon salt

2½ cups fresh or frozen peas

2 tablespoons minced parsley

In a small bowl, dissolve the tomato paste in the water. In a heavy saucepan, heat the olive oil over the heat and add the onion, garlic, oregano, and salt. Cook until onion is limp. Add the peas and the diluted tomato paste. Cook over very low heat for 15 minutes, or until the peas are very tender. Transfer the peas to a serving dish and sprinkle with the parsley.

Serves 4

Salad with Walnuts and Pecorino Cheese

Salads were very simple in Italy, dressed with olive oil and Balsamic vinegar. Pecorino or other sharp Southern Italian cheeses were typically used in salads of this type.

Mixed greens
1 cup walnuts, chopped
¼ cup olive oil
3 tablespoons balsamic vinegar
Salt and pepper
Shaved Pecorino cheese

Divide the salad greens among four plates. Sprinkle with the walnuts. In a small bowl, whisk together the olive oil, balsamic vinegar and the salt and pepper. Drizzle over the salads. Garnish with the shaved pecorino.
Serves 4

Red Pepper Salad

Red and green bell peppers flourished in the hot climate of Sicily. They and their counterpart, the chili pepper, form the basis of many sauces and salads.

3 large red peppers, seeded and sliced
2 tablespoons capers, rinsed
2 tablespoons raisins
2 tablespoons minced parsley
½ cup olive oil
4 tablespoon lemon juice
1 garlic clove minced
Salt and pepper to taste

Place the red peppers in a serving bowl; add the capers and raisins. Sprinkle with the parsley. In a bowl, whisk together the rest of the ingredients, adding salt and pepper to taste. Pour over the salad. Let it marinate at room temperature for 1 hour.

Serves 4

Cassata De Siciliana

Rich cakes like this one were served in Sicily at weddings and other festive events.

1 pound cake
½ cup orange liqueur
1 32oz container, ricotta cheese
½ cup candied orange peel
½ cup candied fruit, diced
8 oz bittersweet chocolate
3 cups confectioners sugar
1 stick butter

Slice the pound cake in three layers, lengthwise. Place the first layer in a loaf pan and sprinkle with the orange liqueur. Grate 4 oz of the bittersweet chocolate. Mix the ricotta in a bowl, with the candied fruits, 1 cup of the confectioner's sugar and the grated chocolate. Spread 1/3 of the mixture on top of the first layer, continuing with another layer of cake sprinkled with liqueur. Finish with a layer of cake. Chill in the refrigerator for 1 hour. Remove from the loaf pan, and place on a serving dish.

Melt the rest of the chocolate in a double boiler, with the butter. Place in a bowl and allow to cool slightly. Sift the powdered sugar into the chocolate mixture and mix until thick frosting forms. Spread on top of the cake and on the sides. Decorate with candied fruit. Refrigerate until ready to serve.

Serves 6

Coffee Granita

In Italy, the making of ice cream reached the level of art during the late 19th century. Sicily was especially known for its making of granitas. During the hot summer months, it was a pleasure to sit at a café and eat one of these sumptuous ices.

1½ cups water
1 cup granulated sugar
¾ cup espresso
½ cup whipping cream
3 tablespoons granulated sugar

Stir the water and the sugar together over medium heat, until the sugar has dissolved. Boil for 1 minute. Remove from the heat and cool the syrup. Add the coffee. Pour the mixture into a medium size bowl and freeze. Using a fork, scrape the ice to form flakes. Return to the freezer. Whip the cream until stiff and whip in the sugar. Pile the ice flakes into individual dessert dishes. Top with the whipped cream.
Serves 4

*   *   *

Sarah Bernhardt

1844 to 1923, Actress, France

I was the daughter of an unmarried milliner, who was so beautiful that she rose through the heights of Parisian society to become a successful courtesan. I was so sickly as a child suffering from tuberculosis, I was not expected to live past my teenage years. I begged my mother to buy me a coffin, ahead of time, so I could be assured I would have a beautiful resting-place. However, I survived and my mother's lover the Duc De Morny, decided the perfect career for me, the Theatre. I studied at the Conservatoire and at the Comedie Francaise. By 1880, I became so successful that I formed my own troupe and traveled the world doing productions. I had many lovers, but the real love of my life was my son Maurice.

My lifestyle included many grand parties with fabulous food, in opulent Art Nouveau settings, but I never made any of my men eat in my coffin with me. Today I shall present a meal to you, attended by many of my favorite men, Henri de Ligne, Victor Hugo, Oscar Wilde, Emile Zola, King Umberto of Italy, and my dissolute but loved husband, Aristides Jacques Damala. All my lovers found it rather disconcerting to sleep with me in my coffin, but after a while they found it exhilarating.

There will be many flowers, rich Damask tablecloths, candelabras shining with a thousand lights, and of course the food. The food of Paris in the 1890's, created by Auguste Escoffier and Cesar Ritz. By the time they had arrived on the scene, Paris was starved for new and exciting creations in food and luxurious living. Escoffier revolutionized the whole scheme of French cookery, while Ritz created fabulous watering holes for the rich and famous in Monte Carlo, at the Savoy in London, and the Paris Ritz Carlton. This was the era of *La Belle Epoche*, a constant movement from one fashionable place to another.

The English imported French chefs, and at Buckingham Palace one might dine on hot and cold consommés, followed by fillets of trout, quail and chicken, then by salad. Later a dessert course of pastries, soufflés, fancy bavarians and creams. At Maxim's in Paris, one might find the Grand Duke, Sergi of Russia, presenting his current mistress, Augustine De Lierre, with a twenty-million-franc pearl necklace, served on a bed of oysters. The elite of Paris were game for a party at any time, with each one costing as much as a poor man earned in a year. Such an event could be held for the strangest of reasons, such as a celebration for the christening of a cat. It was a time when the most aristocratic and wealthy could be found mingling in the foyer of the Paris Ritz, with some of the highest paid Courtesans of the century. When I gave a party, the house would be overflowing with Camellias, in honor of my success in Duma's play, Le

Dame Aux Camellias. I would have enough champagne to float an army and course upon course of rare and exotic foods, while my pet leopard sat waiting patiently for scraps. What a time! Vive Le Belle Epoche!

*   *   *

The Dinner of a Thousand Camellias

French Country Pate with Pistachios
Cream Soup with Herbs of the spring
Tarragon Chicken Breasts
Lamb Fillet with Morels
Gratins Dauphiniois
Glazed Green Beans with Shallots
Almond Meringue with Hazelnut Praline Buttercream

*   *   *

French Country Pate with Pistachios

Hot pates were all the rage in Paris during the 1890's. They would have been served with toast or brioche. How I loved a good Pate, slathered on a buttery brioche.

1 tablespoon butter
½ cup shallots, coarsely chopped
½ pound pork liver, diced
¼ teaspoon thyme

1 bay leaf, crumbled

¾ pound lean veal cut into 1-inch cubes

¾ pound lean pork cut into 1-inch cubes

½ pound ham, cooked, cut into ½ inch dice

½ cup roasted pistachios

1/8 teaspoon allspice

1/8 teaspoon ground cloves

¼ teaspoon ground nutmeg

1/8 teaspoon ground cumin

1 pinch ground cinnamon

1 pinch cayenne pepper

½ cup dry white wine

Salt to taste if desired

4 bacon slices, cut in half

Preheat the oven to 425°F. Heat the butter in a heavy skillet and add the shallots. Cook briefly. Add the liver and sprinkle with the thyme and the bay leaf. Cook for 2 minutes. Remove from the pan and place in a food processor. Puree until as fine as hamburger. Remove to a bowl. Add the veal and pork to the food processor and repeat the process. Add to the bowl with the spices, pistachios, ham and dry white wine. Mix well. Place a small patty of the mixture in a frying pan. Cook until done. Check for seasoning and adjust if necessary. Pack the mixture in a 6-cup, loaf pan. Smooth the top. Rounding it slightly. Place the bacon slices on top, and cover with foil. Place in a pan, surrounded by boiling water. Bake for 45 minutes. Remove from the oven and unmold. Place on a serving platter and garnish with gerkins and sprigs of fresh herbs.

Serves 8

Cream Soup with Herbs of spring

This delicate cream soup is similar to the soups prepared by the great Paris chef Auguste Escoffier.

2 tablespoons unsalted butter

1 cup chopped sorrel leaves

¼ cup chopped basil leaves

2 tablespoons minced chives

2 tablespoons minced tarragon leaves

2 cups chicken stock

1 teaspoon salt

½ teaspoon white pepper

6 large egg yolks

2 cups whipping cream

2 tablespoons lemon juice

Sorrel leaves for garnish

Heat the butter in a saucepan and add the sorrel. Stir over the heat until wilted. Add the basil, chives, and tarragon. Stir for 2 minutes. Add the stock and bring to a boil. Simmer for 5 minutes. Season with the salt and pepper. In a bowl, combine the egg yolks and the whipping cream. Very gradually beat the egg yolk mixture into the herb mixture. Reduce the heat to very low, and simmer, whisking constantly until thickened. Do not boil. Pour into a very large bowl. Chill in the refrigerator, until ready to serve.

Ladle into soup bowls and garnish with shredded sorrel leaves.

Serves 4

Tarragon Chicken

Tarragon continued to be a favorite French herb since its introduction during the middle ages to the Pope's Court at Avignon, by St. Catherine of Sienna. I particulary liked it in this cream sauce for chicken breasts.

4 skinless, boneless chicken breasts

½ cup dry white wine
1½ cup chicken broth
1 tablespoon dried tarragon
1 clove garlic, minced
¾ cup whipping cream
1 tablespoon chopped fresh tarragon
1 tablespoon minced parsley
Salt and pepper to taste

Season the chicken breast with salt and pepper. Put them in a saucepan, just large enough to form a single layer. Pour in the wine and the broth. Add the garlic and the tarragon. Poach for 8-10 minutes. Remove chicken breasts from the liquid and put into oven, on low heat to keep warm. Strain the poaching liquid into a small saucepan. Skim off the fat. Cook until reduced by half. Add the rest of the ingredients. Simmer for 5 minutes. Return chicken breasts to cook in the sauce for an additional 5 minutes. Slice each chicken breast and fan out on a plate. Spoon the sauce over the top.
Serves 4-6

Lamb Fillet with Morels

The best lamb was produced in the salt marshes of the South of France. The lamb fillet was considered an epicurean delight and appeared on many of the finest tables in 19th century France.

12 dried morels, soaked in water overnight, stems removed
1 (2 pound) fillet of lamb
Salt and pepper
½ cup butter
1/3 cup beef stock
1 cup port wine

½ cup shallots, minced

1 tablespoon minced chives

Preheat the oven to 350°F. Heat one-tablespoon of the butter, in an ovenproof casserole dish and brown the lamb fillet. Transfer to the oven and bake for 20 minutes. While the lamb fillet is cooking, dice the morels. Heat 2 more tablespoons of the butter, in a saucepan and add the morels and the beef stock. Cook for 5 minutes. Then add the Port wine and the shallots. Salt and pepper to taste. Cook for 10 minutes. Whisk in the rest of the butter. When the lamb is done, slice and fan out on serving plates. Serve with sauce spooned over the top.

Serves 4-6

Gratin Dauphiniois

Potatoes continued to appear on the tables of France. As a result, rich dishes composed of cream, cheese and potatoes were perfected.

1 garlic clove, minced

2 cups whipping cream

1 cup milk

1 cup Gruyere cheese, grated

1 teaspoon salt

½ teaspoon pepper

2 pounds russet potatoes, peeled and thinly sliced

Freshly ground nutmeg

Preheat the oven to 425°F. Butter 6 ramekins, and sprinkle with some of the garlic. In a large bowl, mix the whipping cream, milk, ¾ of a cup of the cheese and the salt and pepper. Add the potatoes and toss to combine. Spoon into the ramekins. Cover with foil and bake 34 minutes. Uncover and sprinkle with the remaining cheese and the nutmeg, Bake uncovered for 15 additional minutes.

Serves 6

Glazed Green Beans with Shallots

We the French had always eaten more vegetables than our English neighbors. Green beans, asparagus and spinach were cooked with garlic, shallots, cream, cheese and herbs, during the 20th century in France.

1½ pounds green beans, trimmed
1 cup shallots, minced
½ cup butter
1 teaspoon salt
½ teaspoon pepper
½ teaspoon dried thyme

Place the beans in a saucepot and add water and salt. Bring to a boil. Boil for 3 –4 minutes, or until the beans are just tender. In a saucepan, melt the butter and add the shallots. Cook until the shallots are limp. Add the salt, pepper and dried thyme. Drain the beans and transfer to the saucepan, with the shallots. Toss until coated with the butter mixture. Cook for 1 minute. Transfer to a serving bowl and serve.
Serves 6

Almond Meringue with Hazelnut Buttercream

We never lost our love of rich sweet desserts. In the households of the wealthy, desserts like this almond Meringue would have appeared as every day fare. Pastry shops were very popular during Le Belle Epoche. These shops, with their painted and gilded walls, marble topped tables, mirrors and waiters in impeccable livery, were places were the rich could meet and sample luxurious pastries and cakes, sip coffee and gossip about their neighbor's latest escapades.

Cake:

6 large egg whites, room temperature
¾ cup almonds, blanched and ground
3 tablespoons granulated sugar
2½ cups confectioners sugar, sifted

Hazelnut Butter-cream:

1cup milk
4 large egg yolks
½ cup granulated sugar
1 cup butter, unsalted, room temperature
1 tablespoon granulated sugar
4 oz hazelnut praline paste
1½ cup almonds, toasted

Preheat the oven to 425°F. Cut out three, 10-parchment paper circles and one, 10-inch cardboard circle. Set the parchment circles on baking sheets. Beat the egg whites to soft peaks and gradually add the 3 tablespoons of sugar. Continue beating until stiff. Then fold in the almonds and confectioners sugar. Spoon mixture into a pastry bag fitted with a no. 6, round tip. Pipe the meringue onto the parchment circles, in a spiral. Dust lightly with the powdered sugar and bake until very crisp and lightly golden, about 25 minutes. Cool on racks.

Butter cream: Place a medium bowl in a larger bowl of ice. Set aside. Bring the milk to a boil, over medium heat. Meanwhile, beat the egg yolks, until smooth. Gradually add the sugar and continue to beat, until the mixture forms a ribbon. Gradually add the boiling milk to the egg yolk mixture, beating constantly to avoid curdling. Return to the saucepan and cook over low heat for 30 seconds. Pour the custard into a bowl, set over the ice. Cool. Beat the butter and the praline paste in a large bowl until smooth and creamy. Gradually add the cooled custard.

Trim the meringues to even circles. Carefully peel off the parchment paper. Choose 1 meringue with a smooth bottom and place it on a cake plate. Top with 1/3 of the butter cream mixture, top with the next meringue and then 1/3 of the butter cream. Top with the remaining meringue and cover the top and the sides of the cake with the remaining butter cream. Gently press the sliced almonds on the sides and top.
Serve in wedges
Serves 8

        *   *   *

Anne Wood Besant

1847-1933, Socialist and Theosophist, England

My father and mother were both Irish. When my father died, a rich relative paid for the education of my brother at Harrow and I was able to go to a home school of a friend of the family. At a time when women were only supposed to get married and raise a family, I did exactly that, marrying at 19 to a Vicar I had met through my family. By the time I was 23, I already had two children and my marriage was a Victorian horror. I was in complete disagreement with my husband's religious viewpoints and when I refused to attend communion any more, he demanded that I leave our home. I was legally separated from my husband and took my daughter Mabel to live with me. In 1874, I joined the Secular Society, and began to write articles along with Charles Bradlaugh, about women's rights and marriage. Because I published articles advocating birth control, I was charged with moral depravity and my daughter was taken away from me.

I had many prominent friends in London, including George Bernard Shaw, who shared many of my socialist ideals. I was very concerned about the working conditions for women in factories during the 1880's, and so I helped women at match companies form the Matchgirls Union, which was concerned with better wages and less dangerous working conditions. In 1889, I was elected to the London School Board, where I worked diligently to provide free meals for the undernourished children of London.

In 1890, I found my true love, Theosophy, a religious movement founded by the great Madame Blavatsky. In Theosophy, I found true religious freedom. I was profoundly moved by the eastern concept of reincarnation, so I moved to India to pursue my quest for religious illumination.

While living in London, I found the food provided to the poor was less than nourishing. They lived in circumstances that can only be described as appalling, with no heat, or sanitation, infested by rats and vermin. Although writers like Charles Dickens had started their quest for social reform, it would be well into the 21st century before many changes were made. It was galling to see the well-meaning ladies of means trying to promote a cookbook for the poor, written by the famous chef Alex Soyer, when the poor couldn't even read. A recipe for poor man's pie, created by Soyer, consisted of tapioca, onions and suet with a piecrust. Although well intentioned, the meal had no nutritional value.

So while on the London School Board, I tried to institute meals with many vegetables and a large addition of meat. I was also successful in getting better medical treatment for the people of the East End in London, for I believed medical treatment of consumption and other diseases, might prevent the early death of so many children. In a middle class house, cooking was made easier by the development of the cast iron range, the icebox and better food with less adulteration. As more men were going to the office or to their clubs, breakfast became a bigger event, followed by a light lunch, a large tea and dinner at a later hour. The amount of food served at a Victorian dinner was prodigious and now there was an order to the way the meal was served. Soup and fish started off the meal, followed by a meat and vegetable course, finishing with sweets and savories. Below is a dinner I would have given for my fellow social reformers, reflecting the tastes of middle class Victorian England.

*   *   *

The Social Reformer's Dinner

Stilton Potato Soup
Lamb chops with lemons and Capers
Carrot puree with Cinnamon and Orange
Potatoes Baked in Sage Sauce
Braised Celery Salad
Lemon Balm and Elderflower Sorbet
Apricot Flan
Anchovy Toasts

*   *   *

Stilton Potato Soup

With the development of a better railway system, faster transportation meant that certain products such as Stilton cheese, before only common in the countryside, now graced the dining tables of London.

1 pound russet potatoes, peeled and diced
8 cups Beef broth
1 cup dark beer
1 teaspoon salt
1 teaspoon pepper
1 tablespoon minced parsley
1 teaspoon marjoram leaves
½ teaspoon thyme
1½ cups Stilton cheese, crumbled
Additional minced parsley

Cook the potatoes in the beef broth with salt and pepper until tender. Remove from the heat and cool. Then puree in a blender. Return to the pot and add the herbs, parsley, and beer. Cook for 10 minutes. Add the cheese and let melt. Whisk until smooth. Ladle into soup bowls and garnish with additional minced parsley.

Serves 4

Lamb Chops with Lemon and Capers

While mutton became more of a working class food, lamb chops were still served on the tables of the middle class and the affluent. Sauces with sharp tastes continued to be a favorite accompaniment to meat.

    4 large loin lamb chops
    3 tablespoons unsalted butter
    1 teaspoon freshly grated lemon zest
    2 teaspoons, drained, bottled capers
    2 tablespoons fresh lemon juice

Pat the lamb chops dry and sprinkle them with salt and pepper to taste. Broil on a broiler pan for about 6 minutes. Turn and broil for another 4 minutes. While the lamb chops are broiling, combine the rest of the ingredients, in a small bowl. Whisk lightly. Remove the lamb chops to a serving plate and drizzle with the sauce.

Serves 4

Carrot Puree with Orange and Cinnamon

Carrot's remained a preferred vegetable of Victorian and Edwardian England. Appearing in stews glazed with butter and pureed with fruit, they never lost their appeal from their first appearance back in Roman times..

    2 pounds carrots, peeled and chopped
    4 tablespoons butter
    1 cup chicken stock

1/3 cup orange juice

1 teaspoon ground cinnamon

¼ teaspoon ground nutmeg

1 teaspoon salt

¼ teaspoon pepper

1 tablespoon minced chives

1 tablespoon minced parsley

Place the carrots in a large pot. Cover with water and bring to a boil. Reduce the heat and simmer until the carrots are very tender. Drain the carrots and toss them in a mixing bowl with the remaining ingredients. Place in batches in the food processor and puree. Return the puree to the pan and reheat. Serve sprinkled with chives and parsley.

Serves 4

Potatoes Baked in Sage Sauce

Unlike the French, who created rich and delectable sauces for the humble potato, we preferred to serve them plain. Either mashed or in a sauce of breadcrumbs and herbs. Sauces with breadcrumbs still appear in the English cuisine today.

4 large russet potatoes, peeled and diced

Sauce:

1 tablespoon olive oil

1 large garlic clove, minced

¼ cup minced parsley

10 large sage leaves, torn

1 teaspoon thyme, dried

1 teaspoon salt

¼ teaspoon pepper

½ cup dry white wine

½ cup fine white breadcrumbs

Preheat the oven to 350°F. Grease a large casserole dish. In a skillet, heat the olive oil and add the garlic. Sauté until golden. Then add the sage leaves, thyme, salt and pepper and white wine. Cook for two minutes. Place the potatoes in the casserole and add the sauce. Cover with the breadcrumbs. Bake for 30 minutes, or until the potatoes are tender.

Serves 4

Braised Celery Salad

By the late 19th century, salads became a main part of the meal. Usually they were served European style, after the meat and vegetable course.

2 cups chicken broth
1 large celery, stalks trimmed, diced into two inch pieces
1 cup mayonnaise
2 tablespoons minced parsley
1 tablespoon minced chives
2 tablespoons red wine vinegar
1 tablespoon Dijon mustard
Salt and pepper to taste
Butter lettuce
Additional minced chives

In a large saucep an, bring the chicken broth to a boil. Add the celery and simmer for 30 minutes, or until the celery is tender. Remove from the heat and cool. Wash the butter lettuce and divide among four plates. In a bowl, combine the mayonnaise, parsley, chives, red wine vinegar, Dijon mustard and the salt and pepper. Mix well. Drain the celery, and combine it with the dressing. Spoon onto the salad plates. Garnish with the minced chives.

Serves 4

Lemon Balm and Elderflower Sorbet

To clean the palate before tackling the rich desserts and savories, Victorian cooks created delicate sorbets and ices. The frequent use of herbs in sorbets and ices seen today has come full circle, back from their use in Victorian times.

3 large lemons
1 cup granulated sugar
2½ cups water
1 sprig of lemon balm
4 branches of Elderflower sprays
1 egg white

Remove the Elderflower's from the branches and place in a saucepan. Pare the lemons and place the rinds, sugar water, lemon balm in the saucepan with the Elderflower's. Set over a low heat and stir until the sugar has dissolved. Bring to a boil, and heat for an extra 5 minutes. Add the lemon juice. Then strain the liquid through several thicknesses of cheesecloth, and place in a container. Freeze until slushy. Remove from the freezer and place in a food processor. Blend until smooth. Beat the egg white until stiff and fold into the mixture. Return to the freezer and freeze until the edges are firm. Beat by hand, and replace in the freezer. Place one scoop in each dessert dish and garnish with twists of lemon peel, and sprigs of lemon balm.
Serves 4

Apricot Flan

Our love affair with the pie and the tart began back in the Middle ages with the first cheese tart and continued through Victorian times.

1 recipe Short Crust Pastry, page 391
1 pound apricots, pitted and diced

½ cup granulated sugar

3 large eggs, separated

1/3 cup whipping cream

¼ cup granulated sugar

Cook the apricots until soft. Transfer the apricots to a mixing bowl, and cool. Beat in the eggs yolks, sugar and whipping cream. Roll out the pastry to fill a 9-inch tart or Flan Pan. Fill with the apricot filling. Bake at 350°F. for 35 minutes. Beat the egg whites until stiff, then fold in the sugar. Beat again until glossy meringue forms. Pile on top of the apricot pie and bake for an additional 15 minutes. Remove from the oven. Serve either hot or cold.

Serves 8

Anchovy Toasts

Here is the quintessential English savory. Anchovies appeared in certain dishes of the 18th century and began to assert their flavor and taste in Victorian England.

8 toast points

1 tablespoon butter

½ cup butter

1 tablespoon minced parsley

1, 2 oz tin anchovy fillets, drained

1 teaspoon pepper

Take four slices of white bread and trim the crusts off. Toast. Then cut the toast into triangles.

Spread the toast points with butter and set aside. In a food processor, combine the rest of the ingredients and spread on the toast points.

Make 4 servings

*   *   *

Lillie Langtry

1853-1929, Actress, England

I was born in the Channel Islands, on the isle of Jersey. Life was very peaceful and oh so boring. So when I met Edward Langtry, I found the ticket for my escape to the bright lights of London. I was hell bent on climbing the ladder of success and this meant cultivating rich lovers, which I was more then able to do with my masses of red gold hair, and porcelain complexion. Among those who loved and courted me as their mistress where: The Prince of Wales, the American Millionaire Frank Gebhard and of course, the great love of my life Prince Louis Alexander of Battenberg. It was by him that I gave birth to my only child, Jeannie Marie.

After I had Jeannie Marie, I began to think of other ways of making money besides being the paramour of rich men. So I decided to go on stage. I made my debut in 1881, and while I must admit I was not a great actress, I was still the toast of Europe and America, winning the hearts of Oscar Wilde, George Bernard Shaw and Mark Twain.

Let me give you a sample dinner prepared for Bertie, the Prince of Wales, on one of the country estates of an English lord. The Prince was a monumental eater. Dinner consisted of a great many courses, with wine and champagne flowing. Tables were set with several different kinds of silverware and a huge epergne or centerpiece composed of many levels, topped with flowers and fruit. Hugh candelabras were also placed on the table, which could seat as many as 50 people. Bone china had replaced the heavier china of the past century, painted with exquisite patterns. This kind of dinner was served at the large estates, which Edward visited to shoot game and attend balls. The expense of having the Prince of Wales visiting you for a weekend was immense and the arrangements might take weeks getting in place. Arrangements also had to be made for his latest mistress, making sure her room was close to his, for discreet visits at night. Dinners like this might happen 4 times a month and the cooks might be asked to create as many as 30 different dishes.

I must say, I had a most interesting life. What a bore it would have been if I had married a local man on Jersey and raised a parcel of children.

*   *   *

Dinner with Bertie

Oyster Cocktail
Cream of Chervil Soup
Stilton Stuffed Tomatoes
Medallion of Beef with Truffles
Guinea Fowl Breast Stuffed with Mushrooms
Lamb Cutlets with Red Currant Sauce
Victoria Pie
Raspberry Ice Cream
Charlotte Russe
Potted Beef
Sardine Spread
Assorted English Cheeses and crackers
Port

*   *   *

Oyster Cocktail

By the time Sir Arthur Nan Doyle was writing about Sherlock Holmes and his penchant for oysters, the oyster had made its return to the tables of the wealthy. Bertie could consume dozens of these at one sitting and then consume huge servings of every other thing on the menu.

3 tablespoons mayonnaise

1 tablespoon horseradish, grated

3 tablespoons tomato sauce

1 tablespoon lemon juice

1 teaspoon Worcestershire sauce

4 drops Tabasco

1/3 teaspoon salt

1/8 teaspoon pepper

20 oysters

Mix together the mayonnaise, horseradish, tomato sauce, lemon juice, Worcestershire sauce, Tabasco, salt and the ginger. Remove the oysters from their shells and add 16 of them to the sauce. Chill in the refrigerator for at least 1 hour. Pour into 4 champagne glasses. Top each glass with an oyster. Serve immediately.

Serves 4

Cream of Chervil Soup

Cream soups still continued to grace the table of Edwardian England, while the poorer classes had their vegetable and meat potages thickened with oatmeal or barley.

1 Bunch leeks, trimmed and chopped

2 medium onions, chopped

1 cup celery leaves

4 tablespoons butter

2 quarts chicken stock

1 pound potatoes, peeled and sliced

1 teaspoon salt

½ teaspoon pepper

1 cup heavy cream

1 cup chervil, chopped finely

Melt the butter in a large soup pot. Add the vegetables and cook for several minutes. Then add the chicken stock, the potatoes and the salt and pepper. Bring to a boil. Reduce the heat and simmer for 1¼ hours. Remove the soup from the stove and puree in a food processor in batches. Return to the pot. Add the cream and the chervil and reheat. Serve in soup bowls, with additional chervil.

Serves 6-8

Stilton Stuffed Tomatoes

Tomatoes were now firmly ingrained in the British Menu, having finally removed the suspicions associated with its membership in the nightshade family.

8 large tomatoes
Salt and pepper
1 cup Stilton cheese, crumbled
¼ cup butter
1 tablespoon minced chives

Cut the tops off the tomatoes. Turn upside down. Drain for 30 minutes. With a serrated spoon remove some of the insides of the tomatoes. Reserve. Sprinkle the insides of the tomatoes with salt and pepper. Mix together the insides of the tomatoes, cheese, butter and chives in a large bowl. Preheat the oven to 350°F. Butter a large casserole dish. Stuff each of the tomatoes with some of the cheese mixture and place in the greased pan. Bake for 20 minutes.

Serves 6-8

Medallion of Beef with Truffles

The Prince of Wales was a man who loved his meat. Expensive items like truffles were eaten daily in the houses of the well to do.

8 (4 oz) filet Mignons
3 tablespoons butter
8 asparagus spears, trimmed and cooked

3 shallots, minced

½ cup white wine

1 cup Brown Sauce, page 388

8 grinds of pepper

1 teaspoon salt

½ cup diced black truffle

Salt the fillets. Heat two tablespoons of the butter and sauté the fillets. Cook them to medium rare. Remove them from the pan. And keep warm in the oven. Add the shallots to the pan and sauté for 1 minute. Then add the white wine, brown sauce, the pepper and the salt. Cook until reduced. Strain and return to a clean skillet. Add the butter and the truffles. Cook for 1 minute or until the butter is melted. Place two fillets on each serving plate. Cover with two asparagus tips. Spoon some of the truffle sauce on top.

Serves 6

Guinea Fowl Breast stuffed with Mushrooms

The Prince of Wales was an avid hunter. His favorite weekend was to stay at the Duchess of Grenville's and shoot, shoot, shoot!

4 guinea fowl breasts

1 cup diced morels

2 garlic cloves, minced

2 tablespoons minced parsley

¼ cup butter

Salt and pepper to taste

2 tablespoons whipping cream

2 shallots, minced

1 cup dry red wine or port

Melt the butter in a skillet and add the mushrooms, garlic, parsley, and season to taste with salt and pepper. Cook until the mushrooms are tender. Add the whipping creme and the shallots. Cook for 2 more minutes. Stuff some of the mixture under the skin of each breast. Fasten with toothpicks. Place in a greased baking pan. Cover with the red wine. Bake at 400°F. for 12 minutes. Remove From the oven and place each guinea fowl breast on a serving plate. Spoon some of the pan drippings on top of each guinea fowl.

Serves 4

Lamb Cutlets in Red Currant Sauce

The lamb cutlet began to appear as an alternative to the roasted joint of meat during Edwardian times. Fried to a golden brown, it could be glorified with a multitude of different sauces.

8 lamb cutlets

Flour

Salt and pepper

2 tablespoons butter

2 tablespoons oil

1 cup button mushrooms

4 tablespoons red currant jelly

1 tablespoon Worcestershire sauce

1 tablespoon flour

½ cup beef broth

¼ teaspoon ground nutmeg

1 tablespoon minced parsley

Trim the cutlets of fat and dip in flour, seasoned with salt and pepper. Heat the butter and oil together and fry the cutlets, until golden brown on both sides. Remove from the pan and place in a large casserole dish.

Add the mushrooms to the pan and sauté until just soft. Add to the casserole. In a small saucepan, melt the jelly and add the rest of the ingredients. Whisk until smooth. Pour on top of the meat. Bake at 350°F., for 45 minutes. Remove from the oven. Place 2 cutlets on each plate and spoon the sauce over the top.

Serves 4

Victoria Pie

Pies began to be served with an accompaniment of ice cream, such as the following recipe for raspberry ice cream. Many dishes were named for prominent people of the age and it is quite humorous to think of the Prince of Wales downing this pie, named for his mother, who was the bane of his existence.

10 large Granny Smith apples, peeled, cored and sliced
½ cup water
½ cup raisins
1 cup granulated sugar
1 unbaked 10 inch pie shell
½ cup sugar
1 cup almond paste
6 egg yolks, beaten
1 cup whipping cream

Combine the apples and water in a saucepan and cook until tender. Add the raisins and the sugar. Stir until the sugar is dissolved. Cool slightly. Preheat the oven to 400°F. Turn the apple mixture into the pie shell. Bake for 20 minutes. Meanwhile, add the ½ cup sugar to the almond paste and mix in a food processor. Blend in the cream and the egg yolks, beating after each addition. Remove the pie from the oven

and reduce the heat to 350°F. Spread the almond mixture on top. Bake for another 15 minutes. Remove from the oven and cool.
Serves 8

Raspberry Ice Cream

    1 pound raspberries
    1 cup granulated sugar
    2 tablespoons lemon juice
    2½ cups Custard, page 387

Mix the sugar, raspberries and lemon juice together. Let it sit for 1 hour, then pour the juice off. Mix the fruit with the custard. Pour into an electric ice cream maker and freeze according to directions.
Serves 6-8

Charlotte Russe

It was never just enough to have one dessert at these dinners, especially if you were entertaining the Prince. Bavarian cremes, made popular by Chef Alexis Soyer, were one of the elaborately iced and molded desserts, which were an essential part of a formal Victorian dinner.

    1 recipe Custard-page 389
    3 tablespoons brandy
    1 sheet gelatin
    ¾ cup whipping cream
    1 package ladyfingers
    ¼ cup brandy
    Additional whipped cream
    Candied Violets.

Heat the brandy in a saucepan and add the gelatin, stirring until it dissolves, but do boil. Stir mixture into the cooled custard. Then beat the whipped cream until stiff and fold into the custard. Line a round mold with ladyfingers. Sprinkle them with the brandy. Spoon the custard filling into the middle. Place in the refrigerator and chill until set. Remove from the mold, by running the bottom of the mold under warm water. Then take a small knife and run it around the sides of the mold, loosening the lady fingers. Unmold on a serving platter. Garnish it with whipped cream rosettes piped around the mold, and for a real Victorian touch decorate the mold with candied violets.

Serves 8

Potted Beef

Little pots of beef, cooked with butter and fish, were spread on toast or crackers, to go with the port that was served at the end of the meal. There were endless variations on the savory theme, potted shrimps, potted kippers, chicken pates, cheese dishes, all washed down with a copious about of claret, port or brandy.

This recipe and the one following are examples of several kinds of savories served at the end of a meal.

2 Pounds rump roast

2 cups Beef stock

6 cloves

1 teaspoon anchovy paste

1 teaspoon salt

1 teaspoon pepper

2/3 cup clarified butter

Put the meat in an ovenproof baking dish, with the stock, cloves, anchovy paste, salt and pepper. Cover with foil and bake at 350°F. until the meat is tender. Remove from the oven and discard the cloves. Strain the cooking liquid, and set aside. Shred the meat and then place in a food processor, with 1/3 cup of the clarified butter and ½ cup of the cooking liquid, processing until smooth. Place in a pot and cover with the rest of the clarified butter.

To clarify Butter: Place two sticks of butter in a small saucepan, and gently heat, until the butter separates from the solids. Place a layer of cheesecloth in a strainer, and pour the butter through it, into a small crock.

Makes 8-10 servings.

Sardine Spread

½ cup butter

1,can (3-½ oz) sardines

1 tablespoon lemon juice

4 drops Tabasco sauce

1/8 teaspoon paprika

Remove the skins from the sardines and place in a food processor. Add the rest of the ingredients and process until smooth. Serve with crackers.

Makes 1 cup

*   *   *

Annie Oakley

1860-1926, Shootist and Feminist, America

Due to the extreme poverty of my childhood, I learned to shoot a gun early on. Going out to the woods when I was but ten, I watched and listened for the call of the birds, and the soft footpads of the deer. I could often find myself a filling dinner. I became such a good shot that by the time I was 15, I was entering shooting matches. It is there that I met Frank Butler, who said that when I defeated him in a match, he fell in love with me. In 1884, I joined Buffalo Bill's Wild West Show, with Frank as my manager and husband. For 16 years, we traveled all over the United States and Europe. I became a star, with European royalty clamoring to see me perform. In 1901, I was in a serious train accident, ending my career with the Wild West Show, but I was still able to continue my shooting demonstrations. I was a woman who believed in the emancipation of women, like many of the other great feminists of my time. I gave lessons to women on how to shoot a gun, to protect themselves. I donated money to charities that supported women and children and was also responsible for putting more then 20 women through college. The horrible poverty and separation I endured as a child was always in the back of my mind, and if I could make it better for others, then I vowed to do so.

Many members of the Wild West Show were American Indians and cowboys from the Western United States. Wild Bill knew that they would be uncomfortable with the fancy foods provided by our European hosts. So in order to keep everyone happy, he retained several cooks capable of rustling up a good western meal when necessary.

Especially well loved were grits, beef stew, shoofly pie, pinto beans and of course, biscuits to sop it all up with. Since we had people from all over the United States in the show, we would have food from every region, We even had some adventurous members of royalty admit that it was mighty good eating!

*   *   *

The Wild West Show Dinner

Beef Stew
Ham in Coffee Gravy
Baked Grits
Black Eyed Peas Southern Style
Creole Green Beans
Country Biscuits
Shoofly Pie
Apple Pan Dowdy
Indian Pudding

Note: Some Recipes Adapted from the *Original Fanny Farmer Cookbook, 1896,* and *the Horizon Cookbook.*

*   *   *

Beef Stew

By the 19th century, cattle runs from the West to Chicago were a normal occurrence. Beef had become the major meat of the time, appearing in every conceivable form. Beef stew was a favorite of both the eastern part of the United States, as well as the West. Cooks, who manned the chuck wagon, usually provided a hearty meal like this for the cowpunchers that were herding the cattle.

2 pounds beef stew meat
4 tablespoons butter
3 large carrots, peeled and diced
3 medium sized onions, cut into hunks
2 stalks of celery, diced

2 bay leaves

1 sprig of thyme

1 teaspoon salt

½ teaspoon pepper

3 cups of beef broth

1 tablespoon flour

Roll the beef in the flour and brown in the melted butter in a large saucepot. Add the bay leaves, celery and onions. Season with salt and pepper and add the beef broth. Bring to a boil and then cover with a lid. Simmer on low heat for 2 hours and then add the carrots. Simmer for 30 minutes, or until the carrots are tender. Make a paste with the flour and water and add to the stew. Stir until thickened. Serve in bowls.

Serves 4

Ham in Coffee Gravy

When coffee was added to gravy in the south it was called Red Eye, because the ham appeared like a red eye starting up from the plate. A plate of buttery grits, and a vegetable dish such as the green beans usually accompanied Ham with Red Eye Gravy.

1 large slice center cut ham, about 2 pounds

1 cup meat stock

1 cup black coffee

1 teaspoon salt

½ teaspoon pepper

Preheat the oven to 350°F. Remove some of the ham fat and cube. Set aside for use in the gravy later. Place the ham in a large baking dish and cover with 1 cup of the meat stock. Bake for 1 hour. Remove the ham from the pan Place some of the fat cubes in the pan and cook until the fat is rendered. Add the coffee and cook for 2 minutes. Slice the ham lengthwise, into thick pieces. Pour some of the gravy over the top and serve.

Serves 4-6

Baked Grits

1 cup quick cooking grits,
½ pound sharp cheddar cheese, grated
8 tablespoons butter
3 eggs, well beaten
½ cup milk

Preheat the oven to 350°F. Cook the grits according to the package directions. Remove from the heat and stir in the cheese, butter, eggs and milk. Mix well. Pour into a greased baking pan. Bake for 40 minutes.

Serves 6

Black Eyed Peas Southern Style

Most dried bean dishes and those containing greens were cooked with salt pork. When I was growing up, salt pork was the only meat we might had, except for an occasional rabbit or deer, which I had shot.

1 pound black eyed peas
1 pound salt pork, diced
Bouquet Garni:
(1 bay leaf, 1 sprig of thyme, 8 sprigs of parsley and 8 peppercorns tied in a cheesecloth bag)
1 medium sized onion, peeled and quartered
½ teaspoon salt
1 quart of water

Soak the black-eyed peas overnight in water. Drain and place in large soup pot with the rest of the ingredients. Place the Bouquet Garni in the pot.. Bring to a boil, and then skim off the foam that forms on the top. Reduce the heat and simmer for 2 hours or more, adding more water if necessary. Remove the Bouquet Garni from the pot. With a slotted spoon transfer the beans to a serving bowl.

Serves 6

Creole Green Beans

Green beans cooked in a spicy Creole sauce was a common recipe for vegetables during the late 19th century, when food from Louisiana was making itself known to the rest of the United States.

1 pound green beans
2 cups Creole sauce, page 391
Salt and pepper to taste

Clean the beans and snap them in half. Place in a saucepan, with the Creole sauce. Bring to a boil and simmer for 30 minutes. Add the salt and pepper to taste if necessary.

Serves 6

Country Biscuits

Biscuits were eaten with almost every meal. They sopped up all the good juices from the stew and the coffee gravy.

2 cups flour
2 tablespoons baking powder
1 teaspoon salt

¼ teaspoon baking soda

2 tablespoons lard or shortening

¾ cup buttermilk

Preheat the oven to 400°F. In a mixing bowl, combine the flour, baking powder, salt and soda. Mix well. Then cut in the shortening, until the mixture resembles breadcrumbs. Add the buttermilk and mix lightly. Lightly flour a cutting board and roll out the biscuits to 1 inch thick. Cut out with round cookie cutters. Place the biscuits on a greased cookie sheet. Bake for 10-12 minutes.

Makes 10 Biscuits

Shoofly Pie

Shoofly pie used the most common ingredient found in the West for sweetening, molasses, which was easier to come by then its more expensive counterpart, sugar.

1 recipe Short Crust Pastry, page 391

¾ cup fine white breadcrumbs

¼ cup flour

¼ cup butter

1 teaspoon ground cinnamon

¼ teaspoon ground nutmeg

1/8 teaspoon ground ginger

¼ cup hot water

¾ cup light molasses

6 well beaten eggs

Preheat the oven to 400°F. Line a 7-inch pie plate with the pastry. Trim and then prick all over and bake for 10 minutes. While the crust is baking, mix the first six ingredients together with your fingertips to make a crumb. Then beat the molasses and the water into the eggs. Beat well. Remove the piecrust from the oven and pour the egg mixture into it. Then sprinkle with the crumb mixture. Reduce the heat to 350°F., and bake for 30 minutes.

Serves 6

Apple Pan Dowdy

Apple pan dowdy is as American as the covered wagon. It could be made over a campfire in a pan, suspended over a cauldron, or in an oven as well. Again the main sweetening agent was molasses, although a small amount of sugar was used as well.

1 recipe Short Crust Pastry, page 391
2 pounds apples cored, peeled and thinly sliced
½ cup granulated sugar
½ teaspoon ground cinnamon
½ teaspoon salt
¼ teaspoon ground nutmeg
½ cup light molasses
¼ cup water
3 tablespoons melted butter
Half and half

Preheat the oven to 350°F. Line a deep dish with pastry and trim. Toss the apples in a bowl with the sugar, salt and spices. Place in the dish. Then mix together the water, molasses and the butter. Pour over the apples. Roll out the rest of the pastry and cover. Trim and cut slashes on the top. Bake for 35 minutes. Remove from the oven and chop the pastry and apples to pieces with a knife. Add more butter and water if it seems dry. Bake for an additional 30 minutes. Remove from the oven and serve in bowls, with cream.

Serves 6\

Indian Pudding

The origins of the name of this dish are unknown. It is more than likely left over from our English ancestry and the suet puddings they started to make in the 17th century.

6 tablespoons cornmeal
1 quart milk
½ pint cold water
½ cup suet, chopped.
2 teaspoons salt
3 tablespoons brown sugar
1 cup molasses
1 teaspoon baking soda
1 tablespoon ground ginger
½ teaspoon allspice
½ teaspoon ground nutmeg
4 eggs
Sweetened whipped cream

Boil the milk. Moisten the cornmeal in the water. Add to the boiling milk with the salt and the suet. Boil for 15 minutes, stirring constantly. Remove the pan from the fire and add ½ cup of cold milk, the sugar, molasses, baking soda and the spices. Beat the eggs yolks separately and fold into the pudding. Beat the egg whites until stiff and fold in also. Butter a 2-quart pan and bake in the oven at 350°F. for 1 hour. Spoon into dessert dishes and serve with whipped cream.

Serves 8-10

*   *   *

Chapter 5

Emma Goldman

1860 to 1940 Anarchist

I believed in the freedom of the people. Born in Russia, I immigrated to the United States in 1885. While living in New York, I became the head of the anarchist movement. During the 1890's, I was arrested for inflammatory speeches against the Government. After my release, I went to Europe and gave lectures on anti-imperialism. I also published a newspaper called *Mother Earth*, which expressed strong anti-government views, especially during World War 1. I was imprisoned in 1917 for my anti-conscription views and then deported to the USSR in 1919. At first I loved the new Soviet Regime, but later I became disillusioned, when I saw it was biased against the Jews and other minorities of the country. I began to speak out against the government and was then expelled from Russia.

In order to live in England, where I hoped the power of free speech would be honored, I married a Welsh coal miner who was an anarchist also. I was allowed to live in London for many years. During the Spanish Civil War, I felt that I needed to help, so I worked for the Spanish Republican Government in London and Madrid. I spent the last years of my life in Toronto, disenchanted with the duplicity of the so-called, communist governments.

When I was young, my father told me that women were only good for creating Passover dinner, a project I rejected for many years, But when I saw the imprisonment of Jews in Russia for their beliefs, I began to search for discoveries of my own heritage. While not religious, I enjoyed the cultural significance of Jewish food and customs Though I never celebrated the Sabbath, I certainly relished the chance to relive the traditions of my heritage and often hosted meals during Passover. The meal below includes traditional foods of both the Sabbath and Passover. During the 19th century the earliest known Jewish food came from the northern part of Europe, especially Russia, Poland and Czechoslovakia. It wasn't until the establishment of Israel that Sephardic cuisine became known. Since Sephardic Jews came from Arab countries, Spain, Italy, Yemen, Ethiopia, India and even China, their food incorporated more of the spicy and exotic tastes of their respective countries. The Jewish cooking from Poland and Russia concentrated on using chicken, beef, chicken fat, sour cream, noodles and vegetables. Come enjoy the religious event that has a most poignant significance for Jewish people all over the world, the Passover. This is the great Jewish holiday that celebrates the liberation of the Jewish people from their bondage in Egypt. It lasts for a total of 8 days, during which one cannot eat any leavened bread. This is because the Jews had no time to make leavened bread for their flight, making do with the unleavened kind. I have also included an alternate menu, containing Sephardic foods served at Passover.

*   *   *

Eastern Passover Dinner
Chopped Liver
Chicken Soup with Matzo Balls
Challah (Included because it is traditional Sabbath bread)
Unleavened Matzo crackers
Gefilte Fish
Haroseth

Potato Carrot Kugel
Cholent
Passover Chocolate Nut Torte

Sephardic Passover Dinner
Golden Potato Soup, Egyptian
Stuffed Artichoke Bottoms, Egyptian
Stuffed Trout, Russian, Georgian
Eggplant Caviar, Georgian
Halek, Turkish Haroseth
Lamb and Fava Beans, Turkish
Beet and Coriander Pickle, Georgian
Orange and Coconut Cake, Egypt
Coconut Jam-Egyptian, Turkish, Greek

*   *   *

Eastern European Passover Dinner

Chopped Liver

Chopped liver was one of the most favored Sedar appetizers; usually served to start out a Friday night. Since the Passover meal is so substantial, oftentimes one would not eat again until Saturday after services.

3 tablespoons chicken fat
1 large onion, chopped
2 garlic cloves, minced
1 pound chicken livers
3 hard-boiled eggs, quartered
1 tablespoon minced parsley

Melt the chicken fat in a large frying pan. Add the onion and the garlic. Cook until the onions are tender. Add the chicken livers and cook until they are no longer pink. Pour the mixture into a food processor and add the hard-boiled eggs. Chop coarsely. Season with salt to taste. Add a little more chicken fat, if too dry.

Transfer to a serving bowl and garnish with parsley

Serve with crackers.

Serves 4

Chicken Soup with Matzo Balls

Matzo meal was made from unleavened bread, and was used as the only source of flour during Passover. In Eastern European countries such as Poland, dumplings were very common in soups. The chicken soup served at Passover contained dumplings made only of matzo meal.

2 pounds chicken breasts, diced

9 cups cold water

1 large onion, peeled and quartered

1 parsnip, peeled and cut into hunks

1 large carrot, peeled and cut into hunks

2 celery stalks, diced including the leaves

5 sprigs parsley

5 dill sprigs

1 teaspoon salt

½ teaspoon pepper

Matzo Balls:

2 large eggs

2 tablespoons vegetable oil

½ cup matzo meal

2 tablespoons water

1 teaspoon salt

2 quarts salted water

1 tablespoon minced chives

Combine the chicken breasts, cold water, onion, parsnip, carrot, celery, parsley and dill, in a large soup pot. Bring to a boil, and skim. Then reduce the heat and simmer, covered, for 2 hours. Remove the meat from the broth, and then strain into a bowl. Dice the meat. Return the meat and the broth to the pot. Add salt and pepper. While the soup is cooking, make the matzo balls.

Matzo Balls: In a medium bowl, combine the eggs with the oil. Add the matzo meal and the salt and stir until smooth. Stir in the water. Let the mixture sit for 30 minutes. Bring the salted water to a boil. Wet your hands and roll about 1 teaspoon of the mixture between your hands, to make a ball. With a rubber spatula, carefully lift the balls into the boiling water. Cover and simmer, until the soup is ready.

Ladle the chicken soup into soup bowls; garnish with the matzo balls and snipped chives.

Serves 6-8

Challah (Golden Egg Bread)

Challah or golden egg bread is the traditional bread eaten on the Sabbath. This bread would not have been eaten on Passover as it contained yeast. Serve some unleavened matzo crackers if you are making this meal for Passover.

2 tablespoons yeast

3 cups all purpose flour

4 tablespoons granulated sugar

2 eggs

6 tablespoons vegetable oil

1½ teaspoons salt
¾ cup warm water
  1 egg, beaten with 1 tablespoon of water
  1 tablespoon poppyseeds

In a bowl, combine the yeast with the warm water. Let the yeast mixture sit for 10 minutes. Then add the rest of the ingredients. Mix well. Then turn out onto a floured board and knead for 10 minutes. Place in a greased bowl and cover with a cloth. Let rise for one hour. Return to the floured board, and knead 4 times. Divide into 3 ropes and braid the ropes together. Place on a greased cookie sheet and cover with a cloth. Let rise for another hour. Preheat the oven to 350°F. Make an egg wash with the egg and water. Then paint the bread with it. Dust with the poppy seeds. Make for 40 minutes or until golden brown.
Serves 16

Gefilte Fish

Gefilte fish is said to have originated in Holland, as a dish created by the Spanish Jews who fled there during the inquisition.

1 pound whitefish
1 pound pike fillets
2 onions sliced
4 cups water
2 carrots, sliced
1 teaspoon salt
½ teaspoon ground white pepper
2 eggs
¼ cup matzo meal

Place the fish fillets in a large pan, with the water, onions, carrots and salt. Cook over high heat until the fish is cooked. Drain the fish and place in the food processor with the salt, white pepper, eggs and matzo meal. Mix until well blended. Make balls with your hands and return to the pot with the fish stock. Cook for 10 minutes. Remove from the pan. Cool. Place on a platter. Add the sliced carrots to the platter. Strain the fish stock over the Gefilte fish, and chill in the refrigerator until ready to serve.

Serves 9

Harsoeth

Haroseth, a dried fruit dish, is part of the ritual plate containing a hard boiled egg, bitter herbs and a lamb bone. These items symbolize the Jewish flight from Egypt This particular recipe was a common one found in Poland and the Eastern part of Europe.

¾ cup raisins, chopped

2 pounds dates, chopped

1 apple, peeled, cored and diced

1 cup red wine

Combine all the ingredients in a large bowl. Chill until ready to serve. Makes 6 cups

Potato and Carrot Kugel

Kugel is made with potatoes or carrots, or sometimes a combination of both. They are a Passover food, using matzo flour as their thickening agent.

6 large potatoes, peeled

4 large carrots, peeled

1 large onion, peeled

2 medium eggs

4 tablespoons chicken fat, melted

1½ teaspoons salt

1 teaspoon sugar

4 tablespoons matzo flour

½ teaspoon black pepper

2 tablespoons minced parsley

Paprika

Preheat the oven to 375F. Grease an 8-inch pan. Break one egg into the food processor. Add half of the onion. Next add three of the potatoes, cut into 1-inch pieces. Cut the carrots into 1 inch pieces and blend until smooth. Repeat with the rest of the onion, potatoes and carrots. Place in a large mixing bowl and add the chicken fat, salt, matzo flour, black pepper and parsley. Pour into the pan and sprinkle with paprika. Bake for 1 hour or until browned.

Serves 6-8

Cholent (Beef Brisket)

Cholent was the main dish of the Sabbath. Cooked slowly; it could be eaten on Saturdays, having been kept warm in the oven overnight, since cooking on Saturday was not allowed

2 large onions, sliced

4 tablespoons margarine

3 pounds brisket of beef

1 teaspoon salt

½ teaspoon pepper

6 medium potatoes, peeled and halved

1½ cup dried lima beans

3 garlic cloves, minced

1 bay leaf

Preheat the oven to 250°F. In a Dutch oven, melt the butter and sauté the onion until translucent. Then add the meat and brown on all sides. Add the rest of the ingredients. Then add enough water to cover the meat. Cover tightly with a lid. Bake for 12 hours.

Makes 6-8 Servings

Passover Chocolate Torte

Many cakes and tortes were created at Passover using matzo flour and a non-dairy source of fat.

Torte:

¾ cup margarine

¾ cup granulated sugar

7 eggs, separated

4 oz bittersweet chocolate, melted and cooled

1 cup almonds, ground

1 teaspoon baking powder

¼ cup chopped almonds

Icing:

4 eggs, lightly beaten

½ teaspoon potato starch

4 oz bittersweet chocolate, melted

4 oz margarine, softened

½ cup finely ground almonds

Preheat the oven to 350°F. Grease a 10 inch spring form pan. Cream the butter with the sugar, until light and creamy. Beat in the yolks, one at a time. Blend in the chocolate and add the ground almonds and the chopped almonds. Beat the egg whites until stiff but not dry. Fold into the egg yolk mixture, a third at a time, very gently. Pour into the spring form pan and bake for 30 minutes.

Frosting: Mix together the eggs, sugar and potato starch, in the top of a double boiler. Stir until the mixture thickens. Do not boil. Cool and then stir in the chocolate. Beat in the butter, one-tablespoon at a time, until all the butter is incorporated.

Cool the cake and remove from the springform pan. Place on a cake plate or serving platter. Spread the icing thickly over the cake and then sprinkle with the ground almonds.

Serves 10-12

*   *   *

Sephardic Passover Dinner

Golden Potato Soup

This soup is eaten by the Egyptian Jews, for their Friday Sabbath dinner. Its main flavor is that of lemon juice.

   1 large carrot, sliced
   3 stalks celery, sliced, leaves chopped finely
   6 cups chicken broth
   1 tablespoon corn oil
   2 cloves garlic, minced
   2 pounds russet potatoes, peeled and cubed
   2 teaspoons salt
   ¼ cup lemon juice
   ¼ teaspoon turmeric
   2 tablespoons cilantro, minced

In a food processor, combine 3 cups of the chicken broth, with the carrot and the celery. Puree. Pour the puree into a soup pot and add the remaining 3 cups of chicken broth. In a skillet, heat the oil and add the garlic, cooking until the garlic is slightly golden. Add to the soup pot. Then add the potatoes and cook over low heat, for 45 minutes. Add the salt, lemon juice and the turmeric. Cook for another 30 minutes, or until the potatoes are very soft. Ladle into soup bowls and garnish with minced cilantro.

Serves 6

Stuffed Artichoke Bottoms

This Jewish Egyptian dish can be served as an appetizer, or as part of the main course.

1, 14oz package artichoke bottoms, frozen

1 large onion, finely chopped

3 tablespoons sunflower oil

2 tablespoons Pine nuts

1 pound ground beef

2 tablespoons Italian parsley, minced

1 teaspoon salt

¼ teaspoon pepper

¼ teaspoon ground cinnamon

1 teaspoon ground cumin

1 egg beaten

2 tablespoons lemon juice

Defrost the artichoke bottoms. Fry the onion in the sunflower oil, until golden. Add the pine nuts and stir well. Mix in the meat, the parsley, the salt, pepper and the spices. Then add the egg. Mound the meat mixture into the artichoke bottoms. Place them in an oiled baking dish. Mix the lemon juice with 2/3 cup of water and pour over the dish. Bake at 350°F. for 30 minutes. Remove from the oven. Serve at room temperature.

Serves 6

Stuffed Trout

This Georgian dish is reserved mainly for special occasions, such as weddings and Passover.

    1 large trout, about 1 pound
    1 teaspoon salt
    ½ cup walnuts, chopped fine
    1 teaspoon hot chilies, minced
    ¼ cup pomegranate seeds
    ¼ teaspoon ground cinnamon
    ¼ teaspoon ground cloves
    Flour
    4 tablespoons corn or sunflower oil.

Rinse the trout and dry. Remove bones. Rub with salt and let stand for ½ hour. Lightly mix the walnuts, chili, pomegranate seeds, cinnamon, and cloves. Stuff the trout with the filling. Close the fish with toothpicks. Roll in the flour. Heat the oil and fry the fish for 3 minutes on each side. Drain on a paper towel. Remove to a platter and surround with fresh cilantro springs.
    Serves 4

Georgian Eggplant Caviar

Many Sephardic Jewish cultures have recipes for eggplant. Here is one of the most delicious, an eggplant salad from Georgia, in Russia.

    4 cups water
    2 large eggplants
    2 large tomatoes, quartered
    2 red bell peppers, seeded and sliced
    2 tablespoons corn oil

3 medium onions, minced

3 garlic cloves, minced

1 teaspoon salt

1 teaspoon pepper

2 tablespoons minced Opal basil

2 teaspoons red wine vinegar

Bring the 4 cups of water to a boil, in a large pot. Put the eggplants in the water and cook for 15 minutes, or until the eggplants are soft. Drain and cool the eggplants. Skin and dice them. Process the tomatoes, onions and pepper in the food processor, until pureed. Add the eggplant and process, until pureed. Heat the oil in a frying pan and add the garlic and the pureed eggplant and tomato mixture. Fry for 5 minutes. Transfer to a serving bowl and stir in the pepper, salt, opal basil and wine vinegar. Refrigerate until ready to serve.

Serves 6

Halek

Halek is the Turkish equivalent of Haroseth. It includes many more nuts and fruits then the Northern European version. The making of Halek was a very special procedure, and each family had its own recipe, handed down through the generations.

¼ cup almonds

¼ cup pistachio nuts

1/8 cup pitted dates, chopped

1/8 cup golden raisins

1/8 cup dark raisins

1/8 cup pitted prunes, chopped

1/8 cup pitted, dried apricots, chopped

1/8 cup pitted, dried sour cherries, chopped

½ cup red wine

2 teaspoons red wine vinegar

½ teaspoon rosewater

Chop all the nuts in a food processor. Mix the nuts, fruits, wine, vinegar and rosewater together. Chill until ready to serve.

Serves 6

Lamb with Fresh Fava Beans

This Turkish Passover dish uses only the most simple of ingredients, to allow for the fresh flavor of the fava beans to shine through.

2 cups water

3 pounds lamb shanks

2 cups water

3 pounds fresh fava beans

1 teaspoon salt

1 teaspoon sugar

4 scallions, sliced into ½ inch pieces

Cook the lamb in a large pot, with the two cups of water for 5 minutes, stirring several times Then add the rest of the water to the pan and cook the lamb for 2 hours. Trim the fava bean pods on both ends. Cut the pods into three pieces. Add them to the lamb with the salt, the sugar and the scallions. Cook for 20 minutes, or until the favas are tender.

Serves 6

Beet and Coriander Pickle

Here is a Georgian recipe to be served on the side, with the Passover meat dish.

1 pound of beets, cooked and peeled
1/8 teaspoon cayenne pepper
½ teaspoon salt
4 garlic cloves put through a press
½ cup finely chopped cilantro
3 tablespoons red wine vinegar

Dice the beets and mix together with the rest of the ingredients. Refrigerate in a jar for up to two weeks. Serve with meat dishes.
Makes 1 pint

Orange and Coconut Cake

This is a sweet cake made with no flour. This Egyptian Passover Cake is lightly perfumed with orange blossom water.

8 extra large eggs, yolks and whites separated
1 cup sugar
4 tablespoons grated orange zest
1 teaspoon ground cinnamon
1 teaspoon allspice
1 cup almonds, ground finely
1 cup unsweetened coconut

Syrup:

2½ cups fresh orange juice
1 teaspoon orange blossom water
1 cup granulated sugar

Preheat the oven to 350°F. In a large mixing bowl, beat the egg yolks with the sugar, until light and lemony. Then add the orange zest, the spices, the almonds and the coconut and stir well. Beat the egg whites until stiff, and then fold into the egg yolk mixture, a third at a time. Pour into a greased springform pan. Bake for 1 hour. While the cake is baking, make the syrup by boiling the orange juice and the sugar together, until thick. Add the orange blossom water and remove from the heat. Remove the cake from the oven. Poke holes in the top of the cake and pour the syrup over the top. Leave to sit several hours or overnight.

Serves 8

Coconut Jam

One speciality of Sephardic cultures is their ethereal and delicate jams. These jams are served at the end of a meal as a sweet, with tea or coffee. Sometimes they are put on a plate with several other jams, or swirled into a glass of ice water. This coconut jam with almonds is an Egyptian style jam.

    1 pound unsweetened coconut
    2 tablespoons rosewater
    2½ cups sugar
    2 tablespoons lemon juice
    ½ cup almonds, chopped finely

Mix the coconut with the rosewater. Leave overnight to swell and soften. Make a syrup, combining the sugar with 2/3 cup of water and the lemon juice. Add the coconut and bring to a boil. Boil for 5 minutes.

Remove from the heat and cool.

Place in a bowl and cover with the almonds.

Makes 1 pint

*   *   *

Maria Sklodowska-Curie

1867-1934, Polish Scientist, Discover of Radium

Warsaw, Poland was my place of birth. My mother was a pianist, singer and teacher and my father was a professor of mathematics. Early on, I displayed unusual intellectual talents and at 16 I won a gold medal, upon completion of my secondary education. Because my father had made some bad investments, I was unable to continue at school and had to go to work as a teacher. From my earnings, I was able to send my sister Bronia, to medical school, with the understanding that she would later help me to continue my education. So in 1891, I was able to go to Paris to continue my education at the Sorbonne. In 1883, I graduated at the top of my class and began to work in a research laboratory. While there I met Pierre Curie, and started a scientific partnership and marriage that lasted until his death.

While Pierre devoted his studies to the physical effects of the newly discovered concept of radiation, I resolved to find pure radium in the metallic state. This I achieved in 1903. Also in 1903, Pierre and I shared the Nobel Prize for Physics, with the German physicist Becquerel. I also found time to give birth to two daughters and believed in keeping a clean house and cooking meals, while continuing to work in the laboratory. In 1906, Pierre died and I vowed to continue his work by myself. In 1911, I was awarded the Nobel Prize for Chemistry, for the isolation of pure radium. During World War I, my daughter Irene and I worked on development of the use of x-radiography.

As for food, I always remembered the wonderful meals of my native Poland, and made sure my girls were well fed with all kinds of good food. Poland is a country with distinctive tastes and flavors. On one hand there are recipes passed down from generation to generation from the tables of Polish aristocracy, on the other hand we have the healthy food of the Polish peasant, consisting of good cheeses, rye breads, borsch, and simple stews. Polish cuisine combines many sweet and sour tastes. Cabbages are a very important crop in Poland and can be found in various soups, stews and sauerkraut. Desserts are finished with either a pastry or fruit soup. Even though I lived a majority of my life in Paris, I never forgot the simple food of my childhood.

*   *   *

The Nobel Prize Dinner
Cottage Cheese with Chives and Radishes
Black Bread
Sauerkraut with Mushrooms
Beets with Dill
Bread Dumplings
Pork chops with Pickles
Clear Rhubarb and Prune Soup

*   *   *

Cottage Cheese with Chives and Radishes

Polish food includes the use of many dairy products such as cottage cheese, farmer's cheese and sour cream. I loved this creamy appetizer that could be spread on black bread.

2 ½ cups cottage cheese
½ cup sour cream
10 radishes, sliced
2 tablespoon chives, minced
1 teaspoon salt

Cream the cheese and the sour cream together. Fold in the radishes and the chives. Then add the salt. Mix well. Chill until ready to serve. Serve with black bread.

Serves 4

Sauerkraut with Mushrooms

Sauerkraut is a major vegetable in Eastern European countries and combined with a bounty of mushrooms growing wild in the forests of Poland provided a basis for many savory dishes.

5 cups sauerkraut, drained and rinsed
½ cup dried mushrooms, soaked in water, diced
1 teaspoon caraway seeds
1 bay leaf
3 tablespoons vegetable oil
½ onion, minced
3 tablespoons flour
1 teaspoon pepper
1 tablespoon minced parsley

Place the sauerkraut in a sauce pan, with 1 cup of water. Add the mushrooms, caraway seeds and the bay leaf. Simmer for 10 minutes. In a skillet, heat the vegetable oil and add the onion. Brown lightly. Then add the flour, and cook for 2 minutes. Add a little water to dilute. Combine the cabbage with the onion and cook for 5 minutes. Stir in the pepper. Garnish with minced parsley.

Serves 4

Beets in Dill

Another major crop of countries Poland and Czechoslovakia, and Bulgaria are beets. They were pickled in brine, included in soups and smothered in sour cream.

2 pounds baby beets
¼ cup vegetable oil
1/3 cup white wine vinegar
2 tablespoons dill, minced
1 teaspoon salt
¼ teaspoon pepper

Cook the beets in a pot of boiling, salted water, until tender. Drain. Dice. In a bowl, whisk together the rest of the ingredients. Pour over the beets. Refrigerate for several hours.

Serves 4-6

Bread Dumplings

In Poland, the normal accompaniment to meat would have been either been noodles or a dumpling similar to this bread dumpling.

3 tablespoons butter
¼ cup minced onion

2 tablespoons minced parsley

1 teaspoon dried dill

8 slices white bread, crusts removed, diced

2 cups flour

2 large eggs

1¼ cup milk

1 teaspoon salt

Heat the butter and sauté the onions, parsley and dill, until the onion is soft. Add the diced bread and continue to sauté, until the onions and bread turn brown. Cool. Combine the flour, eggs, milk and salt. Beat vigorously for 5 minutes, until the batter is bubbly. Mix the bread into the batter and let stand for 30 minutes. Boil 8 to 10 cups of salted water in a deep pot. With wet hands, shape the batter into balls and drop into the boiling water. Simmer for 15 minutes or until the dumplings float. Reduce the heat and simmer for 5 more minutes. Drain and serve with butter.

Serves 4-6

Pork Chops with Dill Pickles

We are particulary fond of sweet and sour tastes, like our neighbors, the Germans. We included pickles in many of our recipes, to provide that sour taste.

4 large loin pork chops

3 tablespoons onion, chopped

1 cup tomato sauce

½ cup sour cream

1 small dill pickle, minced

3 tablespoons sweet sherry

1 teaspoon salt

½ teaspoon pepper

In a lightly greased skillet, brown the chops. Cover and reduce the heat. Cook until almost tender, (about 20 minutes). Add the onion and cook, until the onions are soft. Add the rest of the ingredients and mix well. Do not boil.

Serves 4

Clear Rhubarb and Prune Soup

Dessert often consisted of soup made from major Polish fruit crops, such as rhubarb, plums, and apples.

2 cups rhubarb cut in 1-inch pieces

2 cups prunes, pitted and diced

6 cloves

1 cinnamon stick, 1 inch long

6 cups water

1 cup sugar

1 tablespoon cornstarch

In a large pot, combine the rhubarb and prunes with two cups of water. Add the cloves and the cinnamon stick. Cook until soft. Press through a sieve. In a pot, combine the sugar and the water and heat until the sugar is dissolved. Add the pureed fruit. Cook for 10 minutes. Make a paste of the cornstarch with some water. Add to the fruit soup and stir until thickened. This soup can be served hot or cold.

Serves 6

*   *   *

Queen Mary

1867-1953, Queen of England, Wife of George the V

I was born Mary of Teck, the daughter of the Duke of Teck. I was of royal blood, my mother being Princess Mary Adelaide, the youngest child of Prince Adolphus, one of the sons of George III. Although I was a royal, my earliest memories are of living a penurious existence, with my family spending a good deal of time abroad because it was cheaper. In 1891 Queen Victoria, summoned me to Balmoral as a possible candidate for marriage to her grandson, the Duke of Clarence, or Prince Eddy. I passed the test and Eddy and I were engaged. Unfortunately he died before I could marry him. Queen Victoria decided that I should then be affianced to George, the next son. So George and I courted and were married in 1893. I loved George, even though we were very different. I adored intellectual pursuits and had a fantastic memory, but George possessed no interest in the opera, or theatre. He was a sailor, whose main hobby was collecting stamps. Duty to the crown soon became my main focus. While married to George, I did my best to foster the necessary feelings of responsibility for the Crown to the people.

Since the epoch I lived in straddled the Victorian, Edwardian and modern ages, I sometimes found it difficult to adjust. I refused to change the way I dressed, partially because George liked it a certain way and partly because I didn't agree with the new fashions. I suffered a great deal when my son David abdicated the throne for Wallis Windsor. My entire life had been about responsibility, and now he shunned it.

Even dinner was a strictly regimented affair. We were always served and dressed by an order of servants. The meals changed over the years, from the very elaborate Edwardian feasts, to the wartime meals on ration cards.

While at Windsor, we had fresh vegetables and food, provided by the estate and when we wanted a special product, we would patronize certain establishments, still carrying the royal warrant today. By the time of Queen Victoria, dinner was eaten at eight, and could last for two hours or more. To fill in the gap, afternoon tea reached ritual proportions in some houses. High tea that included hot dishes sometimes replaced the necessity for dinner. Dinner now was served A la Russe style. Instead of many dishes of both meat and sweets presented at the same time, the meal was divided into various courses. Starting with soup, followed by fish, meat and vegetables, desserts and fruits, cheese or a savory. However, George and I were very shy and even if we ate such a meal, we would have been too tongue-tied to remark on it to each other.

*   *   *

The Buckingham Palace Dinner
Chilled Cucumber Soup
Rib Eye Roast with Madeira Sauce
Grouse baked with bacon
Champ
Leeks in soured Tarragon sauce
Peach Ice
Balmoral Tart
Watercress savory

*   *   *

Chilled Cucumber Soup

Now thanks to the introduction of the refrigerator, soups could be served cold as well as hot.

1 large seedless cucumber, peeled and seeded
3 cups light cream

3 tablespoons tarragon vinegar

1 garlic clove, minced

Salt and pepper to taste

¼ cup fresh mint leaves, chopped

Grate the cucumber and place in a bowl. Add the cream and the rest of the ingredients. Stir well. Then chill in the refrigerator, until ready to serve. Serve in soup cups, with a sprinkling of fresh mint.

Serves 6

Rib Eye Roast with Madeira Sauce

Roast beef continued to be one of the preferred meats of my era. It was usually served with a sauce containing some kind of wine or spirits.

5 pound rib eye roast

1 garlic clove, crushed

1 teaspoon salt

1 teaspoon black pepper, cracked

1 teaspoon dried thyme leaves

½ teaspoon dried tarragon leaves

¼ cup shallots, finely minced

1 cup beef broth

½ cup Madeira wine

1 tablespoon tomato paste

Preheat the oven to 350°F. Combine the garlic, salt, thyme and tarragon, to form a paste. Rub all over the roast. Place the roast on a rack, in a shallow roasting pan. Insert met thermometer into thickest part of the roast, not touching the fat. Roast to 135°F for rare, or 155°F. for medium. Remove the roast from the oven and tent with aluminum foil. Let stand for 15 minutes. Meanwhile, skim the fat from the drippings in the roasting pan. Add the shallots to the drippings and cook over medium heat for 2 minutes. De glaze the pan by adding beef broth and Madeira wine, stirring to dissolve the browned meat juices attached to the pan. Add the tomato paste and continue cooking, until the liquid is reduced to one half its original amount. Serve the roast with the sauce.

Makes 8-12 servings

Baked Grouse with Bacon

My husband, George the V, was a great huntsman, taking after his father Edward the VII. Grouse or some other wild bird was on the menu for everyday meals at Buckingham Palace.

1 grouse per person
Apple
Butters
Salt and pepper
Bacon

Core and cut the apples into quarters. Place one quarter of an apple and a knob of butter inside each grouse. Season with salt and pepper. Wrap with bacon. Preheat the oven to 300°F. Roast the birds in a roasting pan, in 1 inch of water, for 45 minutes. Pour the liquid from the pan. Increase the oven temperature to 450°F. Roast for 10 minutes to brown the birds.

Makes one serving per person

Champ

Champ extended itself from origins in Ireland to England, where it became a much loved potato dish.

1½ pound Yukon gold potatoes, peeled and diced
1 cup scallions, minced

1 cup milk
2 tablespoons butter
Salt and pepper

Bring the potatoes to a boil in a large pot of boiling water. Cook until tender, about 15 minutes. Drain and return to the pot. Add the scallions, milk, butter and salt and pepper. Mash until fluffy.
Serves 4

Leeks in Soured Tarragon Sauce

Vegetables served in creamed sauces remained a favorite vegetable dish in the early 1900's. Tarragon was an herb used mainly by the French, but started to appear in English recipes for vegetables, eggs and poultry dishes.

8 small leeks
1 teaspoon salt
1 cup sour cream
1 tablespoon minced tarragon
1 small garlic clove, crushed
1 tablespoon apple cider vinegar
1 pinch sugar
2 tablespoons minced parsley

Clean the leeks, and trim. Place in a large saucepan. Pour in enough boiling water to cover. Add the salt. Cook over low heat for 10 minutes or until just tender. In a bowl, combine the rest of the ingredients. Transfer leeks to a serving platter. Pour the sauce over the top.
Serves 4

Peach Ice

The 19th century saw the advent of the hand cranked Ice Cream Maker. Many cooks of the 19th century had a large repertoire of ices and ice creams, often served at dinner parties.

8 small peaches, peeled, pitted and sliced
1 tablespoon lemon juice
1 cup confectioners sugar

Place all the ingredients in the food processor and puree. Pour into an ice cream maker and freeze according to directions.
Serves 4

Balmoral Tart

This recipe comes from the area around Balmoral Castle in Scotland, where we spent every summer. This tart could be served both as an afternoon snack during Tea or as a dessert after dinner.

1 recipe Short Crust Pastry, page 391
½ cup butter
1 cup sugar
2 large eggs
¼ cup stale bread crumbs
1 tablespoon candied orange peel, finely chopped
2 tablespoons glaceed cherries, finely chopped
1 tablespoon brandy
1 egg white, stiffly beaten

Roll out the pastry and line 16 tart pins. Preheat the oven to 350°F. Cream the butter with the sugar until fluffy. Add the eggs and beat well. Then add the breadcrumbs and the fruit. Mix well. Fold in the brandy

and the egg whites. Spoon the filling into the tart pans. Bake for 25 minutes. Remove from the oven and cool. Remove pastry from the tart pans.
    Makes 16 tarts

Watercress Savory

A savory would be served at the end of the meal, a fitting climax to a royal feast.

1 bunch watercress, cleaned, the tough stems removed
4 ripe pears, peeled, cored and sliced
12-oz Stilton cheese, crumbled
1 teaspoon freshly ground pepper

Preheat the oven to 450°F. Grease a casserole dish. Lay the watercress on the bottom of the pan and place the pear slices on top. Cover with the Stilton cheese and sprinkle with the black pepper. Bake for 5 minutes, or until the cheese melts. Serve on small dessert plates.
    Serves 4-6

*   *   *

Colette (Sidonie Gabrielee Colette)

1873-1954, Writer, France

My life really started at twenty, when I married Henry-Gauthier-Villars, a friend of the family who was a notorious womanizer. With his urging I came to write, and within three years had produced the Claudine novels, which he had the audacity to sell as his own. Needless to say, I became entirely disillusioned by his affairs and dishonesty, and finally left him. I went to live with a woman, the Marquise de Belboeuf, and had a lesbian affair. This started a whole series of lesbian lovers, until I met Henry de Jouvenal, who encouraged my writing. He had me write a series of articles for the French paper *Le Matin*. I eventually married Henry, and had my only child. Later I went on to write *Cheri* and *The Ripening Seed*. When his infidelities got to be too much, I divorced him. At 52, I met the man with whom I would spend the rest of my life, Maurice Goudeket. He became my third husband and I continued writing my next title, *Gigi*. I was considered to be one of the most celebrated French authors of the 20th century. I wrote 73 books in all, all centered on the subject the French know best: love.

Life in France during the early 20th century was sophisticated for those who were fortunate enough to possess money. Food, dancing and drinking became national past times. If you were an artist or an author, you would find yourself spending endless evenings in world-class restaurants, bistros, cafes, and dance halls, where a full meal could be provided while watching people dance the Can Can. The *Moulin Rouge* was one of the most famous nightclubs of all time. I would go there with my lovers, dressed as a man and drink Champagne all through the night. The incredible cuisine included succulent fish dishes with exquisite sauces, ingenious salads, and elegant desserts. A revolution in French food that had started in the 19th century was firmly entrenched in the 20th as well. I reaped the endless bounty, surrounded by the finest my culture had to offer.

*   *   *

A Left Bank Dinner

Shrimp, Avocado and Citrus Salad
Gratin of Oysters with Calvados Cream
Moules Marinieres
Frites
Mushrooms in Oil and Garlic
Fig Claflouti
Fromage Blanc Ice Cream

*   *   *

Shrimp, Avocado and Citrus Salad

Salads were taking on new heights, progressing from the simply dressed lettuce or escarole, to combined salads of many ingredients.

Dressing

1 tablespoon fresh lemon juice
1 tablespoon fresh lime juice
1 tablespoon honey
3 tablespoons olive oil
3 tablespoons walnut oil
2 tablespoons fresh minced chives
Salt and pepper to taste
24 large shrimp, cooked and shelled
1 large avocado, peeled and diced
1 pink grapefruit, peeled and segmented
1 naval orange, peeled and segmented
2 tablespoons toasted walnuts, chopped

Make the dressing first. Blend all the ingredients in a food processor. Then pour into a small bowl and refrigerate. On six salad plates, arrange the shrimp, avocado, grapefruit and orange sections. Drizzle with the dressing and sprinkle with the toasted walnuts.

Serves 6

Gratin of Oysters with Calvados Cream

Appetizers such as this gratin of oysters were the usual starters at a French bistro or nightclub like the Moulin Rouge.

16 large oysters, shelled
2 tart apples, peeled, cored and diced
1 cup whipping cream
3 egg yolks
½ cup Calvados

Preheat the oven to 350°F. Butter a large casserole dish. Place the diced apples on the bottom of the pan. Whip the cream until soft peaks form, then whisk in the egg yolks and the Calvados. Place the oysters over the apple and cover with the Calvados cream. Bake for 15 minutes. Remove from the oven and serve immediately.

Serves 4

Moules Marinieres ET Frites

The mussel gained great heights in the France of the 1920's, appearing in classic Bistro dishes still enjoyed today.

Vegetable oil
¼ cup unsalted butter
4 large shallots, finely chopped
2 garlic cloves minced

2 pounds fresh mussels, well cleaned and de-bearded

2 cups dry white wine

2 tablespoons lemon juice

1 cup half and half

2 tablespoons minced flat leaf parsley

4 potatoes, peeled and cut into long sticks

Melt the butter in a large soup pot. Add the shallots and the garlic and cook until soft. Then add the mussels, white wine and lemon juice. Place a lid on the pot and cook until done. Discard any unopened mussels. While the mussels are cooking, fill a deep fryer with oil. Heat the oil until smoking, add the potato sticks, or Frites and fry until brown. Stir the half-and-half into the mussels with the parsley, but do not let boil. Ladle into soup bowls and place on plates, ringed with the Frites.

Serves 4-6

Mushrooms with Garlic and Oil

When Morel season hit France, this mushroom appeared on countless occasions.

1 pound fresh morels

3 tablespoons olive oil

1 cup minced parsley

2 garlic cloves, minced

Salt and pepper

¼ cup bread crumbs

Clean and slice the mushrooms. Sprinkle with one tablespoon of the oil and set aside. Heat the rest of the oil in a skillet. When the oil is hot, add the mushrooms. Sauté gently for a few minutes. Add the garlic and the parsley and season with salt and pepper. Then add the breadcrumbs. Turn up the heat for 1 minute. Serve the mushrooms hot.

Serves 4

Fresh Fig Claflouti

A Claflouti is an old time cake with a pudding quality to it. It is usually made with cherries.

 1½ cups milk
 3 large eggs
 ¼ cup flour
 ½ cup sugar
 ½ cup melted butter
 4 large figs, cut in half
 Vanilla sugar

Preheat the oven to 350°F. In an bowl, beat the milk and the egg together with ¼ cup of the melted butter. Then add the sugar and the rest of the melted butter. Pour into a greased, 9-inch square-baking dish. Place the fig halves on top. Sprinkle with vanilla sugar. Bake for 30 minutes, or until puffed and golden.
 Serves 4

Fromage Blanc Ice Cream

Ice cream became a French obsession, as it had long been for the Italians. Ice cream shops dotted Paris and unusual ingredients were used to create new flavors.

 4 cups milk
 5 egg yolks
 ¾ cup granulated sugar
 4 oz cream cheese
 4 oz mascarpone cheese
 1 teaspoon vanilla

Heat the milk in a double boiler. Whisk together the sugar and the egg yolks. Add the milk slowly. Rinse out the pan and return the mixture to it. Heat until thickened. Strain and cool. Add the cheeses and the vanilla. Mix well in a blender. Freeze in an ice cream maker, according to directions.

Serves 8

*   *   *

Gertrude Stein

1874-1946, Writer, American

I was born in Allegheny, Pennsylvania, the child of a well-to-do family. By the time I was in college, I realized I was a restless spirit who loved women, a very alternative lifestyle for the age I came from. Realizing that living in America would be very difficult, I moved to Paris, living off the money left to me by my parents. I first lived with my brother Leo, an art critic. Through him I began a life-long appreciation for Cubist paintings. This allowed me to meet and form friendships with the great artists of the 20th century. While in Paris I began to write, which was to become my greatest source of pleasure, besides my life long companion and lover Alice B. Toklas. Alice provided the security I craved; creating a home for me, organizing my books, becoming an expert cook; and presiding over the many dinner parties we gave. Our house was always filled with great writers and artists. Alice accepted the fact that I was a genius, and as such, needed to have the environment run smoothly.

A dinner at our house for a guest like Picasso was based on an elegant menu, which Alice worked out with the help of our cook. There would be soup that only the French could excel at, a fish dish that Alice made into a work of art and some sinfully rich dessert. Dinner overflowed with conversation and wine. Ernest Hemingway might expound on his latest novel, Picasso talking about his latest exhibitions or Max Ernest about his gallery. During the war, it was life threatening to be a Jewish woman in France, but I refused to leave my home and for some reason the Nazis left me alone. Living with me led Alice to create a cookbook of the recipes she had produced during our time together. Her cookbook has become very famous, as is only fitting of her, since she was an excellent chef. Alice could create a dish out of anything, which she was called upon to do quite often during World War II. Luckily, we lived in the country and could count on finding fresh eggs, a ham, a pound of potatoes, or a piece of lamb that the Germans had overlooked. With these Alice would produce gastronomic delights. She grew vegetables in our garden, which she bartered for a supply of cigarettes. Alice could suffer through without coffee, but not without her cigarettes. The menu for the dinner given below would have come from happier days before the war, when there was an unlimited supply of food and my dear Alice could have created it without stinting.

*   *   *

The Dinner of Bass for Picasso

Brandade De More
Flageolet Bean Soup
Bass for Picasso
Wild Mushroom Potato Galette
Salad De Escarole
Bitter Chocolate Truffle Cake

*   *   *

Brandade De Morue

Brandade de Morue is a traditional French appetizer, made of cod-fish, cream and garlic.

2 pounds cod fish, dried
3 garlic cloves, crushed
1 cup olive oil
1 cup half and half
Salt and pepper
Toast points

Soak the cod overnight in cold water. After 24 hours, remove from the water and place in a pan. Cover with fresh water and simmer for 8 minutes. Remove the cod from the water and discard the bones. Then flake the fish. Add the crushed garlic. Heat the olive oil and the half and half together until just warm. Gradually add the mixture to the fish, beating until the fish is smooth. Season with salt and pepper
Serve with toast points.
Serves 8

Flageolet Bean Soup

This creamy bean soup made with flageolets was an excellent starter to a meal. Alice learned to make such soups, having gathered a multitude of recipes from French neighbors and cooks we hired.

1 ½ cups dried flageolet beans
1 small onion, quartered
1 garlic clove, halved
1 tablespoon minced fresh thyme
1 tablespoon sea salt
3½ cups chicken broth

½ cup half and half

¼ cup minced parsley

3 fresh plum tomatoes, peeled, seeded and cut into small cubes

1 cup croutons

In a medium bowl, soak the beans overnight, covered in cold water. Drain the beans and transfer them to a soup pot. Add the onion, garlic, thyme and 6 cups of water. Bring to a boil. Reduce the heat and simmer, covered for 1 hour. Add 2 teaspoons of the salt and continue simmering, until the beans are tender. Drain. Transfer the beans, onion and garlic to a food processor and puree. Then strain into the soup pot. Add the chicken broth and simmer for 10 minutes. Then add the rest of the salt. Drain the tomato cubes in a colander. Right before serving, add the half and half and if the soup is too thick, add a little more chicken stock. Heat until just warm. Ladle soup into soup plates and garnish with parsley, tomato cubes and the croutons.

Serves 6

Bass for Picasso

Alice created this recipe for a dinner where Picasso was the guest of honor. It comes from the *Alice B. Toklas Cookbook*. The finished product looked like one of Picasso's paintings.

1 recipe Court Bouillon, page 388

1,stripped bass (3-4 pounds) the head removed and boned

2 cups mayonnaise

1 ½ tablespoons tomato paste

3 hard-boiled eggs, whites and yolks separated and chopped

3 tablespoons fresh, fine herbs, (combination of tarragon, thyme and parsley)

4 black olives, sliced

Simmer the court bouillon for 30 minutes and cool. Place the fish in a fish poacher, with the court bouillon. Preheat the oven to 350°F. Poach the fish for 30 minutes. Remove from the oven and let the fish cool in the poacher. Remove fish from the poacher and dry thoroughly. Coat the fish with half the mayonnaise. Add the tomato paste to the remaining mayonnaise and mix. Spoon the mixture into a pastry bag and decorate the fish with squiggles. Then garnish with the chopped egg whites and yolks, the fine herbs and the olive slices.

Makes 6-servings

Wild Mushroom and Potato Galette

By the 1930's, Galettes made of potatoes or leeks and mushrooms had started to be a standard recipe of French Cuisine.

6 medium potatoes, peeled and sliced thinly
1/3 cup olive oil, divided in two equal portions
1½ cup morels, chopped
6 garlic cloves, minced
¼ cup minced chives
Salt and pepper to taste

Preheat the oven to 325°F. Heat 2 tablespoons of the oil in a cast iron skillet. Add the mushrooms, garlic and salt and pepper to taste. Cook over medium heat until the mushrooms are tender. Transfer to a bowl and add the chives. Set aside.

Lightly brush a 12-inch piece of aluminum foil with oil, and place the rest of the oil in the skillet. Arrange half of the potato slices in overlapping circles. Cover with the mushrooms and arrange the rest of the potatoes in overlapping circles on top. Cover with the aluminum foil and then weight down with pie weights. Bake in the oven for 35 to 45 minutes or until the potatoes are tender. Remove from the oven and remove the pie weights. Remove the aluminum foil carefully. Then invert on a serving plate.

Serves 6-8

Salad De Escarole

Alice always provided a simple salad after a meal of rich foods, such as the bass and potato Galette.

1 large head of escarole, washed and broken into bite size pieces

Dressing:

½ teaspoon Dijon Mustard

3 tablespoons white wine vinegar

1/3 cup olive oil

1 teaspoon minced parsley

1 hard-boiled egg

Place the escarole in a salad bowl. In a small mixing bowl, combine the rest of the ingredients, except for the egg and whisk. Then sieve the egg and fold into the dressing. Pour onto the escarole and toss.

Serves 6

Bitter Chocolate Truffle Cake

Needless to say, I loved my sweets. I suffered bitterly during the war when chocolate disappeared from the stores. But Alice was very ingenious and managed to secret away some from under the noses of the Germans. She saved up enough to make an occasional soufflé, a tart with walnuts, or a cake such as this bittersweet truffle cake for a special occasion.

Sponge Base:

4 eggs

½ cup granulated sugar

¼ cup cocoa and cornflower, sifted together

Syrup:

¼ cup rum
¼ cup granulated sugar
¼ cup water

Truffle:

1 pound dark, bittersweet chocolate
2 cups whipping cream

Preheat the oven to 350°F. On the top part of a double boiler, whisk the eggs and the granulated sugar, until a thick ribbon forms and it has doubled in volume. Remove from the heat and place in a serving bowl. Add the sifted cocoa and cornflower, being careful not to break down the volume. Pour into a greased sponge cake baking tin. Bake for 7-8 minutes, until the mixture is firm and springy.

Cut the cake into 2 circles to fit the bottom of a deep spring form pan. Use one of the circles and freeze the other for future use. Make the rum syrup by dissolving the sugar and the rum with the water. Boil until heavy syrup is produced. Brush the sponge base with the syrup. Set aside. Grate the chocolate and let stand in the cream, in a warm place for 30 minutes. Then heat on top of a double boiler, until the chocolate is melted. Do not boil the water, or the mixture will become grainy. Let the mixture cool, then whisk until soft peaks form. Pour into the cake tin, over the prepared sponge. Smooth and leave to set in the refrigerator. Before serving dust the cake thickly with cocoa.

Makes 8-10 servings

Mata Hari (Margaretha Geertruida MacLeod)

1876-1917, Exotic Dancer and World War I Spy, Dutch

My real name was Gertrude Margarita Zelle and I was born in Amsterdam. When I was eighteen, I answered an ad for an officer who was seeking a wife. He was Rudolph Mc Leod and I married him. We went to the Dutch East Indies, where I got the ideas for my later career from the Javanese temple dancers. Mc Leod was a horrible man, who drank and beat me, as he was insanely jealous. By 1904 I had left him and moved to Paris. I met the owner of an Oriental art museum and convinced him to let me dance there, dressed in Eastern clothes. I was an immediate sensation and all of Paris began to flock to see me. It was then that I changed my name to Mata Hari. The illusion was furthered by the story I created about my past. I was the daughter of a temple dancer and the priests who raised me taught me how to dance. As for my spying activities, I became involved in spying for the French, if they would give me a million Francs. When they refused, I decided to spy for the Germans and was arrested in 1917 and brought to trial. Many people testified to my innocence, but it was not enough to save me from the horrible sentence of death by firing squad.

From my time spent in the Dutch East Indies, I became very fond of Indonesian food. Many Dutch men had traveled to the East Indies and found Indonesian wives for themselves, whom they brought back to the Netherlands. These women brought their recipes for food with them. Indonesian food is a myriad of tastes: hot, salty, pungent and sweet. Complex spice mixtures add to the unusual tastes. Peanut butter, coconut milk and Sambel, a fiery chili paste, are just some of ingredients used in Indonesian cooking. There is an emphasis on freshness, exhibited by the artful salads and delicate noodle and rice dishes. Meat is eaten in small quantities as an accompaniment, rather than the main course. Eating Indonesian food brought me back to the days I spent watching the graceful dancers, flirting with officers in my husband's regiment and eating on verandas surrounded by swaying trees.

*   *   *

A Spy's Dinner

Indonesian Pork Sate
Gado Gado
Fish with Garlic and Scallions
Indonesian Fried Noodles
Fried Bean Curd with Sambel
Chicken in Chili Sauce
Indonesian Spiced Rice
Sambel
Mango and Yogurt
Beer

*   *   *

Indonesian Pork Sate

Satays are a common Indonesian way of preparing meat. They are little skewers of beef, chicken or pork, accompanied by a peanut sauce with chili peppers for dipping. Pork is not eaten in the Muslim part of Indonesia.

½ cup peanut butter, plain
1 tablespoon coriander seeds, crushed
½ tablespoon garlic, minced
½ teaspoon ground dried chili
1 medium red onion, quartered
4 teaspoons dark brown sugar
½ teaspoon fish sauce
2 tablespoons fresh lime juice
2 tablespoons soy sauce
¼ teaspoon black pepper
1/3 cup orange juice

¼ cup peanut oil

1 pound lean pork, cut into 1-inch cubes

12 small bamboo skewers

In a food processor, combine all the ingredients except for the pork. Puree Place the mixture in a saucepan, and bring to a boil. Let boil for 2 minutes. Remove from the heat and cool. Reserve 1/3 of the marinade for basting. Pour the remaining marinade over the pork. Marinate in the refrigerator for at least 3 hours or overnight. Soak the bamboo skewers in water for 1 hour before broiling. Drain the meat from the marinade and thread on the skewers. Broil for about 8 minutes. Place the marinade in a saucepan and heat until boiling. Boil for 2 minutes. Remove from the heat and place in a serving bowl. Use the marinade for dipping the sates.

Serves 4

Gado Gado

Gado Gado is a way of preparing vegetables, which are cooked separately and placed on a serving platter, to be served with a sauce.

2 pounds boiling potatoes, peeled and cut into I inch cubes

1 pound green beans, trimmed

8 carrots, peeled and cut diagonally into 1 inch chunks

1 pound broccoli, separated into small florets

Sauce:

½ cup plain peanut butter

2 cloves garlic, crushed

½ teaspoon red pepper flakes

1 tablespoon brown sugar

¼ cup lemon juice

1 tablespoon soy sauce

¾ teaspoon salt

1 cup hot water

Garnish:

2 cucumbers, peeled, seeded and cut into ½ inch strips

1/3 cup chopped peanuts

2 scallions, chopped

Bring two medium saucepans of salted water to a boil. Add the potatoes to one of the pans and cook until tender. Remove with a slotted spoon and drain well. Meanwhile, cook the green beans in another pan, until tender. Remove with a slotted spoon and drain well. Place the carrots and the broccoli in the pans and cook until tender. Drain. While the vegetables are cooking, puree the peanut butter in a blender with the rest of the ingredients. Then place in a saucepan and heat. Stir in the scallions. Divide the vegetables among six plates and drizzle with the sauce. Garnish with the chopped peanuts and the cucumber.

Serves 6

Whole Fish with Garlic and Scallions

When I lived in Indonesia with my husband, I was taught to make many of the dishes in this menu, but none was so dramatic as this whole fish fried to a golden crispy brown and served with a dark brown sauce.

1 Snapper (3–4 pounds) boned and left whole

Flour

Vegetable oil

6 cloves garlic, minced

3 tablespoons Indonesian Soy Sauce, (Kecup Manis)*

1 cup scallions, sliced lengthwise

Clean and trim the fish, leaving the head on. Pat dry. Flour on both sides. Heat at least ½ cup vegetable oil in a wok, until very hot. Fry the fish on both sides, until brown and crispy. About 10 minutes total. Remove from the oven and set aside. Remove most of the oil from the wok, except for about 2 tablespoons. Add the garlic and the scallions. Sauté for 2 minutes. Then add the soy sauce. Let the sauce cook for 1 minute. Return the fish to the wok and reheat for 2 more minutes. Remove to a serving platter and pour the sauce over the top. Garnish with scallions.

Serves 4

Indonesian Fried Noodles

Indonesians stir-fry noodles or rice to serve with the meal. Sometimes it is a simple preparation, unless served with a rijsttafel or rice table, when it becomes a complex creation, mounded like a pyramid and topped with strips of omelet, chilies and chopped cilantro.

1 pound uncooked soba noodles

1 tablespoon peanut oil

3 tablespoons soy sauce

1 tablespoon brown sugar

2 teaspoons red pepper flakes

1 cup onions, finely chopped

1 tablespoon garlic, minced

1 tablespoon gingerroot, peeled and grated

1 teaspoon lime zest

8 green onions, minced

8oz tofu, cut into 1-inch cubes

1 tablespoon lime juice

¼ cup chopped cilantro

---

*Note: Kecup Manis is an Indonesian Soy sauce found in Asian markets. It has a sweet taste due to the addition of brown sugar. If you cannot find it, mix 3 tablespoons of soy sauce and add 2 teaspoons of brown sugar. Stir well to dissolve.

Cook the noodles until tender. Drain. In a skillet, heat the peanut oil and add the soy sauce, brown sugar, red pepper flakes, onions, garlic, gingerroot and lime zest. Cook for several minutes. Then add the green onion, and the tofu. Sauté for several minutes. Add the noodles and sauté, tossing lightly. Transfer to a serving dish and sprinkle with the lime juice and the cilantro.

Serves 4

Fried Bean Curd with Sambel

Bean Curd fried until crisp and combined with sweet soy sauce, Sambel and scallions, was one of my favorite dishes.

    2 packages Tofu (8oz) sliced
    3 tablespoons vegetable oil
    4 tablespoons sweet soy sauce
    2 teaspoons Sambel, (chili paste)*
    2 tablespoons minced cilantro
    3 scallions, minced

Pat the tofu dry and heat the vegetable oil in a pan. Fry the tofu on both sides, until crisp and brown. Remove from the pan. Drain on paper towels. In a bowl, mix the rest of the ingredients together. Place the tofu in a shallow bowl and pour the sauce over the top. Chill until ready to serve.

Serves 6

---

*Note: Sambel is a hot chili paste found in Asian markets and also in gourmet food stores.

Chicken in Chili Sauce

Chicken is common meat in Indonesia, as pork is forbidden for eating by the majority Muslim population.

4 boneless chicken breasts cut into 1-inch cubes
2 garlic cloves, minced
2 teaspoons ground coriander
2 teaspoons, ground ginger
1 tablespoon chili paste or Sambel
3 tablespoons dark soy sauce
3 tablespoons rice wine vinegar
2 tablespoons peanut oil

In a large bowl, combine the chicken breasts with the rest of the ingredients, except for the peanut oil. Refrigerate overnight. Drain the chicken breasts. Heat the oil in the wok and stir-fry the chicken breasts for two minutes. Then add the marinade and stir-fry for another 3 minutes, or until the chicken is done.

Serves 4

Indonesian Spiced Rice

Any Indonesian dinner would be incomplete without spiced rice or Nasi Goreng. This rice dish could be very simple with a few extra ingredients, or an elaborate cone-shaped mountain of rice with a slivered omelet, peanuts and chilies as a garnish.

3 tablespoons peanut oil
1 large onion, chopped
2 jalapeno chilies, seeded and chopped
1 teaspoon turmeric
½ teaspoon ground cinnamon

2 cups long grain rice
4 cups Chicken broth
½ cup green onion, minced

Heat the oil in a large saucepan. Add the onion and the chilies and sauté, until the onion is translucent, about 8 minutes. Add the turmeric and the cinnamon and stir. Then add the rice and stir for two minutes. Next add the chicken broth and bring to a boil. Reduce the heat to low and cover. Cook until the water is absorbed, about 20 minutes. Mound on a serving platter and sprinkle with the green onions.
Serves 6

Mango and Yogurt

Desserts are not commonly eaten in Indonesia. Fruit is generally served at the end of a meal.

2 cups yogurt, plain
1 tablespoon ginger root, grated
1 teaspoon ground cardamon
2 tablespoons granulated sugar
½ cup whipping cream
½ teaspoon vanilla

Combine the yogurt with the ginger. Finely dice one mango and add to the yogurt. Puree the other mango in a food processor and add the cardamon to it. Fold into the yogurt. Whip the cream until stiff and add the sugar and the vanilla. Fold into the mango yogurt. Spoon into dessert glasses.
Serves 4

* * *

Eleanor Roosevelt

1884 to 1962, First Lady, American

I was never very interested in food. Perhaps this stems from the fact that when I was first married; I lived in adjoining houses with my mother-in-law Sarah Delano Roosevelt. Mother Roosevelt took care of everything, from the planning of menus to the disciplining of our children, of which Franklin was never very good at. However, after Franklin contracted Polio, I was able to assume more responsibility and insisted that certain domestic arrangements be turned over to me.

When Franklin became President, I was much too busy being his eyes and legs to worry much about dinners at the White House. I was the sponsor of an experiment in West Virginia to help train the numerous coal miners in other professions more fitting to the changing Depression era economy. One of the most important tasks I undertook during those years was to have Marian Anderson sing at the Lincoln Memorial, when she was denied the use of Constitution Hall by the Daughters of the American Revolution.

I was content to let the competent household chefs make the arrangements for our meals. However, one ritual during our years at the White House was Franklin's Martinis. The gin, vermouth and cracked ice, along with pimento stuffed green olives were wheeled into his office every evening, so he could make the perfect martini for his guests. When the King and Queen of England came to visit before the war, I decided we should have a typical American meal. I remember the King and Queen were especially taken by the barbecue we served them at Hyde Park. I can still see Queen Elizabeth, munching daintily on a hot dog.

The food at the White House during the 1930's and 1940's was very good yet plain, with an emphasis on meat and potatoes, chicken, turkey, and cornbread and other American dishes. We had an abundance of wonderful seafood from the coastal areas of Maryland and Virginia. We especially loved the wonderful crabs from Maryland, which we had prepared in every conceivable way, from soups to Gratins. Besides the shortcake recipe below, Franklin loved devil's food cake or a good peach pie. When a foreign dignitary was to visit, such as Winston Churchill, there might be a fancy meal in his honor. But more than likely his visits took place during the war when food was rationed, so they tended to be very plain. We were very strict during the War about rationing and made sure we had a Victory Garden planted in a corner of the White House grounds. We were allowed a larger amount of sugar, butter and other staples for state functions, such as the Teas for wounded servicemen that I gave.

After the war, I again had very little to do with the art of cooking as I was too busy setting up the *Universal Declaration of Human Rights* for the United Nations and writing many books. I am afraid many of my meals were eaten in a hurry or out in restaurants, as I had very little time to spare.

The White House Dinner

Franklin's Martinis
Maryland Crab Soup
Jerusalem Artichoke Salad
Savory Mushroom Stuffed Steak
Twice Baked Potatoes
Red White and Blue shortcake

*   *   *

Franklin's Martini's

Franklin loved to make his own Martini's. I can remember Churchill
visiting and Franklin stopping work, to mix a Martini for him.

1 jigger gin
2 drops vermouth
Cracked ice
Olives

In a cocktail shaker, place the gin, vermouth and cracked ice. Shake
well. Strain into a martini glass, and garnish with olives.
Makes 1 serving

Maryland Crab Soup

The cooks at the White House made use of products grown in the vicinity. Purveyors of different foods would make their rounds to the White House, and meals would be prepared from what was available, that day.

8 cups vegetable broth
1 large onion, minced
2 large celery stalks diced
1 32 oz can tomatoes, diced with liquid
2 cups carrots, peeled, and diced small
2 cups green beans cut into 1inch dice
2 teaspoons salt
¼ teaspoon black pepper
¼ teaspoon cayenne pepper
2 pounds crab meat cooked
2 tablespoons minced parsley

In a large soup pot bring the vegetable broth to a boil. Add the onion, celery stalks, tomatoes, carrots, green beans, salt, pepper and cayenne pepper. Cook until the carrots are tender. Then add the crab-meat. Cook for 15 minutes. Ladle into soup bowls and sprinkle with chopped parsley.
Serves 6-8

Jerusalem Artichoke Salad

The Jerusalem Artichoke is a tuber that when cooked blends perfectly with strong flavors like the apple cider and mustard seeds of the recipe below. It is indigenous to the United States.

1 pound Jerusalem artichokes, peeled and diced

½ cup apple cider vinegar
¼ cup honey
2 tablespoons vegetable oil
½ teaspoon mustard seed
1 tablespoon chopped dill
Mixed salad greens

Mix the Jerusalem artichokes with the rest of the ingredients except for the salad greens. Chill until ready to serve. Serve on a bed of lettuce.
Serves 4-6

Savory Mushroom Stuffed Steak

During the 1930's and 1940's, beef was a common feature on the menus from the White House. Of course, during World War II, steak would become a treat for a special occasion.

3 pounds boneless top sirloin steak, cut into 2 pieces
1 tablespoon olive oil
1 cup fresh mushrooms, finely chopped
¼ cup shallots, minced
1 tablespoon red wine
¼ teaspoon salt
¼ teaspoon pepper
¼ teaspoon dried thyme

Heat the oil in a large skillet. Add the mushrooms; dry red wine, salt pepper and thyme. Sauté for several minutes or until the mushrooms are soft. Remove from the heat and cool. Cut pockets into the steak pieces. Stuff each steak piece with ½ cup of the mushroom mixture. Close with toothpicks. Broil the steak on a rack, placed 4-5 inches from the broiler. Broil 20 minutes to 30 for rare or medium rare. Remove to a platter, and carve into slices.

Serves 6

Twice baked Potatoes

Potatoes native to the Americas, became one our most loved foods. Next to the Irish and the English, we ate potatoes almost every day in some form or another.

6 large russet baking potatoes

½ cup cream

4 tablespoons butter

1 cup shredded cheddar cheese

1 tablespoon minced parsley

Salt and pepper to taste

Preheat the oven to 375°F. Scrub the potatoes and prick all over. Bake on a rack, for 35 minutes or until soft. Remove from the oven and cool. Slice a top off the potato lengthwise and scoop out the flesh. Place in a food processor with the rest of the ingredients, and process until blended. Stuff the potato skins with this mixture. Place in a baking pan and bake for 15 minutes.

Serve immediately.

Serves 6

Red White and Blue Shortcake

Shortcake is another American institution. Filled with luscious fruits native to America such as the blueberry, it has remained a summer dessert that is eaten as soon as the fresh fruits are ripe.

Biscuit:

2 cups all purpose flour
2 teaspoons baking powder
1 teaspoon salt
2 tablespoons sugar
1 stick plus 2 tablespoons butter, chilled
2/3 cup milk

Filling:

1 pint ripe strawberries
1 pint ripe blueberries
6 tablespoons sugar

Whipped Cream:

1 cup heavy cream
4 teaspoons sugar
1 teaspoon grated lemon zest

Preheat the oven to 375°F. In a large mixing bowl, sift the flour, baking powder, sugar and salt. Cut the butter into pieces, and cut into the flour, until it resembles coarse crumbs. Then blend in all but 2 tablspoons of the milk. Mix until the dough just holds together, and then add the rest of the milk. Lightly flour a board, and knead the dough lightly for 1 minutes. Roll out to 1 inch thick. Cut into 6 biscuits. Put the biscuits on an ungreased cookie sheet and chill for 20 minutes. For the filling, wash and hull the strawberries, then cut them in half. Mix them with the blueberries and the sugar and then set aside. Whip the cream until soft peaks form, and then add the sugar and the lemon zest, whip again until stiff peaks form. Chill in the refrigerator until ready to use. Bake the biscuits until golden brown, about 12 to 15 minutes. Split the biscuits, and spread with butter if you want. Fill with the fruit filling and top more fruit and the whipped cream.

Serves 6

*   *   *

Agatha Christie

1890-1976, Mystery Writer, Dame of the British Empire

My family lived in Torquay, and were fairly well off for that time. My father didn't need to work, having inherited some money, which was invested for him. My earliest remembrances of food, were the smell of the kitchen, presided over by the indomitable Kate. Kate was always good for a handful of raisins or a piece of pastry, to tide me over until the next meal. We had a large pantry, which was filled with all sorts of preserved fruits, candy, vinegars and syrups, which Kate used in cooking. Meals were elaborate, sometimes having as many as 10 courses, when my mother and father entertained.

Later, even after I married Archibald Christie had a child and starting my writing career, I loved to cook. I liked to create various dishes when my friends came to visit, and many of these are mentioned in my murder mysteries, such as anchovy toasts, which was a favorite of mine. In 1928, I divorced Archie and to heal from the pain of it, I decided to travel. It was fate that led me to change a ticket to the West Indies, for one on the Orient Express to Baghdad, which led me to meet my beloved second husband Max Malloween, the archeologist. For many years, he led archeological expeditions, in Iraqi, and I learned about the food of the Middle East.

While teaching, the Arab cooks how to make a decent soufflé, they taught me the subtle nuances of spices in Arab food. Arab food can be greasy and the meat tough, but it also can rival the beauty of a sunset, at Nippur. Arabs eat much the same as their ancestors did in Babylonia and Assyria. Salads of herbs, purslane, dandelion, cos lettuce and leeks, vegetables stuffed with meat, rice and lentils, and soups of beans all are part of the modern Arab diet. There is a code of etiquette for serving and presenting particular dishes that is according to the social, family status and age. A dignitary or head of the family is served the best helping, and the same code applies to a visitor. Hands are washed both at the beginning and the end of a meal. Adherence to Muslim codes derived from the Koran, forbids the eating of blood, pig flesh and the drinking of Alcohol.

Food on an expedition was a combination of European and Arab cuisine's. Many times, I would pack a picnic lunch and walk to the excavation, to share it with Max.

During World War II, it was hard to get good food, and so when one of my circle of acquaintances, had a special treat, such as a tin of Lobster, sent from America, we would meet for a dinner and share it as if we were at a banquet. Even after the war, food was still rationed but I had my kitchen Garden at Greenway, which supplemented our meals. Being a very private woman, I am reluctant to share my special food loves, but it won't hurt I guess. I love to drink double and single cream, and I love to eat apples in the bathtub. I even gave my character, Ariadne Oliver, a penchant for eating bags of apples and having apple cores lingering in strange places on her body.

I thought that I would take you on a journey through an Iraqi meal, where the contrasts of flavors are truly exceptional.

*　　　　　*　　　　　*

Dinner at the Tell

Chickpea and Bean Soup

Purslane Salad with Garlic Yogurt Dressing
Or-
Fattoush (Toasted Bread Salad)
Cucumbers and Sultanas in Yogurt
Flat Bread or Pita Bread

Chicken in Pomegranate Sauce
Lamb Meatballs in Garlic Mint sauce
Green Beans in Olive Oil
Rice with Vermicelli
Middle Eastern Date Cake
Iraqi Coffee

*   *   *

Chickpea and Bean Soup

Even though it is extremely hot in Iraq, soup is a traditional start to a meal and is actually thought to cool one down. This soup of chickpeas and fava beans is similar to soup prepared in ancient Assyria, except for a few additions like potatoes and tomatoes..

6 cups water
1 cup skinned fava beans, rinsed and drained
2 medium sized potatoes, peeled and diced
¼ cup olive oil
2 medium sized onions, minced
4 garlic cloves, minced
¼ cup cilantro
1 can (28oz) stewed tomatoes
1 can (16oz) chickpeas
1 teaspoon oregano
2 tablespoons lemon juice
1 teaspoon salt

Place the fava beans and the water in a large pot and bring to a boil. Cover and cook over medium heat for 1 ½ hours. Then add the potatoes, and cook for another 25 minutes. While the potatoes are cooking, heat the olive oil in a frying pan and saute the onions and the garlic until golden. Add the cilantro and the tomatoes, and cook for 5 minutes. Then pour this mixture into the soup. Simmer for 5 minutes. Add the lemon juice, and salt right before serving. Ladle into soup bowls.

6 servings

Purslane Salad with Garlic Yogurt Dressing

Purslane is a wild green that is used in many salads in the Middle East. It has a slightly bitter taste like Dandelion leaves.

4 cups purslane rinsed and dried*

2 scallions, minced

3 tablespoons extra virgin olive oil

2 tablespoons fresh lemon juice

1 cup whole milk yogurt

2 cloves of garlic, minced

Salt and pepper to taste

Place the purslane and the scallions in a large salad bowl. In a blender combine the rest of the ingredients and blend until smooth. Add the dressing to the salad and toss. Serve immediately.

Serves 4

Fattoush (Toasted Bread Salad)

Fattoush is a famous Arab salad, eaten by the Iraqi's, Syrians and the Lebanese. Each region has its own variations of this theme.

---

*Note: You can find Purslane in gourmet grocery stores, or you can substitute Dandelion or any other wild green that you might like.

4 pita breads, torn into pieces and toasted

6 leaves of romaine lettuce, shredded

1 large cucumber, peeled and sliced lengthwise

2 medium tomatoes, chopped

½ cup green onions, chopped

½ cup chopped parsley

¼ cup chopped mint leaves

1 cup bell peppers, seeded and chopped

1 cup purslane or mache

Salad Dressing

1 garlic clove, minced

1 teaspoon salt

½ cup lemon juice

½ cup olive oil

Place all the ingredients for the salad in a large bowl and toss. Whisk together the ingredients for the salad dressing in a small bowl. Pour over the salad and toss. Serve immediately.

Serves 6

Cucumbers and Sultanas in Yogurt

Another favorite Iraqi dish consisted of cucumbers, with green onions and Sultanas, it gives an interesting contrast of pungent and sweet tastes.

2 large cucumbers, peeled and sliced thinly

2 cups plain yogurt

4 green onions, minced

½ cup golden sultanas

¼ cup walnuts, chopped

1 teaspoon salt

½ teaspoon black pepper

1 tablespoon minced mint leaves

Sprinkle the cucumber with the salt and leave in a colander to drain. Pat dry, and then combine with the yogurt in a bowl. Stir in the green onions, sultanas, and the walnuts. Mix well, then season with salt and pepper. Add the mint and chill the mixture for 1 hour. Serve with flat bread.

Serves 4

Chicken in Pomegranate Sauce

Pomegranate juice and syrup still figure prominently in Middle Eastern Cuisine. While many times the cooks were heavy handed on the spice and grease, an expertly prepared meat dish would be exquisite.

2 large onions, chopped

5 tablespoons butter

3 pounds of chicken cut into serving pieces

1 cup chicken broth

1 cup water

½ cup finely ground walnuts

4 tablespoons pomegranate syrup

½ teaspoons sugar

½ teaspoons salt

½ teaspoon saffron dissolved in boiling water

¼ teaspoon ground cinnamon

¼ teaspoon ground nutmeg

¼ teaspoon black pepper

2 tablespoons lemon juice

Sauté the onions in 2 tablespoons of the butter until golden brown. Remove from the pan. Add the rest of the butter and sauté the chicken pieces until light brown. Add the chicken broth and sautéed onions. Cover and simmer gently for 30 minutes. Remove the chicken from the stove and cool. Then remove the chicken from the bones, and dice into bite size pieces.

To prepare the sauce: Add the water to the walnuts in a saucepan. Then add the pomegranate syrup and the sugar and simmer gently over low heat for 10 minutes. Then add the chicken and most of its drippings to the walnut sauce. Add the rest of the ingredients and simmer for 10 minutes. The chicken pieces will be coated with a rich dark sauce. Serve with rice.

Make 6 servings

Lamb Meat Balls with Garlic Mint Sauce

Lamb is a major meat source in Iraq, where it is presented ground, stewed and roasted.

1 ½ pounds ground lamb
1 teaspoon salt
½ teaspoon black pepper
½ cup minced Italian parsley
1 ½ cups onions, finely chopped
3 tablespoons vegetable oil
8 garlic cloves, minced
4 tablespoons lemon juice
1 ½ tablespoons sugar
1 cup minced mint leaves

Make the meatballs first. Mix the meat with the salt, pepper and parsley. In the food processor until a fine paste is formed. Roll the paste into meatballs the size of walnuts. Fry the onions in the vegetable oil and add the garlic, and the meatballs. Turning the meatballs to brown. Then add 2 cups of water, and reduce the heat. Simmer for 25 minutes. Then add the lemon juice, sugar and mint leaves. Cook for 15 more minutes.

Serves 6

Rice with Vermicelli

Sautéing rice with vermicelli, and then adding liquid is the basis for the Middle Eastern dish of rice pilaf. It is a major accompaniment to all meat dishes. It is usually served mounded on a communal platter with the meat surrounding it. Rice is scooped up with the fingers of the right hand, as eating with the left is considered taboo.

½ cup vermicelli, broken up

3 tablespoons sunflower oil

1 ¼ cup rice

2 cups water

1 teaspoon salt

Toast the vermicelli in a dry frying pan. Stirring Constantly. Then add the oil. Add the rice and brown for 5 minutes. Then add the water and the salt. Stir well. Lower the heat and cover. Simmer for 18 minutes, or until the rice is tender and the water absorbed. Turn off the heat and steam for 5 more minutes. Fluff and serve.

Serves 6

Green Beans with Olive Oil

Vegetables such as this green bean recipe are served at room temperature. The green beans are blanched and then cooked until soft with tomatoes and onions.

¾ cup extra virgin olive oil

2 large onions, minced

3 garlic cloves, minced
2 pounds green beans, trimmed and cut into two-inch lengths
3 medium sized tomatoes, peeled, seeded and chopped
½ cup water
2 teaspoons salt
1 teaspoon black pepper
3 tablespoons minced parsley

In a large skillet, heat the olive oil and cook the onions until they are light brown. Add the garlic and cook for 1 minute longer. Reduce the heat and add the green beans, tomatoes, water, salt and pepper. Cover and cook for 1 hour or until the beans are soft. Remove from the heat and transfer to a serving bowl. Garnish with minced parsley. Allow the beans to come to room temperature before serving.

Serves 6

Middle Eastern Date Cake

Cakes usually consist of fruit, or layers of honey soaked pastries, with nuts. I did so love to cook in the kitchens along with the camp chefs. I would teach them such esoteric mysteries as making a Flan and they would teach me how to pastries with layers and layers of fragile dough., or a simple spice cake such as this.

1 cup flour
1 cup sugar
½ teaspoon salt
¼ teaspoon ground cloves
½ teaspoon ground nutmeg
½ teaspoon ground cinnamon
2 teaspoons baking powder
4 eggs slightly beaten

¼ cup butter, softened

4 cups dates, chopped

2 cups walnuts or almonds, chopped

1 teaspoon vanilla

Preheat the oven to 350°F. Grease a 10-inch baking pan. Mix the flour, sugar salt and spices together. Add the eggs, butter, dates, nuts and vanilla. Mix well. Pour into a baking pan. Bake for 30 minutes. Remove from the oven and let cook for 10 minutes. Sprinkle with confectioner's sugar and cut into squares.

Serves 8

Iraqi Coffee

Besides mint tea, coffee was served after a meal in tiny cups. It was usually flavored with spices such as cardamon and heavily sugared.

4 cups of freshly brewed expresso

4 pods cardamon, cracked

4 tablespoon sugar

In the bottom of each expresso cup place one of the pods of cardamon. Cover with the coffee. Then add one tablespoon of sugar to each cup and stir until dissolved. Serve immediately..

*   *   *

Pearl Sydenstricker Buck

1892-1973 China, Novelist

My mother and father where Southern Presbyterian missionaries who were stationed in China. My father roamed the countryside looking for new Christian converts, while my mother took care of the medical side of things, dispensing medicine, to Chinese women. I grew up speaking Chinese as fluently as English. After the Boxer Uprising, my family returned to the United States, where I entered college. I was going to stay in America, but my mother became seriously ill in China, and I had to return. While there I met my first husband, John Lossing Buck whom I married in 1915. In 1921 I had my daughter Carol, who was retarded. Because of this and due to unfortunate female problems, I was unable to have any more children. In 1925 we adopted our second daughter Janice. Our marriage was unhappy one, so I devoted myself to teaching at Nanking University. Due to the political unrest in China, we had to be evacuated by the Americans in 1927 and even though we went back to Nanking, the situation there was dangerous.

I began to take my mind off my marriage and the unsettling events in China by writing. In 1930 I published my first novel, *East Wind, West Wind*. In the course of publishing this novel, I met my second husband Richard Walsh. In 1931, *The Good Earth* was published, and I won the Pulitzer Prize for it. After I divorced my first husband, I moved to America, and Richard and I adopted more children. While I would like to be remembered for the novels and essays that I wrote, I am most proud of *Welcome House*, an adoption agency that I established in 1949. This was to aid in placing interracial children. I also founded *The Pearl S. Buck Foundation*, which provided sponsorship for Amerasian children in Asian countries. For you see in my mind a child is always to be loved, no matter what race.

My days in China left me with a deep love for China and its people, culture and food. Even though my parents were missionaries, we always had a cook and I even had a Chinese tutor. Later when I lived in Nanking, I loved to present an excellent Chinese meal, and many times would work side by side with the chef we had. China is a country with many different regions, and each region has a different repertoire of food. I remember savory rolls called won tons, filled with bean sprouts, and shrimp. Sweet and sour soups, with rice noodles and eggs. Succulent pork roasts glazed with soy sauce. Pickled thousand year old eggs and Tofu cooked in chili or black bean sauce. From the Spicy dishes of Hunan, to the Noodle dishes of Canton, Chinese food is a work of Art that I appreciated until the end of my days.

*   *   *

The Good Earth Dinner

Egg Flower Shrimp Soup
Ginger Garlic Shrimp
Rice
Drunkards Noodles
Chinese Roast Pork
Chinese Lemon Chicken
Bok Choy in Black bean Sauce
Szechwan Eggplant
Eight Precious Pudding

*   *   *

Egg Flower Shrimp Soup

Light soups such as this Egg Flower Shrimp Soup, usually start out a Chinese Meal.

1 pound large shrimp, peeled and deveined
8 slices fresh ginger
5 cups Chicken broth
2 teaspoons soy sauce

1 cup frozen peas, defrosted

½ cup green onion, minced

2 large eggs slightly beaten

Pepper to taste

Rinse the shrimp and pat dry. Pound the ginger slices with a mallet, so the juice can seep out. Combine the ginger, broth and sauce in a medium saucepan. Cover and bring to a boil. Reduce the heat and simmer for 5 minutes. Discard the ginger. Return to a boil and stir in the shrimp, peas and green onion. Drizzle the eggs over the soup, and cover. Take the pan from the heat, and let stand until the shrimp is opaque, from 3 to 10 minutes, depending on their size. Stir the soup to break up the eggs. Season to taste with pepper.

Serves 4

Ginger Garlic Shrimp

A Chinese meal might include seafood, meat and a chicken dish. Shrimp are especially loved, and are usually prepared lightly, in a sauce to be served with rice.

16 jumbo shrimp with the shell

¼ cup vegetable oil

1 piece ginger, peeled and thinly sliced

3 cloves of garlic, crushed

2 large green onions, sliced

Salt and pepper to taste

Heat the vegetable oil in a skillet or wok. Add the ginger and the garlic and stir-fry for 1 minute, then add the green onions and stir-fry again for 1 minute. Add the shrimp and stir-fry until the shrimp are pink. Season with salt and pepper. Serve immediately.

Serves 4

Drunkard's Noodles

This recipe comes from Hunan, were chilies are used in many dishes. You can find the Sen Yai noodles in a Chinese Grocery store.

    4 tablespoons vegetable oil
    2 garlic cloves, minced
    4 small red chilies, finely chopped
    8-oz sen yai noodles
    2 small onions cut into segments
    12 sweet basil leaves, shredded
    6 tablespoons dark soy sauce
    1 teaspoon sugar
    2 small red bell peppers, chopped

In a wok or a skillet, heat the oil until a light haze appears. Add the garlic and the chilies and fry until the garlic is golden. Add the noodles and stir, then add the remaining ingredients, and stir until the peppers began to cook. Transfer to a serving dish.
Serves 4

Chinese Roast Pork

Pork roast is usually slow roasted and served with a sauce on the side. The Hoisin sauce in this recipe is a sweet spicy mixture, of soybeans, garlic and chili peppers. It can be found In Chinese or Asian markets.

    3 tablespoons soy sauce
    3 tablespoons dry sherry
    2 tablespoons Hoisin Sauce
    2 tablespoons honey
    2 cloves of garlic, minced
    1 tablespoon finely grated gingerroot

1 boneless pork tenderloin (1 ½ pounds)

Mix all the ingredients for the marinade together in a bowl. Add the pork tenderloin, and marinate for 24 hours in the refrigerator turning often. Preheat the oven to 350° F. Remove the pork tenderloin from the marinade, and place on a roasting rack over a pan of hot water. Bake for 50 minutes. Baste frequently with the marinade. Serve cut in thin slices, with additional Hoisin or Plum sauce.

Serves 4

Chinese Lemon Chicken

Chicken stir-fried in a wok, with rice wine, honey and lemon, is another favorite Chinese dish.

2-pound boneless chicken breast cut into serving pieces
1 tablespoon rice wine
1 tablespoon light soy sauce
1 tablespoon honey
3 tablespoons lemon juice
2 tablespoon vegetable oil
2 slices ginger root

Combine the rice wine, soy sauce, honey and lemon juice in a bowl. Add the chicken and toss to coat. Marinate in the refrigerator for at least 2 hours. Heat the vegetable oil in a wok or a skillet, add the gingerroot, and stir-fry for 1 minute. Then add the chicken and stir fry until the chicken, is cooked. Add the sauce and stir-fry for 1 minute. Transfer to a serving bowl.

Serves 4

Bok Choy in Black Bean Sauce

Black Bean Sauce is made of salted black beans. It is used in many dishes, including vegetable ones, like this recipe for bok choy.

    2 tablespoons black bean sauce *
    1 clove of garlic minced
    2 tablespoons, fresh ginger root minced
    ½ cup chicken stock
    1 teaspoon cornstarch
    2 tablespoons oil
    1 pound bok choy, cleaned, trimmed and cut lengthwise

Heat the oil in the skillet or wok and add the garlic and the ginger-root. Stir-fry for 1 minute. Then add the bok choy and stir-fry for 1 minute. Add the chicken broth, and the black bean sauce. Cover and let cook for 4 minutes or until the bok choy is cooked. Mix the cornstarch with water to form a paste and add to the bok choy, stir until thickened. Transfer to a serving bowl.

Serves 4

Szechwan Eggplant

From the area called Szechwan, comes this spicy and hot egg-plant dish.

---

*Note: Black Bean Sauce can be found in Asian Markets.

Sauce:

2 tablespoons spicy bean paste

1 tablespoon dark soy sauce

2 tablespoons dry sherry

1 tablespoon cider vinegar

2 tablespoons sugar

¼ teaspoon crushed Szechwan peppercorns*

1 teaspoon cornstarch

1 tablespoon water

1 teaspoon Sesame oil*

Eggplant:

1 ½ pound, small Japanese eggplants

4 tablespoons vegetable oil

1 tablespoon Chinese chili pepper oil*

1 large clove of garlic, minced

4 slices of fresh ginger, peeled and minced

1 green onion, minced

In a small bowl combine the ingredients for the sauce, stir well and set aside. In another bowl, stir together the cornstarch, water and sesame oil. Set aside. Cut the stems from the eggplants, and cut in half. Then cut in half again. Heat the vegetable oil in a wok, and add the chili pepper oil, garlic, ginger and scallion. Stir-fry for 30 seconds. Then add the eggplant, and immediately start flipping the pieces

---

*Note: Szechwan Peppercorns, Sesame Oil, and Chinese Chili Oil can now be found in most supermarkets and also in Asian Markets.

around in the Wok. Coat each one with the oil. Stir-fry for 2 minutes. Reduce the heat and stir-fry for 4 minutes longer or until lightly browned. Add the sauce and then stir-fry for 2 minutes, then add the cornstarch mixture and stir-fry for another 2 minutes. Transfer to a serving bowl, and garnish with additional minced green onion.

Serves 4

Eight Precious Rice Pudding

Although this is not served at most Chinese meals I have included it in this menu. It is a very special rice pudding, serve at most special occasions.

2 cups rice
½ cup granulated sugar
2 tablespoons lard or Crisco
1 ½ cups combination of dates, and red plums, diced
½ cup honey
1 cup blanched almonds

Cook the rice in 4 cups of water for 30 minutes. Drain and add sugar and lard. While the rice is cooking, oil a heat—proof dish that has a 9-cup capacity. Mix fruit with the honey. Arrange one half of the fruit in a decorative pattern on the bottom of the dish. Spoon half the rice over the fruit. Arrange the remaining fruit over the rice. Top with the remaining rice and cover tightly with foil. Place the dish on a rack in side a large pot. Pour in boiling water to come up to three fourths of the way up the side of the pudding dish. Cover and steam for 45 minutes. Remove cover and let the steam evaporate before removing the bowl. Place serving patter over the rice and invert the bowl in one swift motion so that the fruits will be on top. Garnish with the whole almonds.

Serves 8

*   *   *

Mary Pickford

1892 To 1979, Actress

I was born in Toronto, and came to the United States as a child actress, staring for David Belasco, in his plays in New York. In 1908 I traveled to Los Angeles to begin a career in films. Among my hits, were *Rebecca of Sunnybrook, Farm, Sparrows, Suds* and *Poor Little Rich Girl*. Together with my husband Douglas Fairbanks, and Charles Chaplin, we formed United Artists. I was to become the very first woman in film to earn $1,000,000 per year, a sum that was unheard of in the early 1900's.

My husband Douglas Fairbanks and I were considered Hollywood royalty. We bought this beautiful house, which we named *Pickfair*. It had a stupendous dining room, in which we entertained with great dinner parties. The Hollywood of the 1920's was filled with young people who had struck it rich in the movies, and spared no expense in outfitting their houses, we were no exception. We imported chefs from Paris and London, and paid them huge amounts of money to create meals for us. For most of us, who lived on quick meals snatched at cafes, while working on the stage and in early movies, a sit down meal with many courses, showed that we had a air of sophistication.

Living on the West Coast we were blessed with the freshest produce that was available at that time. Large orange, lemon and grapefruit groves, surrounded Los Angeles, and many of our recipes were based around them. Seafood from the waters off Santa Monica, and Santa Barbara, also constituted are large part of our meals. Hollywood was a melting pot of different nationalities, and we were able to have many recipes from different cultures adapted to our needs. The hotels in Hollywood, such as the Roosevelt, served continental cuisine that reviled that of Paris. During the 1930's the movie studios set up large commissaries that served delectable lunches to the actors. Many times I walked through the commissaries at United Artists and marveled at seeing pilgrims, sitting next to pirates and sophisticated society women, eating a large seafood salad, while discussing the day's shootings.

A meal at my house started with appetizers and moved on to many courses including wine. The woman dressed in their most beautiful evening gowns and the men in Tuxedos. After dinner following the English tradition, the women would retire to the drawing room, while the men had brandy and cigars. Later, Douglas and his cronies would play Billiards until the wee hours. It was not unusual for me to have several dinner parties a week. Even when I was older, my second husband Buddy Rogers and I gave dinner parties quite often, and I turned over *Pickfair* for afternoon, fetes during World War II to raise money, for war bonds.

Pickfair, was a beautiful place, and dinners there were extraordinary.

*   *   *

A Pickfair Dinner

Bronx Cocktail
Whiskey Stinger
Almond mushroom Pate
Whitefish Mousse
Sweet English Peas
Herbed Rack of Lamb
Parsnip Celeriac and Potato Gratin
Blackberry Lemon Ice Cream
Coconut Cream Pie

*   *   *

Bronx Cocktail

During the 1920's unusual cocktails where all the rage in America. The Bronx Cocktail and the Whiskey Stinger are just two kinds of cocktails developed in the 1920's. We always made sure that we had an adequate liquor supply for our fellow thespians loved to drink.

1 Jigger dry gin
1 jigger dry vermouth
1 jigger orange juice

Shake Thoroughly with cracked ice and strain into a martini glass
Makes 1 serving

Whiskey Stinger

2 oz whiskey
1 oz peppermint schnapps
Mint leaves

Fill a cocktail shaker with ice and add the whiskey and peppermint schnapps. Shake well; strain into a Cocktail glass and garnish with mint.

Makes 1 serving

Almond Mushroom Pate

With the introduction of cocktails before dinner, appetizers or starters were moved away from the dining table and served with the drinks.

2 tablespoons butter

1 small onion, minced

1 garlic clove, minced

1 ½ cups sliced mushrooms

1 teaspoon minced fresh tarragon

1 cup blanched whole almonds

1 tablespoon lemon juice

2 drops Tabasco

4 oz cream cheese

In a skillet heat the butter and sauté the onion, and the garlic clove. Add the mushrooms and the tarragon. Sauté until the mushrooms are soft. In a food processor, chop the almonds, with the lemon juice. Add the mushrooms and process until coarsely ground, then add the cream cheese and process for a few seconds. Place in a serving bowl, and garnish with slivered almonds, fresh parsley sprigs, pimiento strips. Chill until ready to serve.

Serves 6

Whitefish Mousse

Mousses pates and dips were typical appetizers of this time. Mousses of lobster combined with other seafood were considered the height of elegance.

½ pound whitefish fillets

½ pound lobster meat

2 tablespoons onion, minced

½ teaspoon salt

2 tablespoons brandy

1 tablespoon tomato paste

½ cup egg whites

¾ cup whipping cream

2 cups Hollandaise Sauce, page 390

2 tablespoons minced parsley, or dill

Combine the whitefish, lobster, onion, salt brandy and tomato paste in a food processor. Blend until well incorporated. Transfer the mixture to a bowl, cover and chill for 30 minutes. Stir in the whipping cream. Whip the egg whites until stiff, and fold into the mousse mixture. Pour into 6 buttered ramekins. Place in a water bath. Bake at 350°F. for 20 minutes. While they are baking, make the Hollandaise Sauce. Remove the Ramekins from the oven, and run a thin knife several times to loosen them. Turn each ramekin out into a serving plate and spoon some Hollandaise sauce over the top. Sprinkle with the minced parsley or dill.

Serves 6

Sweet English Peas

Pickfair looked like an English manor house. This was because Douglas was a decided Anglophile, so many of the meals we served had a decided English ring to them.

1 pound peas fresh

3 tablespoons butter

2 tablespoons chopped mint

1 teaspoon sugar

½ teaspoon freshly ground pepper
½ teaspoon salt

Cook the peas in a small amount of boiling water, until just tender. While the peas are cooking, in a small skillet heat the butter and add the rest of the ingredients. Cook for a 2 minutes. Drain the peas and place in a serving bowl. Add the butter and toss with the peas.
Serves 6

Herbed Rack of Lamb

Since my home was the social center of Hollywood, if we served a certain dish such as this rack of lamb, it was a safe bet that at Theda Bara's next dinner party, the same dish would appear on her table.

2 racks of lamb (1-2 pounds each) trimmed of fat
2 tablespoons Dijon mustard
1 tablespoon Worcestershire sauce
1 teaspoon dried rosemary
¼ teaspoon ground ginger
1 teaspoon dried thyme
1 teaspoon dried marjoram
Ground pepper to taste
2 tablespoons olive oil

Whisk together all the ingredients for the marinade. Paint the marinade generously all over the exposed surfaces of the racks of lamb. Place in the refrigerator and marinate for 2 hours. Preheat the oven to 400°F. Roast the lamb on a rack, for 25 minutes for medium rare. Remove from the oven and carve. Place on a serving platter.
Serves 4

Parsnip, Celeriac and Potato Gratin

During the 1920's vegetables like parsnips and celeriac, were eaten a great deal more then today, with our French Chefs preparing them as a gratin for our dinner parties.

4 tablespoons butter
2 cups parsnips, peeled and sliced
2 cups celeric, peeled and diced
2 cups potatoes, peeled and sliced
1 large onion, sliced
3 large garlic cloves, minced
1 cup aged cheddar cheese
1 cup half and half
1 teaspoon paprika
¼ teaspoon mustard
Salt and pepper

Preheat the oven to 400°F. Butter a large casserole dish. In a skillet, heat the butter and add the onion and the garlic. Sauté until translucent. Add the vegetables, and turn for a minute or two to coat with the butter. Place in the casserole. Shred the cheese, and mix half into the cream. Season the cream with the paprika, mustard, salt and pepper. Pour the cream on top of the vegetables, and then sprinkle with the remaining cheese.

Bake for 30 minutes or until the potatoes are tender and the gratin is golden brown.

Serves 6

Blackberry Lemon Ice Cream

This blackberry lemon ice cream again contains one of the most wonderful ingredients found in California the lemon.

2 cups unsweetened blackberries, fresh or frozen, mashed
1 can (16oz) sweetened condensed milk
¼ cup lemon juice
1 teaspoon grated lemon peel
3 cups half and half

In a bowl combine the blackberries, milk, lemon juice and peel. Mix well, then stir in the half and half. Pour into an ice cream freezer container. Freeze according to directions.

Serves 4

Coconut Cream Pie

Cream pies gained fame during the 1920's. Their popularity started with the pie throwing antics of the Keystone Cops and other great comedies of the 1920's. All joking aside, they started to appear on the dining tables of the very people who threw them.

2 cups milk
1 cup sugar
1 dash of salt
1 cup grated coconut, fresh
4 egg yokes
3 tablespoons cornstarch
3 tablespoons water
3 tablespoons butter
1 teaspoon vanilla
1 9 inch baked pie shell

Meringue:

4 egg whites
¼ teaspoon cream of tartar
1 cup sugar

Combine the milk, ½ cup sugar, salt and ¼ cup grated coconut in a medium saucepan. Cook until the mixture is very hot. Beat the egg yolks, until pale and lemony, and then add in the cornstarch and the water. Add to the milk mixture. Cook until thickened, about 1 minute. Remove from the heat and stir in the rest of the coconut. Add the butter and vanilla, and stir until the butter is melted.

Meringue: Beat the Egg whites until stiff, adding the cream of tartar. Then add the sugar and beat until glossy meringue forms. Spoon the filling to the baked pie shell. Swirl the meringue over the filling. Bake at 400°F. for 10 minutes or until the meringue is browned. Cool completely.

Serves 6

*   *   *

Gala Dali

1984-1982, Wife of Salvador Dali

Although I was born in Russia I was Spanish in my soul. I was born in Kazan Russia. In 1913 suffering from tuberculosis, I was sent to a Swiss Sanatorium in Clavadel for treatment. While there I met the French poet, Paul Eluard, whom I married in 1917. Through my husband and his friends, including the painter Max Ernst, I became acquainted with the Parisian Surrealist movement. In 1929 my husband and I took a trip to Spain to visit the young Spanish painter Salvador Dali at his home in Portilligat. Dali the son of a prestigious notary public of Figueres was encouraged by his father to study painting at a very early age in Madrid. Dali came to Paris in the 1920's and there he was to produce some the greatest surreal paintings of the time. In that summer of 1929, when I met Dali, it was instant love and attraction. I left my husband, and began a journey that was to take me all over the world with Dali. I was his lover, wife and model. No matter where we traveled, Spain was always in our heart. I had a residence of my own during the 1970's Pubol Castle where I stayed when I was not traveling with Salvador. We had many a grand dinner there.

Spanish food is a wealth of tastes from many different regions. It is composed of vivid tastes and flavors that are reminiscent of bullfights, flamenco dancing and the great Spanish painters, such as my husband Salvador. Most of our food is cooked in olive oil and highly spiced, with cumin, garlic, paprika and cinnamon. We also eat almonds, lemons and oranges that are a legacy left to us by our Moorish invaders. We usually eat hot chocolate and a roll for breakfast, followed by a large lunch at around 2pm, consisting of salad, soup, fish, potatoes, chicken, sweets, cheese fruit and nuts. At around 7pm we stop for Tapas or hor-d'oeuvres. Then we might eat a large meal all over again at 9 or 10 at night.

Dali liked long dinners with his friends. While the food was important to him, and we always had a cook versed in Spanish meals wherever we traveled, it was the conversation, jokes and antics that meant the most to him.. Tables loaded with flowers, and set with unusual dishes and glasses, graced our table at Pubol. The following is a meal that I would have had prepared for Salvador and his surrealist painter friends.

Dinner at Pubol Castle

Garlic and Almond Soup
Spicy Potatoes
Spanish Green Beans
Sole in Apple Cider
Lobster Saute from Catalana
Lamb with Pimentos
Salad from Valencia
Baked Stuffed Apples in Rioja Syrup
Almond, Pears and Cheese

*   *   *

Garlic and Almond Soup

This soup has a very aggressive taste, reflecting our love of strong flavors such as the sherry vinegar and garlic.

¾ cup blanched almonds
6 garlic cloves, peeled, whole
3 tablespoons sherry vinegar
½ cup seedless white grapes, peeled
2 pieces rustic bread, the crusts removed
¼ cup extra virgin olive oil
3 cups water
Salt and pepper to taste
12 black grapes for garnish
Additional Sherry vinegar

Place the almonds and the garlic in a food processor and blend until very fine. Add the sherry vinegar, the grapes and the bread. Blend until a smooth paste is formed. With the machine running, drizzle in the olive oil and then add the water a cup at a time. Blending after each addition. Strain into soup tureen and season with the salt and pepper. Ladle into soup bowls, and sprinkle with the black grapes. Sprinkle with the additional sherry vinegar.

4 servings

Spicy Potatoes

One the potato was introduced to Spain from the New World, we embraced it heartily using it in many of our soups and stews, and by itself.In this potato dish there are definite Arab influences.

2 dried red chili peppers

1 pound russet potatoes, scrubbed, and sliced into large wedges. Skins left on

1 large Spanish onion, peeled and diced

6 cloves of garlic, minced

1 teaspoon cumin seeds

1teaspoon salt

½ cup olive oil.

Preheat the oven to 400°F. In the food processor, puree all the ingredients except for the potatoes. Place the potato wedges in a large casserole or baking dish, and spread the puree on top of the potatoes. Bake for 45 minutes or until the potatoes are tender.

4 Servings

Spanish Green Beans

This Green bean dish comes from the area of Andalusa, where ham is included in many of its vegetable dishes.

1 pound green beans, trimmed

1 cup tomatoes, chopped

½ pound ham, cut into strips
1 cloves of garlic, minced
¼ cup olive oil
Salt and pepper to taste

Boil the beans in salted water for 5 minutes, or until tender but still crisp. Heat the olive oil in a large skillet. Add the chopped garlic, the ham, and the tomatoes. Simmer for 10 minutes. Then add the beans, and salt and pepper to taste. Simmer for another 5 minutes. Transfer to a serving bowl.

4 Servings

Sole with Apple Cider

We use apple cider in combination with many fish dishes. It especially pairs well with hake and sole.

4 large filets of sole
Flour
Salt and pepper to taste
½ cup olive oil
1 teaspoon paprika
2 garlic cloves, minced
1 bay leaf
1 cup apple cider
2 tablespoons minced parsley

In a large skillet heat the olive oil and add the garlic. Saute for 1 minute. Pat the sole dry, and dredge in flour. Sprinkle the filets of sole with salt and pepper and paprika. Gently fry in the oil until golden on both sides. Add the bay leaf and the apple cider. Simmer for 5 minutes. Remove the fish from the skillet and place on individual serving plates. Serve with some of the pan juices spooned on top. Sprinkle with the minced parsley.

Serves 4

Lobster Saute from Catalana

In Catalana they have a very simple but sumptuous way of cooking lobsters. We loved having them this way for either lunch or dinner.

2 (1-2 pound) Lobsters, cooked
¼ cup extra virgin olive oil
1 small onion, diced
2 cloves of garlic, minced
4 sprigs of parsley, chopped
½ cup of dry white wine
3 tablespoons of tomato sauce
1 teaspoon salt
½ teaspoon pepper

Remove the meat from the claws and the body of the lobsters. Heat the olive oil and add the onion and garlic. Saute until the onion is golden. Then add the lobster meat, and the rest of the ingredients. Simmer for 10 minutes. Remove from the oven and transfer to serving plates.

Serves 4

Lamb with Pimentos

Our Spanish peppers called Pimentos are used in a variety of dishes from soups to a lamb stew such as this one.

2 pounds lamb stew meat
¼ cup olive oil
3 garlic cloves minced

1 bay leaf

2 tablespoons minced parsley

1 cup white wine

1 teaspoon salt

½ teaspoon pepper

3 pimentos, diced (red bell peppers will be an excellent substitute)

Heat the oil in a large casserole. Add the lamb and the garlic and brown the meat. Add the rest of the ingredients and reduce the heat. Simmer covered for 11/2 hours or until the meat is tender.

Serves 4

Salad from Valencia

This salad combines several of our most loved food, oranges, bell pepper and garlic., and is hails from Valencia.

1 cup garlic croutons

4 cups mixed salad greens

2 oranges peeled, the pith removed and sliced thinly

1 red bell pepper, seeded and thinly sliced

Dressing:

2 hard boiled egg yolks

¼ cup olive oil

¼ cup red wine vinegar

½ teaspoon salt

½ teaspoon pepper

Combine the croutons, salad greens, oranges, and bell peppers in a large bowl. In a small bowl combine the egg yolks, olive oil, vinegar, and salt and pepper. Whisk until smooth. Add to the salad bowl and toss.

Serves 4

Baked Stuffed Apples in Rioja Syrup

A apple with red wine Syrup and stuffed with dried fruit and pine nuts is a very rich and exciting dessert from the region of Asturia.

¼ cup raisins
¼ cup pine nuts
2 tablespoons grated orange zest
1 ½ cup milk
6 egg yolks
2 eggs
8 Macintosh apples peeled, and covered with aciduated water.
3 cups red Rioja wine
3 cups sugar

In a mixing bowl combine the raisins, pine nuts, grated orange zest, the milk, egg yolks and the eggs. Mix well. Create a hollow inside each apple and fill with the egg and fruit mixture. Preheat the oven to 375° grease a large baking pan.. Place the apples in the pan, and make for 40 minutes or until tender. While the apples are cooking, in a saucepan combine the sugar and the wine. Bring to a boil and cook until thick. Remove the syrup from the heat and cool. Pour into a serving pitcher. Place on apple on each dessert plate. Drizzle with the red wine syrup.
6 servings

*   *   *

Golda Meir

1898 to 1978 Prime Minister of Israel

Sometimes I think that I did not live up to my expectations of a good mother and wife. I was a Zionist first and a wife later. In 1921, I married Morris Myerson and we immigrated to Palestine. It was hard at first, we were on a Kibbutz, and Morris and I did not have any experience with any kind of manual labor. In fact, after Morris got sick, he wanted to leave the Kibbutz, and we did. We moved to Jerusalem. The first years there were very tough, I had my children and Morris was the only one working. Sometimes we didn't have enough money for food. When I was offered a job working for the Zionist movement I took it, even though it eventually created a rift between Morris and I causing us to separate in 1945. I then became very active in the creation of an Israeli home state. 1n 1948, I signed the Declaration Of Independence for the State of Israel. I was the first minister to the USSR in 1948 and 1949. In 1956, I changed my name from Myerson, to Meir, because I was to become the Minister of Foreign Affairs. I held that post until 1966. I also was the head of the Mapai party and of the United Israel Labor Party. I was elected Prime Minister from 1969-1974.

Besides all my political activities, I was a firm believer in nurturing of the human body. Food in Israel was very good. The produce was fresh, and we had an abundance of different kinds of fruits and vegetables that we had planted. By the time of Independence for the state of Israel, we had a thriving business in the production of oranges and lemons.We were constantly learning about new techniques in the production of chickens and other meats. Cuisine of Israel is also very unusual, in that it encompasses many different kinds of Jewish cooking. Meals might include, a fresh mixed salad, a grain such as rice or couscous, a fish and a meat dish and some kind of cake or cookies. One dish that has become the national Israeli dish is Falafel, the fried balls of Chickpeas that are served in pita bread with tahini dressing. On many street corners in Jerusalem and other Israeli cities, one finds Falafel stands. Each stand has its own additions, pickled and fried onions, Zhoug, a hot spice mix from Yemen, roasted peppers, herbs and Hummus, might all be part of one Falafel sandwich. In the last 15 to 2 years with the influx of many Jewish people from all over the world, we have begun to form an cuisine that is distinctly Israeli.

When I held cabinet meetings, I always served a cake or cookies that I had baked. During times of stress, such as the Six-Day War, I kept busy by cooking meals for my fellow government officials, while I waited for reports from the Army. Here is a meal that is representative of the many different cultures living together in Israel today. Shalom!

*　　　　　*　　　　　*

The Jerusalem Dinner
Artichoke Hummus
Carmel Avocado Puree
Baked Trout with lemon
Baked Guavas Stuffed with Mushrooms and Olives
Bulgur with Cheese
Stewed Beef Shank
Mixed Israeli Salad
Honey Cake

*　　　　　*　　　　　*

Artichoke Hummus

Israeli food is a combination of many different nationalities, from the Jewish food from Northern Europe, to the exotic dishes of the Yemenite, Ethiopian, Egyptian, Moroccan and Spanish, Italian Jews Hummus is both an Arab and Israeli dish. This one is enhanced by the addition of artichoke hearts.

2 cups cooked garbanzo beans
1 can (12 oz) artichoke hearts
6 garlic cloves, minced
3 tablespoons Tahini *

4 tablespoons lemon juice

½ teaspoon paprika

½ teaspoon cumin

½ Teaspoon Sea salt

½ teaspoon pepper

½ cup olive oil

Combine all the ingredients, except for the oil in a food processor. Puree coarsely. Then add the olive oil in steady drizzle, process to a creamy consistency.

Makes 3 ½ cups Hummus

Carmel Avocado Puree

Climate of Israel is conducive to the growing of citrus crops and Avocados. They have become one of our major exports to European countries.

3 ripe avocados, pitted and skinned

3 tablespoons lemon juice

2 garlic cloves, minced

1 teaspoon salt

½ onion, minced finely

3 tablespoons olive oil

4 tablespoons minced parsley

---

*Note: Tahini or sesame paste can be found in Arab food stores, or in most supermarkets.

Place all the ingredients in a food processor and process until smooth. Serve immediately.

Serves 6

Baked Trout with Lemon

Fish continues to be a favorite Israeli dish, from the northern love of pike, and carp to the Yemenite fiery fried fish.

    4 trout filleted and the heads removed
    3 large lemons, sliced thinly
    3 garlic cloves, minced
    5 tablespoons minced
    1 teaspoon cumin, ground
    2 tablespoons olive oil
    1 cup white wine
    1 teaspoon salt
    ½ teaspoon pepper
    2 tablespoons lemon juice

Preheat the oven to 350°F. Oil a large baking dish with 1 tablespoon of the olive oil. Stuff the fish with the lemon slices. In a small bowl, combine the parsley, garlic and cumin. Mix together. Sprinkle on top of the lemon slices. Close the fish with toothpicks. Place in the baking dish. Cover with the wine, salt, pepper and lemon juice. Bake for 30 minutes. Remove from the oven and serve immediately.

Serves 6

Baked Guavas with Mushrooms and Olives

This recipe comes from the Yemenite Jews, who make a variety of different stuffings for fruits and vegetables.

6 Guavas

1 tablespoon oil

1 cup mushrooms chopped

1 tablespoon onion, chopped

½ cup green olives, chopped

2 tablespoons chopped parsley

4 teaspoons chopped fresh dill

½ teaspoon salt

½ teaspoon cayenne pepper

1 tablespoon lemon juice

To stuff the guavas, cut a thin slice from the top of the guava. Remove the seeds with a melon scoop or a small spoon. Place the guavas in a greased baking dish and set aside. Preheat the oven to 325°F. Heat the oil in a skillet. Add the mushrooms, onion, green olives, herbs and the salt and pepper. Sauté until the vegetables are soft. Remove from the fire. Cool the mixture slightly. Stuff the guavas filling them to the top.

Sprinkle with the lemon juice. Bake for 1 hour or until the fruit is very tender. Remove from the oven and transfer to serving plates.

Serves 6

Bulgur with Cheese

One of the best-loved foods of Israel is bulgur, which we use in salads, and bake in savory dishes like this one with cheese. It is a great accompaniment to the stewed beef shank.

2 large onions sliced

3 tablespoons olive oil

3 cups bulgur

1 teaspoon salt

½ teaspoon black pepper
1 pound mozzarella cheese, diced
¼ cup butter

Fry the onions in the olive oil. Add the cracked wheat and 4 ½ cups boiling water. Season with the salt and pepper. Cook over low heat for 10 minutes. Mix in the cheese, butter and the pepper. Heat until the cheese is soft.
Serves 6

Stewed Beef Shank

This is another wonderful recipe from the Yemenite Jews, who we airlifted out of Yemen. The Yemenite Jews lived the same way as they had since the time of the Queen of Sheba. When they saw an airplane for the first time, they were so frightened that they fell on their knees moaning and wailing.

1 Beef shank (3 pounds)
Water
3 large onions, peeled and quartered
6 garlic cloves, chopped
2 cups tomatoes, chopped
1 teaspoon caraway seed
1 teaspoon turmeric
¼ teaspoon ground Cardamon
1 teaspoon black pepper
1/8 teaspoon saffron
1 serrano chili pepper, minced

Cut the shank into thick slices. Place the meat in a large soup pot, and add water to cover. Bring to a boil, skimming when necessary. When well skimmed add the rest of the ingredients, and bring to a boil. Cover, and reduce the heat to simmer. Simmer for 4 hours or until tender. Serve with rice or bulgur

Serves 6

Israeli Vegetable Salad

Chopped salads such as this one even appear on the breakfast table, with yogurt, bread and olives.

2 heads Bibb lettuce

2 large tomatoes, sliced

1 large cucumber, peeled and sliced

1 large green onion, seeded and diced

10 radishes, sliced

1 large red onion, chopped

4 tablespoons chopped Italian parsley

3 tablespoons olive oil

2 tablespoons lemon juice

Salt and pepper to taste

Tear the lettuce into small pieces and place in a bowl with the rest of the ingredients. Toss well. And Serve immediately.

Serves 6-8

Israeli Honey Cake

The love of honey cakes comes from the cuisine of the Jewish people from Poland, Austria, Germany and Holland. I always made sure that I had a honey cake to serve the cabinet when I met with them.

3 ½ cups all-purpose flour

¼ teaspoon salt

1 ½ teaspoon baking powder

1 teaspoon baking soda

1 ½ cups chopped walnuts

4 large eggs

¾ cup sugar

4 tablespoons vegetable oil

2 cups honey

½ cup extra strong coffee

1 teaspoon ground cinnamon

½ teaspoon ground ginger

½ teaspoon ground cloves

¼ teaspoon ground nutmeg

Preheat the oven to 325°F. Grease a large springform pan. Sift the flour, baking powder, baking soda, salt and spices together. In a bowl beat the eggs until light, adding the sugar. Beat until very thick, then add the oil, honey and coffee. Stir in the flour mixture, and the nuts. Pour into the springform pan, and bake for 50 minutes. Remove from the oven and cool. Then remove from the pan. Cool and cut into squares.

Makes 8-10 servings

*   *   *

Frida Kahlo

1906–1954, Artist, Wife of Diego Rivera

I was born in the Blue House in Mexico City. At 6 years old I was stricken with polio, which left me with a thinner right leg, but that did not stop me from climbing trees and pulling many pranks while I was at school. At 18, I had an accident that changed my life, and perhaps gave me the impetuses to paint. While traveling on a streetcar, a bus hit it, and I was impaled to the wall of the streetcar. I suffered a broken spinal column, broken ribs, a broken pelvis, and eleven fractures of my right leg.

For months, I lay in bed, encased in a plaster cast. This accident was to rear its ugly head all my life. Many times, I was hospitalized with tremendous pain, and more surgeries then I care to count. Bored with the long time I had to spend in bed, I began to paint.

When I recovered an artist friend of mine introduced me to the love of my life, the great artist, Diego Rivera. I fell passionately in love with him, which my friends found hard to understand, as he was very fat, and rather homely. But I didn't care, and we were married in 1929. Our relationship was tempestuous, and several times we separated, and once we even divorced only to come back together again. He was my biggest supporter, encouraging me to dress in native costume, and to create the very best paintings I could. I also provided the cozy home that Diego so needed, as food was a very important part of his life. When he was working on a project, I would fix him lunch, making a very beautiful basket, filled with flowers and all the delicacies he loved.

My paintings may seem narcissistic to the world, but they were the photographs of the suffering I endured in my marriage, the miscarriages I had, and the physical pain I suffered. With these paintings I was able to take myself out of my pain wracked body, and enter another world, where pain did not exist. Besides self-portraits, I painted the beautiful flowers and fruit of Mexico, from which I created exquisite still lives of food, for the many parties, that I loved to give. Mexican food is very sensuous, full of color and spice, it is not just tacos or refried beans, but a combination of very subtle flavors, and textures, that make for a multi level experience. Rich dark red soups, glistening with chilies, deep green salads, burnished barbecued meats and beautiful desserts of mango, papaya and guava, on colorful pottery plates garnished with flowers, were just a few of the works of art I produced.For Diego, I created my own reality in food.

*   *   *

The Blue House Dinner

Agua Fresca De Limon (Lime Drink)

Escabeche (lime Marinated Fish)
Chicken Mole
Carne Mechasa (Steak in spicy sauce)
Frijoles De Olla (Beans cooked in a pot)
Calabacitas
Papaya Relish
Jicama and Avocado Salad
Flan De Vanilla

*   *   *

Agua Fresca de Limon

This is a traditional lime drink served at Cinco de Mayo.

6 cups cold water
1/3 cup granulated sugar
2 large green limes

In a pitcher combine the water, granulated sugar, and the juice of the limes. Stir until the sugar is dissolved. Chill until ready to serve. Then grate the rind of the limes into the pitcher.

Serves 4

Escabeche (lime marinated fish)

This is a national Mexican dish, which has its roots in its Spanish heritage. The raw fish is cooked in the lime juice and then marinated and served on a bed of greens.

    2 pounds white fish, filleted and sliced thinly
    3 cups water
    2 cups lime juice

Marinade

    1 teaspoon pink peppercorns
    1 teaspoon whole coriander seeds
    4 whole cloves
    1 teaspoon whole cumin seeds
    4 whole allspice
    4 cloves of garlic, peeled
    1 cup red wine vinegar
    1 cup water
    1 teaspoon oregano
    2 bay leaves
    4 teaspoons salt
    1 teaspoon sugar
    1 cup salad oil
    Mixed greens
    Cherry Tomatoes

Place the fish in a glass-baking dish. Mix the lime juice and the water together and pour over the fish. Refrigerate until the fish turns opaque. While the fish is cooking, mix the marinade together and set aside. When the fish has finished cooking, drain it, and place it back in the baking dish. Cover with the marinade and let it marinate for 2-3 hours. Remove the fish with a slotted spoon from the marinade and place on individual salad plates with the mixed greens and the cherry tomatoes.

6-8 servings

Chicken Mole

Chicken cooked in mole, sauce is a complex dish consisting of many different spices, peanuts and chocolate.

8 boneless chicken breasts
¼ cup olive oil
1 can chopped green chilies
1 onion, chopped
1 garlic clove minced
1 cup tomato sauce
2 teaspoons chili powder
1 teaspoon salt
2 tablespoons sugar
1 large serrano chili minced
2 whole cloves
1 square unsweetened chocolate
2 tablespoons peanut butter
2 cups of hot cooked rice

In a skillet heat the olive oil and brown the chicken. Remove from the pan and set aside. Then add the onion and the garlic and the green chilies. Sauté until the onion is limp. Then add the rest of the ingredients and cook for 15 minutes. Add the chicken breasts and cook over low heat for 30 minutes or until the chicken is done. Serve over the cooked rice.

Serves 4

Carne Mechasa

Beefsteak, stuffed with peppers, bacon and chilies is usually baked in the oven, in a sweet sour sauce. Some times I would make a dish like this, and pack it up in one of those beautiful baskets that I told you about, taking it to the site where he was working with a love note pinned on the top.

3 pounds of sirloin steak
1 green pepper, sliced into thin slices
6 slices of bacon, cooked and crumbled
4 oz mild green chilies, diced
¼ cup red wine vinegar
1 bay leaf
1 cup tomato sauce
¼ cup brown sugar
1 teaspoon salt
¼ cup flour

Make a deep pocket in the steak. Cook the green pepper, in salted water for 5 minutes then drain. Stuff the steak with the green pepper, chilies, and bacon. Close with toothpicks. Brown the meat in a heavy skillet, then transfer to a large baking dish. Preheat the oven to 350°F. Combine the tomato sauce, sugar, vinegar, salt and bay leaf in the skillet, and stir until the sugar dissolves. Return the meat to the skillet and bake for 11/2 hours. Remove the meat from the pan and keep warm. Skim the fat off the sauce, and make a paste with the flour and some water. Add to the pan, and cook until thickened. Pour the sauce over the steak and serve.

Serves4

Frijoles De Olla (Beans cooked in a pot)

Black beans, cooked in an olla or clay pot, are always part of a Mexican meal, accompanied by rice.

4 ½ quarts water
1 (16oz) package black beans
2 onions, peeled and halved
3 heads of garlic, peeled
1 tablespoon salt
½ cup minced cilantro
Garnishes
Chopped green onions
Chopped tomatoes
Diced serrano chilies
Sour cream

Bring the water to a boil in a large soup pot. Add the beans, onion, and garlic. Cook at a slow boil or until the beans are done. Add the salt after 1 hour of cooking. Remove one cup of the beans, and puree in the food processor, then return to the pot. Stir in the cilantro. Serve in bowls with the garnishes,

Serves 8

Calabacitas

Squash and corn combined together with chilies, make for an interesting side dish.

4 zucchini sliced

1 large onion sliced

3 tablespoons vegetable oil

2 cloves of garlic, minced

4 oz chopped green chilies

One 16 oz cans whole kernel corn

1 cup grated cheddar cheese

2 tablespoons minced cilantro

Sauté the squash and the onion, in the oil for 10 minutes. Preheat the oven to 350°F Transfer the squash mixture to a mixing bowl and add the rest of the ingredients. Oil a large casserole dish and pour the vegetables into it. Bake for 35-40 minutes or until the top is puffed and golden. Remove from the oven and spoon on to serving plates. Garnish with the minced cilantro.

Serves 6

Papaya Relish

Papayas are one of our favorite fruits. We serve a relish like this with our meat dishes.

½ cup red onion, chopped

½ cup red bell pepper, chopped

1 small red chili pepper, seeded and diced

1 tablespoon vegetable oil

¼ cup fresh minced mint leaves

2 tablespoons lime juice

1 extra large papaya (½ pound) pared, seeded and cut into ½ inch cubes.

Combine all the ingredients in a mixing bowl and toss. Chill until ready to serve.

6 servings

Jicama and Avocado Salad

Jicama a tuber with a slightly sweet taste is used in many Mexican Salads, for it's refreshing quality.

1 Jicama, peeled and diced
3 large avocados, peeled pitted and diced
1 large orange, peeled and sectioned
1 tablespoon minced cilantro
3 tablespoons vegetable oil
3 tablespoons lime juice
Salt and pepper to taste

Combine the Jicama, avocados, and orange in a bowl. Add the cilantro and mix. In a small bowl combine the vegetable oil, and the lime juice. Season to taste with the salt and pepper. Combine with the salad ingredients. Toss well and serve.

Serves 6

Flan De Vanilla

Flan originated in Spain and traveled to Mexico with the Spanish Missionaries.

Caramel:

1 cup sugar

Custard:

2 large eggs

2 egg yolks

1 cup sugar

1 can (8oz) evaporated Milk

1 can (8oz) sweetened condensed milk

½ cup heavy cream

2 teaspoons vanilla extract

1 tablespoon rum

Preheat the oven to 350°F. Butter 8 ramekins. In a skillet heat the sugar, over medium heat, as soon as it begins to liquefy, swirl the pot to ensure even browning. When the mixture is amber colored, remove from the heat. With a small ladle, pour about 2 tablespoons of the mixture into each ramekin, coating as much of the sides of each one as you can. Cool.

Beat the eggs and the egg yolks together lightly. Stir in the sugar. In a separate bowl, combine the evaporated milk, the sweetened condensed milk, the heavy cream, vanilla extract and the rum. Stir this gently into the egg mixture. Ladle into the ramekins. Fill a large roasting pan, halfway with warm water. Place the ramekins, in the water. Bake 45 minutes or until the custards are just set. Remove from the oven and cool for 30 minutes. Run a thin knife around the edge of each ramekin to loosen, and invert on a plate.

Make 8 servings

*   *   *

Josephine Baker

1906-1975, Singer, and Actress, Member of the French Resistance

I began my life as a maid working in white homes, as my mother did not have enough money to support us. I was married to my first husband at the age of 14, and left home to travel with a Vaudeville Group. My first real chance at changing my life came, when I starred in *Shuffle Along*, Broadway's first black musical. Four years after this first break, I went to Paris to star in La Revue Negro, where I danced the Charleston, wearing nothing but feathers. I was an instant success, as Europeans loved my very sexual embodiment of the Black Woman. Thus began my life in France, the country that was to become my home. During the 1920's and 1930's I lived a life of luxury, unknown to many black people of my time, traveling around Europe, in Christian Dior clothes, with my pet leopard, Chiquita. I made a brief return to America before the war, but audiences there were not ready for a sophisticated black woman like me. During the war I joined the French Resistance, and worked on Intelligence reports. I officially became a French Citizen in 1937. Unable to have children, I adopted 12 children during the years of 1954-1965, who were all of different races and cultures. Unable to support my children in the style I was accustomed to, I lost my home, and Princess Grace of Monaco, generously gave me a villa in Monaco. In 1973 I launched a successful show in America, and in 1974 I stared in production of Josephine, a show based on my life. One could say that I lived an amazing life for a black woman, born when I was, and this is true, for I achieved heights that no black person had achieved up to then.

I never forgot my roots in America and even though I lived in France for most of my life, I still remembered the food of my native land, especially the great southern food. I was able to have much more elegant and substantial food in Paris then I did back home. At the height of my career, I was able to have a personal chef who could create the southern dishes, whose flavors permeated the houses of the rich that I worked for as a child.. Piquant shellfish dishes, chicken fried and served with mashed potatoes or grits, greens of all sorts, cooked to melting tenderness with salt pork and wonderful dense sweet potato, chess or chocolate pies, all are part of my southern heritage and memories.

*   *   *

The Monte Carlo Dinner
Shrimp Cakes
Chicken Maryland
Corn Fritters
Buttermilk Mashed Potatoes
Mustard Greens
Chocolate Pecan Mud Pie

*   *   *

Shrimp Cakes

A typical appetizer, found in the south, during the 1930's and 40's, in the South where these delectable shrimp cakes, made of shrimps, shallots, peppers and usually served with a spiced mayonnaise.

    1 pound raw shrimp
    2 shallots, peeled and finely minced
    ½ cup finely chopped red or green bell pepper
    ½ teaspoon dried red pepper flakes
    2 tablespoons mayonnaise

½ cup bread crumbs
2 egg whites
Salt and freshly ground pepper
4 tablespoons butter

Mayonnaise

2 tablespoons hot cocktail sauce
6 tablespoons mayonnaise
2 tablespoons capers

Mince the shrimp in a food processor. Place the minced shrimp in a mixing bowl, and add the rest of the ingredients, except for the butter. Mix well and form into 8 cakes. Heat the butter in a skillet, and fry the cakes over medium heat until done. Place two cakes on each plate, and serve with a dollop of the mayonnaise on top of them. Garnish with lemon wedges.

Serves 6

Chicken Maryland

This dish was also made famous by the Duchess of Windsor, who served it to her future husband the Duke at his home, Fort Belevdere The name comes from its association with the State of Maryland. Corn fritters usually accompany this chicken dish.

1 4 ½ pound chicken, cut into serving pieces
3 tablespoons all –purpose flour
¼ teaspoon cayenne pepper
2 eggs beaten
6 tablespoons breadcrumbs
3 tablespoons corn oil
2 cups cream

Corn Fritters:

1 10 oz package frozen corn kernels, defrosted
1 cup flour
½ teaspoon salt
1 egg
1 cup milk
Corn oil

Preheat the oven to 350°F. Pat dry the chicken, and mix the flour and cayenne pepper together on a plate. Dip the chicken pieces into the flour, and into the beaten eggs, and finally into the breadcrumbs. Heat the corn oil in a skillet until very hot; fry the chicken pieces until brown on all sides. Then remove from the skillet and place in a casserole dish. When you have browned all the chicken pieces, add the cream to the skillet, scraping the sides and the bottom of the pan. Season to taste with salt and pepper. Then pour the cream over the chicken and bake for 1 hour or until the chicken is done.

Corn Fritters: About 30 minutes before the chicken is finished, make the batter for the corn fritters, by mixing together the flour, egg, salt and milk. Beat until smooth and let sit. 10 minutes before the chicken is finished, add the corn kernels to the batter, and heat the corn oil to a deep of ½ inch. Drop large tablespoons of batter into the oil, and fry until golden, drain on paper towels. Remove the chicken from the oven, and place on a platter, topped with the sauce. Surround with the corn fritters.

Serves 4

Buttermilk Mashed Potatoes

A typical treat of the Southern States is mashed potatoes made with buttermilk.

6 large russet potatoes peeled and diced
½ cup buttermilk
1 tablespoon butter
Salt and pepper to taste

Cook the potatoes in boiling salted water until done. Drain and add the rest of the ingredients and mash until very fluffy. Transfer to a serving bowl, and add a pat of butter in the middle.
Make 4 servings

Mustard Greens

Greens cooked with salt pork until soft and mellow, are also part of southern cuisine, where in many parts of the south they constitute one of three vegetables served as a lunch time meal. The love of this lowly green never left me, any matter how many gourmet meals I ate in France. During the war vegetable dishes like this sustained the French and me Resistance that I worked for.

2 large bunches mustard greens, washed and shredded
6 cups Chicken broth
½ pound salt pork, diced
1 teaspoon pepper

In a skillet fry the salt pork until the fat is rendered. Remove from the skillet. Add the mustard greens and cook until just wilted. Remove the mustard greens to a soup pot and add the broth, salt pork and pepper. Bring to a boil, and reduce the heat. Simmer covered for 3 hours.
Serves 4

Chocolate Pecan Mud Pie

Pecans are a nut that is native to the Southern United States, and during the late 1890's pies, such as this one began to evolve in the Southern United States.

Crust:

> 1 cup chocolate wafer cookies
> 1 ½ tablespoons granulated sugar
> 3 tablespoons melted butter

Filling:

> ½ Pound bittersweet chocolate
> 2 egg yolks
> 3 tablespoons strong coffee
> ¼ cup granulated sugar
> ¼ pound butter

Caramel Mixture:

> 6-oz pecan halves
> 1 cup light brown sugar
> ½ cup butter
> 1/8 teaspoon salt
> ¼ cup heavy cream
> 2 tablespoons dark rum

In the food processor, process the chocolate cookies, until fine crumbs are formed then add the rest of the ingredients, and process until they are mixed. Pat into an 11 inch fluted tart pan, chill for 10 minutes. Preheat the oven to 350°F. Bake the pie for 5 minutes, and remove from the oven, setting aside.

In a double boiler, melt the chocolate, and whisk in the eggs and the coffee. Whisk for several minutes, then add the sugar, and whisk again. Add the butter, cut in three pieces, and whisk in thoroughly after each addition. Pour into the prepared tart pan. Let cool.

To make the caramel: Chop the pecans coarsely in the food processor. Heat the sugar, salt and butter stirring, until dissolved. Add the cream and the rum. Simmer until the caramel thickens, to a consistency that coats the back of a spoon. Remove from the heat and add the pecans. Then mix well. Spoon on top of the chocolate mixture, and smooth. Chill in the refrigerator until ready to serve.

Serves 8

*   *   *

Carmen Miranda

1909 to 1955, Brazilian Actress and Singer

I was born in Portugal, but my home is Brazil. While I was very young, I became a singer and soon I was a popular star of the radio in Brazil. By the end of the 1930's I was urged to come to the United States, to continue my career and I came to Hollywood.. Soon I was singing and dancing my way into the hearts of America. Who cannot forget *"Down Argentine Way"*, *The Gangs all here, and Weekend in Havana*. They are just a few of my movies. Known for my trademark hats, and colorful costumes, my bubbling personality and comedic skills helped me to remain a fixture even today.

While I loved the United States, it was my native Brazil that caught my heart forever. I had to go home, every once in a while, for a whiff of the sea air around Rio de Janeiro, and to walk on the beaches, and eat wonderful Brazilian food. Brazilian food with it is Portuguese and African roots, is a orgy of sensuous tastes. Brazil is blessed with a wonderful climate that makes for the growing of chilies, garlic, coconuts, limes, oranges, and bananas. Pork and Beef are our main sources of meat. Black beans and rice are two staples that we eat at almost every dinner. From the hot pepper sauces of Bahia, to the Empadao's, Feijoda's, Bahian Shrimp Stew, Kale and mustard greens cooked with garlic and the sweets that the Nuns perfected in the convents, are the recreations the soul of my childhood.

So come with me, and explore a melange of Brazilian food, and soon you will feel the rythum of the conga drum, leading you to the dance floor.

*　　　　　　　*　　　　　　　*

Flying Down to Rio Dinner
Rum Sour
Empadao De Galinha (Brazilian Chicken pie)
Bahian Shrimp Stew
Brazilian Rice
Feijoada (Smoked meat and black bean stew)
Greens Mineira Style
Molho De Pimenta E Limao (Chili and Lime Sauce)
Peanut Cake
Mango Pudding

*　　　　　　　*　　　　　　　*

Rum Sour (Batida Brasileria)

The rum sour is a traditional drink served in Brazil, as a pre dinner drink.

1 jigger rum
1 teaspoon egg white
Sugar

¼ jigger lemon juice
Ice

Shake well in a cocktail shaker. Pour into a glass dipped in sugar.
Makes 1 serving

Empadao De Galinha (Brazilian Chicken Pie)

Empadao, are sometimes small pies, served individually, or large
ones that can be cut into many servings.

Dough

4 cups flour
2 egg yolks
1 cup lard
½ cup vegetable oil
½ cup cold water
1 teaspoon salt

Filling

2 ½ pounds boneless chicken breasts, cut cup
2 medium onions, minced
2 garlic cloves, minced
1 bell pepper, minced
4 large tomatoes, peeled, seeded and diced
1 cup heart of palms, diced
½ cup chicken stock
1 bay leaf
½ teaspoon thyme
¼ teaspoon cayenne pepper
Salt and pepper to taste

2 tablespoons vegetable oil

2 tablespoons flour

To make the Dough: Place the flour and the salt in a mixing bowl and cut in the lard, until it resembles coarse meal. Add the rest of the ingredients and mix. Turn out on a wooden board, and knead for several minutes. Chill for 2 hours.

Season the chicken with salt and let stand 1 hour. Brown the chicken in the oil and add the onions and garlic. Sauté until translucent. Add the rest of the ingredients and simmer for 25 minutes. Remove the bay leaf, and let cool in the sauce.

To Assemble: Preheat the oven to 350°F. Divide the dough into two discs. Roll out the first disc to fit a large Pyrex casserole dish. Trim the edges. Fill with the chicken filling and the roll out the other disc to fit the top. Prick the top all over, and brush with egg yolk. Bake for 30 minutes. Cut into squares and serve.

Makes 8-10 servings

Bahian Shrimp Stew

We call a stew like this a Moqueca. We have many varieties of Moquecas, some are made with eggs and some with chicken. This stew is served over Brazilian rice. Dende is a palm oil that we use as a flavoring in many of our dishes.

1/3 cup extra virgin olive oil

2 medium sized onions, sliced

1 small red bell pepper, seeded and sliced

2 small tomatoes, chopped

1 tablespoon minced cilantro

1 clove garlic, minced

1 tablespoon tomato paste

12 large cooked jumbo shrimp

    2 tablespoons fresh lemon juice
    ½ cup thin coconut milk
    ¼ cup dende (Palm oil)*

Heat the olive oil in a large skillet. Add the onions, pepper, tomatoes, cilantro, garlic and tomato paste. Cook, stirring, until the onions are translucent. Bring the sauce to a boil, then add the shrimp and the lemon juice. Cook for 3 minutes or until the shrimp are heated through. Then add the coconut milk and the dende. Bring to a boil for 1 minute. Remove from the heat and serve with the rice.

Brazilian Rice

Rice always accompanies whatever meat course is being served for dinner.

    6 tablespoons unsalted butter
    1 small onion, minced
    2 garlic cloves, minced
    3 cups rice
    Salt and pepper to taste
    5 cups Chicken stock

In a large pot, melt the butter, and add the onion and garlic, Sauté until golden, then add the rice and salt and pepper and sauté for several minutes. Add the chicken stock and bring to a boil. Cover tightly

---

*Note: Palm oil can be found in Mexican or foods stores specializing in African or South American food.

with a lid and reduce the heat. Simmer for 25 minutes. Remove from the heat, and let it rest for 10 minutes, then fluff the rice and serve.
Serves 10

Feijoada (Smoked Meat and Black Bean Stew)

This is the national meat dish of Brazil, served with rice and sometimes with greens on the side, and a hot sauce. Feijoada is the soul of Brazil, it is Portuguese and African all rolled into one. When I go home to Rio, Feijoada is the one dish I always ask for.

1 pound pork shoulder cubed
1 pound chorizo, sliced
1 pound smoked pork shoulder
1 pound lean bacon, cubed
1 pound beef chuck, cubed
4 cups black beans
2 onions, minced
3 large garlic cloves, minced
2 tablespoons minced parsley
1 teaspoon fresh minced thyme
2 bay leaves
Pepper to taste
3 quarts water
Grated orange peel.

Rinse the salted meats, the night before in cold water. Place them in a large pot and cover with water. Leave them to soak overnight in the refrigerator. In the morning change the water and allow then continuing soaking until you are ready to assemble the dish. Remove the meat from the water and Drain. Place the meat and the rest of the ingredients in a large soup pot, and add the water. Bring to a boil. Reduce the heat and cover. Simmer for 2 ½ hours or until the stew is thick and creamy. Serve in large bowls with the Brazilian rice, and garnish with grated orange peel.

Serves 10

Greens Mineira Style

This side dish traditionally accompanies Feijoada and comes from the region of Minas Gerais in Brazil.

    2 pounds fresh kale
    3 tablespoons olive oil
    1 medium size onion, minced
    2 cloves garlic, minced

Wash the kale thoroughly to remove the dirt and grit. Bunch it together. Take each bunch and roll it tightly and cut it crosswise into thin strips. Wash the strips and dry thoroughly. Heat the oil in a large skillet, and cook the onion and garlic until they are lightly browned. Add the kale strips and cook for five minutes, so that the greens are soft, but retain their bright green color. Transfer to a serving dish.

Serves 6

Molho De Pimenta e Limao (Chili and Lime Sauce)

Malagueta Peppers are a special pepper grown in Brazil, they make up the majority of the hot sauces found in the Bahia region.

    4 malagueta peppers, or 4 serrano chilies minced
    1 teaspoon salt
    1 small onion, minced
    1 clove of garlic minced
    The juice of 5 limes

In a food processor, puree the chilies with the salt, onion and garlic. Add the lime juice. And puree. Remove from the food processor and place in a bowl. Allow standing at room temperature for several hours.

Makes approximately 1 cup

Peanut Cake

Cakes became an art in Brazil, baked by the Nuns in Convents, who sold them to make money for their Orders. The Peanut brought to Brazil by the African slaves, has become a major crop of our country..

2 tablespoons butter
2 tablespoons peanut butter
1 cup light brown sugar
1 cup granulated sugar
3 eggs separated
3 cups all purpose flour
3 teaspoons baking powder
½ teaspoon salt
½ teaspoon ground cinnamon
½ teaspoon ground cloves
1 cup milk

Butter a large springform pan. Preheat the oven to 350°F. Cream the butter, and peanut butter with the sugars. Add the beaten egg yolks. Sift the flour with the baking powder, salt, cinnamon and cloves. Mix into the sugar mixture, alternating with the milk. Beat the egg whites until stiff, and the fold into the cake mixture, gently. Pour into the springform pan, and bake for 1 hours.

Serves 8

Mango Pudding

The Portuguese incorporated the exotic fruits that grew in Brazil, into lovely puddings.

    3 large ripe mangos
    1 teaspoon lemon juice
    ¼ teaspoon salt
    5 tablespoons sugar
    3 eggs separated
    2 tablespoons cornstarch

Peel the mangos, and cut into small pieces. Mix with the lemon juice and salt. Then sprinkle with the sugar and let stand for 10 minutes. Coarsely puree in the food processor. Add the egg yolks and mix. Blend in the cornstarch and beat the egg whites until stiff. Fold into the pureed mango mixture. Pour into a soufflé dish and bake for 30 minutes at 350°F.

Serves 8

Indira Gandhi

1917-1984, Prime Minister of India

I was the only child of Jawaharlal Nehru, the first Prime Minister of India. I was educated in India, and at Oxford in England. In 1938 I joined the National Congress party and became an active participant in lobbying for Indira's Independence. In 1942 I married a lawyer, Feroze Gandhi, who was also active in the movement. When India finally won its independence, I helped my father by being his official hostess, as my mother had died. I held several official posts before I became Prime Minister in 1966. India is a volatile land, and many times during my tenure I was forced to take action my jailing dissenters, and informing states of emergency. I stepped down from being Prime Minister in 1977. But in 1980, the people of India elected me back in. When the Sikh started to rebel I was forced to take action, and that action led to my assassination by Sikh conspirators.

Let me tell you about the meals that were served when my father Jawaharlal was Prime Minister. As I was his official hostess, I wanted people who came to visit our country to have some of the very best of Indian food. Indian food has so many complexes and different tastes. We eat many vegetables from eggplant to potatoes, tomatoes, onions, and spinach. Paneer is a cottage cheese that we eat with spinach in a dish called Sag Paneer. Jaggery is a raw form of Brown sugar that we use to make sweets and confections. The spices we use are cinnamon, cardamon, cumin, cloves, mace, turmeric, and ginger and mustard seeds. Cashew and almonds and pistachios are used in curries, candies, and puddings. From the hot and fiery food of Goa, to the more delicate and subtle dishes from Kashmir, we are a nation with a million ways to prepare food. We would have a spicy dish, cooled by a creamy raita, made of yogurt, chutney, many vegetable dishes and sweets Let me honor you with a meal that would have been served to Viceroy Mountbatten, on the day we were handed our independence.

*   *   *

The Independence Dinner
Yogurt and Cucumber soup
Dhal
Coconut Rice
Chicken Vindaloo
Curried Lamb
Cauliflower Marsala
Cucumber Raita
Naan
Bengali Rice Pudding
Chai

*   *   *

Yogurt and Cucumber Soup

I would start off the meal with very soothing and refreshing soup to contrast with the hot food that is the main part of the meal.

2 cups plain yogurt
4 cups chicken stock
½ tablespoon fresh gingerroot, grated
8 tablespoons cucumber, peeled and finely diced
1 cup tomato peeled, seeded and finely diced
2 tablespoons finely chopped mint
Salt and ground pepper to taste

Put the yogurt in a blender and add the chicken stock and the gingerroot. Blend until well mixed. Remove from the blender and transfer to a large bowl. Stir in the rest of the ingredients. Chill until ready to serve.

Serves 6

Dhal

Dhal is a dish of lentils, with green chilies, that is served with the Naan, to be scooped up. Ghee, which is used in this recipe, is clarified butter.

½ pound split skinless lentils
2 ½ cups water
1 teaspoon salt
½ teaspoon red chili powder
4 cloves of garlic, peeled and thinly sliced
¼ teaspoon turmeric
1 cup chopped fresh tomatoes
2 tablespoons ghee or corn oil, or clarified butter

1 green chili, sliced

2 tablespoons minced cilantro

1 tablespoon Garam Marsala

Soak the lentils in warm water for 30 minutes. Drain and discard the water. Put the lentils into a saucepan, and add just enough water to cover the lentils, add the salt, red chili peppers, turmeric, garlic and the chopped tomatoes. Bring to a boil then simmer covered for 10 minutes, or until the Dhal is cooked but whole. Heat the ghee in the frying pan, the chili slices, cook for 2 minutes, then add to the Dhal and then mix in the cilantro and the Garam Marsala. Transfer to a serving bowl.
Serves 4

Coconut Rice

Fluffy rice, enhanced by coconut and cardamon, is served with the Chicken Vindaloo, and the lamb curry.

1 ½ cups rice

1 ½ cups coconut, fresh and shredded

3 tablespoons butter

1 medium sized onion, minced

1 pinch salt

1 teaspoon ground cardamon,

Soak the rice in water for 30 minutes. Also soak the coconut, for 20 minutes in 2 cups of water. Drain the rice and set aside. Strain the coconut from the water, it has been soaking in and reserve the coconut milk, that has formed. Heat the butter in the skillet. Add the onion and sauté until golden. Then add the rice and fry for a few minutes. Add the coconut milk, and 11/2 cups water. Add the salt and the cardamon, and bring to a boil. Reduce the heat and cook until the rice is done.
Serves 4

Chicken Vindaloo

Every Indian region has its own version of Chicken Vindaloo, a very spicy and hot dish, comprised of many different spices.. This is a very complex dish and requires a great deal of grinding and blending of spices, but the end result is worth all the work involved to make it.

2 teaspoons cumin seeds

1 teaspoon peppercorns, black

1 teaspoon cardamom seeds

1 teaspoon cinnamon

1 ½ teaspoon black mustard seeds

1 teaspoon whole fenugreek seeds

5 tablespoons white vinegar

1 teaspoon salt

½ teaspoon cayenne pepper

1 teaspoon brown sugar

10 tablespoons vegetable oil

2 large yellow onions, peeled and cut into rings

6 tablespoon water

1 tablespoon ginger, peeled and chopped

10 garlic cloves, coarsely chopped

1 tablespoon ground coriander seeds

½ teaspoon turmeric

2 pounds chicken breast, boneless, cut into bit-size pieces

1 can (8oz) tomato sauce

½ pound new potatoes, peeled and quartered

The Vindaloo Paste: Grind the cumin seeds black pepper, cardamom seeds, cinnamon, black mustard seeds, and the fenugreek seeds together in a spice grinder. In a small bowl combine the ground spices, vinegar, salt, cayenne pepper and brown sugar, set aside. Heat the oil in a medium saucepan, and add the onions, stirring frequently until they are a dark brown. Remove the onions with a slotted spoon and put them in a blender. Do not discard the oil. Add about 3 tablespoons of water to the onions, and puree. Add this onion paste to the spices in the bowl.

Put the ginger and garlic in a blender, adding the rest of the water. Puree to form a paste. Heat the remaining oil in the pan, and add the ginger, and the garlic. Stir for a few minutes until the paste is slightly browned. Add the chicken and brown lightly. Then add the Vindaloo paste, tomato sauce and potatoes to the chicken and stir and bring to a boil. Reduce the heat and simmer for about an hour until the potatoes are very tender.

Serves 4

Curried Lamb

Curried lamb made with saffron, and nuts has a different flavor then the Vindaloo, it is richer and has a velvety sauce.

1 tablespoon saffron

4 tablespoons warm milk

1 tablespoon each, cashews, peanuts and raisins

1 teaspoon poppy seeds

1 tablespoon gingerroot, grated

1 cup coconut milk

10 cloves of garlic, peeled and halved

1 small green papaya, peeled, seeded and diced

½ teaspoon ground nutmeg

½ teaspoon ground cumin

1 teaspoon ground coriander

6 serrano chilies, seeded

2 cups plain yogurt

1 teaspoon salt

4 pounds of lamb shanks

4 teaspoons vegetable oil

2 large onions, finely chopped

Saffron Paste: Combine the saffron with the milk and set aside.

To Make the Sauce: Combine the saffron with the milk in a blender and puree. Grind the nuts, and raisins in a food processor along with the poppy seeds, ginger root and coconut milk. Remove from the food processor and set aside. Clean out the food processor, and place the garlic, papaya, nutmeg, cumin, coriander and chilies in the food processor and puree. Set aside. Stir into the yogurt and the salt. Combine both pastes together and marinate the lamb shanks for 30 minutes.

Heat the butter in a large Dutch oven, and add the onions, and sauté until golden. Remove the lamb shanks from the marinade and pat dry. Then add the lamb shanks to the Dutch oven and brown. Add the marinade and bring to a boil. Reduce the heat and cover. Simmer for 50 minutes. Then add the saffron paste, and continue cooking for another 20 minutes, or until the lamb shanks are tender.

Serves 4

Cauliflower Marsala

Cauliflower is a favorite Indian vegetable as its bland texture, lends itself to spices.

½ large cauliflower cut into flowerets

3 large potatoes, peeled and cubed

3 tomatoes, finely chopped

1 large onion, finely chopped

1 teaspoon red chili flakes

1 teaspoon Garam Marsala

1 teaspoon salt

3 tablespoons butter

1 large hot green Chile, seeded and diced

3 tablespoons minced cilantro

Heat the butter in a skillet and add the potatoes, and fry until browned. Then add the cauliflower, the tomatoes, and the onions. Sauté for 5 minutes. Add the Garam Marsala, the chili flakes, and the salt. Cook for 5-8 more minutes or until the potatoes are soft. Transfer to a serving dish, and sprinkle with the green chili and the cilantro.

Serves 4

Cucumber Raita

A Raita is a cooling sauce that is served as a side to the curry dishes.

1 Cup plain yogurt

½ cup cucumber finely chopped

Salt and pepper to taste

1/8 teaspoon cumin

1 teaspoon sugar

1 tablespoon minced cilantro

Combine all the ingredients in a small serving bowl. Chill until ready to serve.

Serves 4

Bengali Rice Pudding

Rice pudding, with nuts such as pistachios, is a common dessert in India. Sometimes we serve this with paper-thin shavings of silver leaf on the top.

½ cup basmati rice
2 teaspoons butter, melted
½ cup pistachios, halved
7 cups milk
½ cup sugar
2 cardamon pods

In a deep saucepot, bring the milk to a boil, and then immediate reduce to low. Simmer until reduced to five cups. Stir constantly, so the milk doesn't burn. Wash the rice and spread out on a plate. Mix with the butter. Add the rice, and keep stirring until it is cooked or about 20 minutes. Pour in the sugar and the pistachios, with the cardamon pods. Cook for another 5 minutes. Remove from the heat and chill. Serve in small dessert dishes.
Serves 6

Chai

Chai is a drink that we serve all day long, with breakfast, lunch, as an afternoon tea, and with dinner. It is made with tea, milk and spices and has a cooling effect,

4 cups water
4 teaspoons loose black tea
4 cardamon pods, cracked
½ teaspoon fennel seeds

1 cup milk
2 tablespoons sugar

Combine the water, tea, cardamon and fennel seeds in a large saucepan and simmer over low heat for 5 minutes. Add the milk and the sugar. Heat until hot. Strain into cups and serve.
4 servings

    *   *   *

Chapter 6

Basics (Supplemental Recipes)

Almond Milk

On days that were Lenten days, Almond milk was an essential ingredient as it replaced sheep and cows milk.

¾ cup blanched almonds
4 cups warm water

Place half the almonds, and 2 cups of water into a blender and blend for quite some time until a smooth, white liquid forms. Do the same with the remaining almonds and water. Line a strainer with a double layer of cheesecloth, washed ad squeezed dry. Strain the almond milk, pressing down on the solids to get as much liquid as possible.

Aspic

The gelatin of the 18th century was made from calf's hooves.

4 cups clear chicken, beef, veal or fish stock
2 envelopes unflavored gelatin

Heat 3 ½ cups stock. Soak the gelatin in the remaining cold stock for 5 minutes. Stir into the stock until dissolved. Cool and use as directed.
Makes 4 cups

Béchamel Sauce

This sauce is named for the chief steward of the royal kitchens of King Louis X1V.

4 tablespoons butter
4 tablespoons flour
1 cup milk
1 small onion, minced
Salt and cayenne pepper

Melt the butter in a saucepan, and add the onion. Stew until the onion is soft but not brown. Remove from the butter with a slotted spoon. Sprinkle the flour over the butter and cook for several minutes. Then add the milk whisking slowly, until it is all incorporated, and it starts to thicken. Then add the onion back to the sauce, and season with salt and cayenne pepper.

Makes 1 cup

Brown Sauce

2 tablespoons butter
2 tablespoons flour
2 cups beef broth
Salt and pepper

Heat the butter in a saucepan, and then add the flour, cook until the flour is medium brown. Add the beef broth slowly whisking in. Bring to a boil, then reduce the heat and simmer for 20 25 minutes.

Makes 2 cups

Court Bouillon

2 stalks celery with leaves, chopped

1 medium onion, chopped

Bouquet Garni (4 sprigs parsley, small bay leaf, 10 crushed peppercorns, 2 thyme sprigs, tied in cheesecloth)

2 pounds white fish trimmings

1 teaspoon salt

1 bottle dry white wine

2 quarts water

Place all the ingredients in a large soup pt. Bring to a boil, and then reduce the heat. Simmer for 25 minutes, uncovered. Strain carefully through double cheesecloth. Cool before using for poaching fish. This bouillon keeps well in the refrigerator.

Makes 2 quarts

Custard

1 quart milk,

1 2 inch piece vanilla bean or

2 teaspoons vanilla extract,

½ cup granulated sugar

¼ teaspoon salt,

4 whole eggs,

2 egg yolks

Scald the milk with the vanilla bean or the extract. Add the sugar and the salt. Mix well. Then cool. Beat the eggs and the egg yolks together. Add the egg mixture to the milk. Beat until smooth, Heat over a double boiler filled with 2 inches of boiling water. Whisk until thickened. Remove from the heat and either bake as a dessert, or use in ice cream or molded desserts.

Creole Sauce

4 tablespoons butter
1 large onion, sliced
1 large green pepper sliced
½ cup mushrooms, sliced
½ cup sliced green olives
1 cup beef stock
1 15 oz can tomatoes, whole
Salt and pepper
¼ teaspoon cayenne pepper
1 small bay leaf
1 small pinch of thyme
1 clove
1 tablespoon of white wine

Melt the butter in a small saucepan, and cook the onion and the pepper in it until soft. Then add the mushrooms and the olives, and cook for another 5 minutes. Add the rest of the ingredients, including the liquid from the tomatoes. Simmer for 20 minutes.

Makes 2-3 cups of sauce

Flaky Whole Wheat Pastry

1 ¼ cups whole-wheat pastry flour
3 tablespoons butter
3 tablespoons lard
3 tablespoons ice water

In a bowl combine the pastry flour with the butter and lard, cut with a pastry cutter until the mixture resembles coarse breadcrumbs. Add the water, and mix until soft pastry forms. With your hands make it into a ball and cover it with plastic wrap and refrigerate until ready to use.

Hollandaise Sauce

> 4 egg yolks
> 1 tablespoon cold water
> 2/3 cup butter at room temperature, cut into small pieces
> ¼ teaspoon salt
> 2 dashes cayenne pepper
> 1 tablespoon lemon juice

Place the egg yolks and the water in the top of a double boiler. Beat well with a wire whisk to mix. Place over I inch of hot water (not boiling) over low heat. Beat the yolks and foamy and light. Add the butter, piece by piece, whisking well between each addition. Keep beating until all the butter has been added. Add the salt, cayenne pepper and the lemon juice. Whisk in. If the sauce separates, add 1 tablespoon of boiling water.

Makes 2 cups

Sauce Espagnole

This sauce originated in France during the 14th century, when sauces became an important part of the cuisine of the French Court.

> 2 tablespoons butter
> 1 onion, finely chopped
> 1 small carrot, diced
> Bouquet Garni (1 bay leaf, ½ teaspoon dried thyme, 4 peppercorns, parsley sprigs tied in cheesecloth
> ½ cup dry white wine
> 3 cups brown sauce

2 cups Beef broth
2 tablespoons tomato paste
Salt and pepper

Melt the butter in a saucepan and cook the onion until soft and browned. Add the Bouquet Garni, wine, brown sauce and 1 cup broth. Simmer for 1 hour, skimming with care. Strain into a clean saucepan. Add the tomato paste and the remaining broth, and stir well. Simmer for 1 hour. Then strain. Used as directed or store covered in the refrigerator.
Makes 4 cups

Short Crust Pastry

2 cups all purpose flour
1 stick butter
1 pinch salt
Ice water

Dice the butter into small pieces. Add to the flour and with a pastry cutter, cut in the butter until it resembles breadcrumbs. Add the ice water a little at a time, until a soft pastry is formed. Gather into a ball and wrap in plastic wrap. Store in the Freezer until ready to use.

Veloute

4 tablespoons butter
1 tablespoon minced onion
4 tablespoons flour
5 cups hot chicken or fish broth

Melt the butter in a saucepan. Add the minced onion and cook without browning for 2-3 minutes. Add the flour and cook for 3 to 4 minutes until barely golden. Add the hot broth, and stir well until smooth and thickened. Lower the heat and simmer very slowly for about 1 hour. Strain; Use a base for sauces.

Makes 2 ½ cups

Vinaigrette Dressing

The French inherited the making of Vinaigrette from the Greeks and Romans, who used it to dip their bread slices in.

1 ½ teaspoons Dijon mustard
½ teaspoon salt
½ teaspoon black pepper
3 tablespoons red wine vinegar
9 tablespoons olive oil

Blend the mustard, salt and pepper in the vinegar, stirring well with a fork. Drizzle the olive oil in. Stir well.

Makes ¾ cup

White Sauce

In the British Isles white sauce formed the basis for many dishes of vegetables and even soups.

2 tablespoons flour
2 tablespoons butter
4 cups milk
Salt and pepper to taste

In a saucepan, heat the butter and then add the flour. Cook for several minutes stirring constantly. Then add the milk slowly, whisking after each addition. Whisk until thickened. Add salt and pepper to taste.

Makes 4 cups

Bibliography

Anon, Ashmole MS 1439-1530 In Austin (ed.) *Two Fifteenth Century Cookery Books*, Early English Text Society, Oxford University Press, Oxford 1964

Apicius, *The Roman Cookery Book*, translated by Barbara Flower and Elizabeth Rosenbaum, 1958, George G. Harrap and Company Ltd. London.

Arano, Luisa Cogliati, *The Medieval Heath Handbook*, George Braizer, New York, New York 1976

Ashby Ruth, Ohrn, Gore Deborah, *Herstory, Women Who Changed the World*, Viking 1995

Baker, Howard G. *Plants and Civilization,* Fundamentals of Botany Series, Belmont, Calif. 1965

Barber Richard, *Cooking and Recipes from Rome to the Renaissance*, Allen Lane, London, 1973

Berriedale-Johnson, Michelle, *The British Museum Cookbook*, The British Museum, Company Ltd. 1998

Black, Maggie, *The Medieval Cookbook*, Thames and Hudson, New York, 1992

Bober, Phyllis Pray, *Art Culture and Cuisine*, University of Chicago Press, London, 1999

Boxer, Arabella, *Mediterranean Cookbook*, Penguin London, 1981

Brears, Peter, Black, Maggie, Corbishley, Gill, Renfrew, Jane, Stead Jennifer, *A Taste of History, 10,000 Years of Food in Britain*, English Heritage in association with the British Museum Press, 1997

Brothwell Don and Patricia Brothwell, *Food in Antiquity, A Survey of the Diet of Early Peoples*. Glyn Daniel No 66, New York, 1969

Casas, Penelope, *The Food and Wine of Spain*, Alfred Knopf, New York, 1984

Cook, Petronelle, *Queen Consorts of England*, Facts on file books, New York, 1993

Cosman, Madeleine, *Fabulous Feasts: Medieval Cookery and Ceremony*. New York, 1976

Cosentino, Lydia, *A Woman Speaks*, Dramaline Publications, Rancho Mirage Ca. 1995

Dalby, Andrew and Grainger, Sally, *The Classical Cookbook*, J. Paul Getty Museum, Los Angeles, 1996

Darby William and Ghaliounghi, Paul, *Food: The gift of Orisis* 2 vols. London, 1977

David, Elizabeth, *A book of Mediterranean Food*,. John Lehmann, London, 1950

De Medici, Lorenza and Passigli, Patrizia, *Italy, the Beautiful Cookbook, Authentic Recipes from the Regions of Italy*, Knapp, Los Angeles, 1988

Edwards, John: *The Roman Cookery of Apicius, A Treasury of Gourmet Recipes and Herbal Cookery*. Point Roberts Washington, 1984,

Farmer, Fanny, *The Original Fanny Farmer Cookbook*, Hugh Lauter Levin Assoc. New York, facsimile, 1896

Faulkner, R.O. *Ancient Egyptian Book of the Dead*, London 1985

Farb, Peter, and Armelagos, George *Consuming Passions, the Anthropology of Eating,* Boston, Houghton, Mifflin 1980

Filer, Joyce, *Disease, Egyptian Bookshelf,* Trustees of the British Museum, London, 1995

Franck, Irene, Brownstone, David, *Women's World, A time line of Women in History,* Harper Collins, New York, 1995

Fraser Antonia, *The Lives of the Kings and Queens of England,* University of California Press, Berkeley, 1993

Glasse, Hannah, *Art of Cookery Made Plain and Easy,* 1747 Facsimile reprint by Prospect Books 1983

Hale, Haran, Mc Kenna, Tatiana, Sheraton, Mimi, *The Horizon Cookbook, and Illustrated History of Eating and Drinking through the Ages,* Doubleday, Publishing Co, New York, 1968

Hazleton, Nika Standen, *The Cooking of Germany,* Food of the World Series, Time Life New York, 1969

Hickman, Peggy *A Jane Austen Household Book with Martha Lloyds Recipes,* David and Charles, Newton Abbot, 1977

Jackson, Glenda, *Women Who Ruled: A Biographical Encyclopedia,* Barnes and Nobles, 1998

Levi Zion, and Agabria, Hani, *The Yemenite Cookbook,* Seaver Books, New York, 1988

Longford, Elizabeth, *Queen Victoria,* Harper and Row, New York New York 1964

Mallo, Tess, *The Complete Middle Eastern Cookbook,* Landsdowne Press, Australia, 1985

Manniche Lise, *An Ancient Egyptian Herbal,* Austin Texas 1989

May Robert, *The Accomplisht Cook,* London, 1660

Mennell, Stephen, *All Manners of Food*, Blackwell Publishing, Oxford England, 1985

Morphy, Countess, *Recipes of all nations*, Wise and Co, New York, 1935

Moss Peter, *Meals through the Ages*, George Harrap and Co. Ltd. 1958

Mc Kendry, Maxime, *Seven Centuries of English Cooking*, Weidenfeld and Nicholson, London 1973

Orga, Irfan, *Turkish Cooking*, Andre Deutsch, London, 1963

Papashvili, Helen and George, *Russian Cooking*, Food of the World Series, Time-Life, New York, 1969

Pasley, Virginia, *In Celebration of Food*, Simon and Schuster, New York, 1974

Pullar, Phillipa, *Consuming Passions*, Little and Brown, Boston, 1970

Redon, Odile, Sabban, Francoise, Serventi, Silvano, *The Medieval Kitchen*, University of Chiacgo Press, 1998

Rodin, Claudia, *The Book of Jewish Food, an Odyssey from Samarkand to New York*, Alfred A Knopf, New York, 1996

Rodin, Claudia, *A New Book of Middle Eastern Food*, Viking 1985

Root, Waverly, *Food*, Smithmark Publications, New York, 1996

Saggs, H.W.F, *Everyday Life in Babylonia and Assyria*, New York 1965

Sahni, Julie, *Classic Indian Cooking*, Morrow, New York, New York, 1980

Santich, Barbara *The Original Mediterranean Cuisine*, Wakefield Press, Australia, 1995

Scott David, *Recipes for an Arabian Night: Traditional Cooking from North Africa and the Middle East.* Pantheon, New York, 1983

Scully, Eleanor and Scully Terence, *Early French Cookery, Sources, History, Original Recipes and Modern Adaptations*, University of Michigan, Ann Arbor, 1995

Sim, Alison, *Food and Feast in Tudor England*, St Martins Press London, 1998

Tannahill, Reay, *Food in History*, Methuen, 1973. Paladin paperback 1975

Tydesley, Joyce, *Daughters of Isis*, Penguin Books, London 1995

Toklas Alice B, *The Alice B. Toklas Cookbook* 1954 Harper and Row, New York

Toussaint-Samat, Magulonne, Translated by Anthea Bell, *The History of Food*, Blackwell Publishers, Oxford, UK 1993

Trager, James, *The Food Chronology*, Owl Books, Henry Holt and Company, New York, New York, 1995

Tzabar, Naomi and Shimon, *Yemenite and Sabra Cookery*, Sadan Publishing House, Tel Aviv, 1966

Vehling, Joseph Dommers, *Apicius, Cookery and Dining in Imperial Rome*, 1977, Dover, New York New York

Williams, Neville, *Henry the VIII and His Court*, Macmillan, New York, 1977

Wilson, Hilary, *Egyptian Food and Drink*, Aylesbury, England, 1988

Wolfe, Linda, *The Cooking of the Caribbean Islands*, Foods of the World Series, Time-life New York, 1969

Wooley Sir Leonard, *Ur excavations* Vol. 2, *The Royal Cemetery: A Report on the Predynastic and Sargonid Graves Excavated Between 1936-1931*. New York, 1934

Index

E

F

N